Globalisation, Market and Rural Consumers

About the Editors

Prof. Suresh Misra is Chair Professor (Consumer Affairs) and Coordinator, Centre for Consumer Studies at IIPA, New Delhi. He holds his Masters in Political Science from Jawaharlal Nehru University, New Delhi, Masters in Human Resource Management from Pondicherry University and D.Phil. from Allahabad University. He had his advance training in Corporate Management at AOTS, Japan, TQM at U.K. Civil Service College and in Training Techniques and Methodology from the Thames Valley University, UK. Dr. Misra has authored/ edited 16 books and contributed several papers in journals of repute. A member of the Central Consumer Protection Council Dr. Misra has done pioneering research in the area of consumer welfare. His major areas of interest include Consumer Welfare, Governance Reforms, Development Administration and Local Governance. He is a member of the Central Consumer Protection Council.

Dr. Sapna Chadah is working as Assistant Professor (Administrative and Constitutional Law) at IIPA. She has done her LLB and LLM from Delhi University and Ph.D. from Jamia Millia Islamia, New Delhi. Dr. Sapna has organised a number of capacity-building programmes in the area of consumer protection and administrative law. She has been associated with the consultancy project on "Involvement of Universities and Colleges in Consumer Protection". She has two books to her credit and published several papers in journals of repute. She has also completed a number of research projects.

Globalisation, Market and Rural Consumers

Edited by

Suresh Misra
Sapna Chadah

CONCEPT PUBLISHING COMPANY PVT. LTD.
NEW DELHI-110059

ISBN-13: 978-93-86682-29-1

First Published 2018

Published and Printed by

Concept Since 1974

Concept Publishing Company Pvt. Ltd.
A/15-16, Commercial Block, Mohan Garden,
New Delhi-110059 (INDIA)
T: +91 11 25351460, +91 11 25351794
E : publishing@conceptpub.com; *W* : www.conceptpub.com

Cataloging in Publication Data--Courtesy: D.K. Agencies (P) Ltd. <docinfo@dkagencies.com>

Globalisation, market and rural consumers / edited by Suresh Misra, Sapna Chadah.
pages cm
"The book is an outcome of a National Seminar on "Globalisation, Markets and the Rural Consumers" organised by the Centre for Consumer Studies, Indian Institute of Public Administration, New Delhi. The Seminar was sponsored by the Department of Consumer Affairs, Government of India"—Introduction.
Includes bibliographical references and index.
ISBN 9789386682291

1. Consumer behavior—India—Congresses. 2. Marketing—India—Congresses. 3. Globalization—Economic aspects—India—Congresses. 4. Rural development—India—Congresses. I. Misra, Suresh, editor. II. Chadah, Sapna, editor. III. Indian Institute of Public Administration. Centre for Consumer Studies, organizer. IV. India. Department of Consumer Affairs, sponsoring body.

LCC HF5415.33.I4G56 2018 DDC 658.83430954 23

Preface

Globalisation aided by information technology has reduced time and space and made it easier for people to travel, communicate, and do business internationally. Today we live in a global village which has integrated the world markets thereby benefiting the consumers in terms of better goods and services. Globalisation has changed the way consumers behave in the market. The world is moving towards a mono culture—of consumerism. In general, as economies become more connected to other economies, they have increased opportunity, but also increased competition. With the entry of a large number of multinational companies and the growth of e-commerce, the problems faced by the consumers are much more complex. The consumers lack knowledge and information to face the challenges of the complex market forces. As a result, the exploitation of the consumers is rampant. The problems are mainly due to unfair business practices and the weakness of the consumer complaint redressal mechanism. Exploitation is more rampant in the rural areas where due to illiteracy and ignorance, it is easy to exploit the rural consumers. They are much more vulnerable to the market mechanisms. Low purchasing power due to poverty and availability of limited choice has added to consumer exploitation.

The rural markets are full of spurious products which not only harm consumers financially, but are also a health hazard. Less said about the service sector the better it is. The services provided in the rural areas lack accountability and transparency in their operations. They have become the victims of globalisation instead of being the beneficiaries. They do not have instruments to protect them which makes them much more vulnerable. The problem is that we see consumers as a homogeneous entity and not a heterogeneous one. Even in the rural areas, the problems of farmers are different from women consumers but we do not have programmes and policies to address their concerns. It is time that specific strategies are adopted to protect and empower the rural consumers who constitute the bulk of the population. The Father of the Nation Mahatma

Gandhi said the India lives in villages. Therefore, if rural consumers are not protected, the consumer movement will not move forward.

In order to understand the problems of the rural consumers in the context of globalisation the Centre for Consumer Studies, Indian Institute of Public Administration, New Delhi organised a National Seminar on "Globalisation, Markets and the Rural Consumers". The present book is an outcome of the papers presented in the National Seminar and contains twenty three papers written by eminent experts working in the area of consumer protection and welfare. Their focus is on how globalisation has changed the Indian markets and how it has affected the rural consumers. Various strategies and policy interventions have been suggested by the authors to address the problems faced by the rural consumers.

We are thankful to the Department of Consumer Affairs, Government of India for sponsoring the Seminar. We would like to thank all the paper contributors for sending their revised papers in time. We are grateful to Dr. T. Chatterjee, Director, Indian Institute of Public Administration for his help and support. We would also like to thank all the members of the Centre for Consumer Studies for their support. Thanks are due to Ms. Deepa for providing excellent secretarial assistance. We hope that the readers will find this book useful in understanding the problems of rural consumer.

Suresh Misra

Place : New Delhi **Sapna Chadah**

Contents

SECTION III

Changing Taste and Preferences of Rural Consumers

SECTION IV

Service Sector and the Rural Consumers

List of Contributors

Aggarwala, Nitish, Engineer, Delhi College of Engineering, New Delhi, 405, Malagiri Apartments, Kaushambi, Ghaziabad-201010, Email: *nitishaggarwala@gmail.com*

Dr. Agrawal, Meenu, Associate Professor and Head (Economics), Ginni Devi Modi Girls PG College, Modinagar, District Ghaziabad-201204, Email: *meenuagrawal2005@rediffmail.com*

Dr. Amir, Zeeshan, Dean, Faculty of Management and Research, Integral University Dasauli, Kursi Road, Lucknow-226026, Uttar Pradesh, Email: *zeeshanamir@sify.com*

Dr. Anand, D. Dev, Secretary, Annai Veilankanni's College, No. 81, VGP Salai, Saidapet, Chennai-600015, Tamil Nadu, Email: *devanand222@gmail.com*

Dr. Baghla, Aditi, Assistant Professor, Department of Commerce, G.C.A.M. College, Abohar, Punjab, Email: *aditigirdhar86@gmail.com*

Dr. Chandra, Suresh Ch, JRF and Faculty on Honorary Basis, Department of Commerce and Business Management, Kakatiya University, Warangal, Andhra Pradesh-506009, Email: *suresh.scholar@gmail.com*

Dr. Choudhury, Sanghamitra, Assistant Professor, Department of Peace and Conflict Studies and Management, Sikkim Central University, 6th Mile, Samdur, PO-Tadong, Gangtok, Sikkim-737102, Email: *schoudhuryassam@gmail.com*

Dr. Christian, Sejalben Ravikant, Assistant Professor, Shri DN Institute of PG Studies in Commerce, MB Patel Science College Campus, Anand-388120, Gujarat, Email: *dr.9825356575@gmail.com*

Dr. Dash, Geetanjali, Associate Professor, P.G. Department of Social Science, F.M. University, Balasore, Odisha-756020, Email: *geetanjali1961@gmail.com*

Dr. Ganesan, K., Head of Department, Business Administration, Annai Veilankanni's College, No. 81, VGP Salai, Saidapet, Chennai-600015, Tamil Nadu, Email: *mail4avc@gmail.com*

Dr. Ganesan, Radhika, President, Association of Health, Food, Nutrition and Dietetics, No. 25, Santhome High Road, Near Light House, Chennai, Tamil Nadu-600004, Email: *info@afnd.in*

Dr. Ghufran, Ali, Assistant Professor, Department of Business Management, Faculty of Management and Research, Integral University, Dasauli, Post Basha, Kursi Road, Lucknow-226026, Uttar Pradesh, Email: *dralighufran@gmail.com*

Dr. Ingole, Aravind Suhas, Lecturer/Assistant Professor, S.G.R.E. F's G.H. Raisoni, Institute of Management and Research, Gate No. 1030, Nagar-Pune Highway, Chas Village, Ahmednagar, TQ. Dist. Ahmednagar-414008, Maharashtra, Email: *aravind.ingole@gmail.com*

Dr. Joshi, Pushyamitra, Research Scholar, 196, VIP Paraspar Nagar, IDA Scheme No. 97, Opposite IDA Auditorium, Indore-452009, Madhya Pradesh, Email: *pushya.josh@gmail.com*

Dr. Kar, Notan Bhusan, Independent Researcher, Milanpally, P.O. Hridaypur, Kolkata-7000127, West Bengal, Email: *notanbhusankar@gmail.com*

Dr. Kasana, Chitra, Professor, Symbiosis Centre for Management Studies, Block 'A', Plot No. 47/48, Sector-62, Noida-201301, Uttar Pradesh, Email: *chitrakasana@yahoo.co.in*

Dr. Kaushal Kishore, Lecturer (Marketing Area), School of Petroleum Management (SPM), Pandit Deendayal Petroleum University (PDPU), Village-Raisan, P.O.–Gandhi Nagar, Dist. Gandhi Nagar, Gujarat-382007, Email: *kaushalk206@gmail.com*

Dr. Kumar, Basanta, Reader and Placement Officer, Department of Business Administration, Utkal University, Bhubaneswar-751004, Odisha, Email: *baghar@rediffmail.com*

Dr. Kumar, Shailendra, Assistant Professor, Department of Management and Commerce, Skkim Central University, 6th Mile, Samdur, PO-Tadong, Gangtok, Sikkim-737102, Email: *shailendra.kumar@sify.com; kumar.shailendra08 @gmail.com*

Dr. Mistry, Snehalkumar H., Professor, C.K. Pithawalla Institute of Management, *Via* Magdulla Port, Near Malvan Mandir, Behind Gariyar Gam, Dumus Road, Surat-395007, Email: *drsnehalmistry@gmail.com*

Dr. Munjal, Sourabh, Assistant Professor, NIMS University, Shobha Nagar, Delhi Highway, Jaipur, Rajasthan, Email: *sourabhmunjal0112@gmail.com*

Parida, Pradip Kumar, Assistant Professor, Indian Institute of Public Administration, New Delhi, Email: *paridapradip1@gmail.com, paridapradip @yahoo.com.in*

Dr. Poojara, Jayesh Gunvantray, I/C Principal, Shri V Z Patel Commerce College, M B Patel Science College Campus, Anand-388120, Gujarat, Email: *dr8866298662@gmail.com*

Prasad, K.S.S. Hari, Executive, BSNL, Tirupati, Guest Faculty in Management Institute, Universities and Academies, First Floor, Ramachandra Nagar, Besides Ramachandra Mission, K.T. Road, Tirupati-517507, Email: *ksshari@yahoo.com*

Raut, Smita, Research Fellow, MS Swaminathan Research Foundation, Koraput, Odisha, Email: *smitaraut78@gmail.com*

Samiulla, Shri, Lecturer, Government. P.U. College Kavalapadoor, Vogga, Bantwal Taluk, Dakshina Kannada, Karnataka, Email: *samiulla7803@gmail.com*

Singh, Anurupa B., 102, F-2, Marketing Department, Amity Business School, Amity University, Noida-201301, Uttar Pradesh, Email: *absingh@amity.edu*

Dr. Singh, P.N., Assistant Professor, Rajarshi School of Management and Technology, U.P. College, Varanasi, Uttar Pradesh,
Email: *pnsinghvns@gmail.com*

Singh, Vijay Kumar, Dy. Director (Law), Competition Commission of India, Hindustan Times House, Room No. 452, 4th Floor, 18-20, Kasturba Gandhi Marg, New Delhi-110 001, Email: *vrsingh.vk@gmail.com*

Tangade, S.F., Principal, Government. First Grade College, Paschapur, TQ. Hukkeri, Dist. Belgaum, Karnataka-591122, Email: *sftangade@gmail.com*

Dr. Uppal, R.K., Head Department of Economics, D.A.V. College, Malout-152107, Punjab, Email: *rkuppal_mlt@yahoo.com*

Introduction

Globalization is the buzzword of today as the economies of the world are being increasingly integrated. Information and communication technology has brought people closer. National boundaries are breaking down and the world is becoming a smaller place. Goods, which were once confined to Western countries, are available across the globe. The world is moving towards a mono-culture which has affected almost every aspect of human life, from economic, social to cultural. It has changed the people—life, eat and think. Widespread exchange of goods, services and ideas have influenced changes around the world. The impact has been more on the emerging new middle class and rural consumers. Globalisation has opened up numerous avenues for making our life more comfortable and convenient. It is by way of exchange of markets, services, products, conveniences, technologies and opportunities that these days assume a seemingly healthy and buoyant look.

Globalisation, in simpler terms means, "global utilisation; utilisation of resources and services, no matter whose resources and what way one is utilising them". Whereas consumerism is a movement or policies aimed at regulating the products or services, methods or standards of manufacturers, sellers and advertisers in the interest of buyers, such regulation may be institutional, statutory or embodied in a voluntary code occupied by a particular industry or it may result more indirectly from the influence of consumer's organisations. The principle of 'Caveat emptor' relieved the seller of the obligation to make disclosure about the quality of the product. In addition, the personal relation between the buyer and seller was one of the major factors in their relations. But with the growth of trade and its globalisation the rule no more holds true. It is now impossible for the buyer to examine the goods before hand and most of the transactions are concluded by correspondence. Further, on account of complex structure of the modern goods, it is only the producer/seller who can assure the quality of goods. With manufacturing activity becoming more organised, the producers/sellers are becoming stronger and organised whereas the buyers are still weak and unorganised. In the age of revolutionised information technology, Internet and with the emergence of e-commerce related innovations the consumers are further deprived to a great extent. As a result buyer is being misled, duped and deceived day in and day out. In India under the auspices of MNCs and trade policies of developed countries which are supposedly formulated to devour the Third World consumer kingdom. Indians seem to imitate what Western nation states do but in context of consumer rights and responsibility we turned out as losers even in this art of ours.

Globalisation means integrating the economy of a country with the world more specifically in the Indian context, this implies removing constraints and obstacles to the entry of Multi National Corporations (MNCs) in India. The Government of India has thrown open the doors to foreign investors. In a globalised world markets for goods and services, capital and labour are increasing. There is free flow of goods from one country to another country. In the present situation, the importance of Consumer Protection Act has its own importance. Consumer Protection Act is safeguarding the interests of consumer against the abuses of marketeers. Government of India has accorded high priority for consumer protection. The focus on consumers gained momentum only after consumers started reacting and voicing their grievances against unscrupulous traders and manufacturers of goods and services.

Furthermore, a country's economy revolves around its markets and when it is a seller's market, the consumer exploitation is the maximum. When there are large numbers of buyers and sellers, consumers enjoy a number of choices. Before enactment of the Consumer Protection Act, 1986, India had a sellers' market. Thus, the year 1986 marks a watershed since then consumer protection in India gained momentum.

Further, liberalisation of our economy in 1991 gave opportunity to Indian consumers to get quality products at competitive prices. Earlier in order to protect our own industries, Government restricted foreign competition. This led to a situation where consumers were getting very few choices and quality-wise also our products were inferior. For purchase of car there used to be a huge booking and there were only two brands available. Nobody bothered about consumer interests and the attitude was towards protecting our own industry. Thus, the need for consumer satisfaction and consumer protection was recognized. As consumer is considered as an inevitable part of a socio-economic-political system, where the exchange initiated and transaction realised between two parties, namely buyers and sellers has an impact on a third party, i.e. society, the inherent profit motive in mass production and sales also offers the opportunity to many manufacturers and dealers to exploit consumers. Problems of defective goods, deficiency in service, spurious and duplicate brands, and misleading advertisements are rampant and often the gullible consumer falls prey to it.[1]

Impact of Globalisation on Rural Consumers

Rural markets have always been seen as an unmanageable territory, due to its vastness and scattered characteristics. Managing this complex market calls for a hard look at available data. For example, going by the concentration and dispersion of population in villages, it is apparent that a marketer need not reach out to every single village. Rural consumers across villages differ with each other. Some of them are as distinct as night and day. A rural consumer in Karnataka will be very different to a rural consumer in West Bengal. With such a vast difference, how does one decide who is the target audience? Before doing that, one must remember that rural consumers though homogenous, are heterogeneous when it comes to buying value-for-money products.

Rural consumers can be broadly categorised into two when it comes to understanding of advertisements. On one hand, we have the consumers who are less literate (even illiterate) and on the other hand we have the educated young population between the age group of 18-35 years. The former group requires a communication message which can be easily understood. While purchasing, this group usually does not specify brand names, because of their inability to read and write. Instead, they choose to demand what they want by mentioning the features or anything that is associated with the brand. They associate their demands (products) with the colours, numerals etc. The youth are more brand conscious due to education, mobility, media exposure etc. because of which they demand the brands of their choices.

Brand Consciousness

Over the last decade, due to globalisation rural India has witnessed substantial improvement in terms of purchasing power, rapid spread of communication network etc. which provide a brilliant opportunity to the corporate sector. Demonstration effect, media exposure etc. have ensured that even remote small villages incorporate the purchasing patterns of the large villages. Recent studies also indicate a remarkable improvement in the types of product used. Rural consumers are shifting from low-priced/local/unbranded to Premium/national brands. Such premium products are penetrating even into the lower socio-economic classes. One reason probably could be because of the belief that branded products stand for quality. Another interesting fact is that there are multiple brand usages within a category for the members of the same family, which prove that there is immense potential for the marketers to promote their products.

Now-a-days, women make brand decisions even if men and children are the ones who actually go to buy the product. However, in some cases like 'Dabur Janam Ghunti' (gripe water) housewives decided the usage of product category while the brand selection and the final purchase was done by the man.

Buying Process

In the urban markets, we are accustomed to one and same individual being the user, purchaser as well as the influencer. However, this is not true in case of rural areas. In rural areas, each intermediary is a different person and hence, a communication message must be customised addressing each of them. For example, in case of a shampoo sachet, the user will be a woman, the one who gives money will be the breadwinner, and the purchaser could be a youth who visits a nearby feeder town to buy it. Finally, the influencer will be the retailer. Because of so many intermediaries, it will be wrong to use the urban communication message as it may not be effective at all.

Coca Cola introduced the Rs. 5 bottle to penetrate deeper into the rural areas. At a time, when the nation's soft drinks sale refused to pump up, Coca Cola decided to turn heads towards the 65 per cent of rural Indian population. By understanding their needs, it decided to introduce 200 ml bottles and price them at Rs. 5, half the price of the conventional size of a bottle. To promote this, the organization used celebrities in their advertising. To prevent the retailers from overcharging and to hit that Rs. 5 concept, the advertisements proclaimed loudly that the small bottle costed Rs. 5, saying "Paanch Matlab Chhota Coke". Low prices are imperative not just because of the desire of 'value for money' but also because the two-thirds of the villagers come under the bottom income band. This also explains why two-thirds of rural income is spent on food, and only after that the poor rural folk can turn their attention to soaps and shampoos.[2]

Consumerism is a movement or policies aimed at regulating the products or services, methods or standards of manufacturers, sellers and advertisers in the interest of buyers, such regulation may be institutional, statutory or embodied in a voluntary code occupied by a particular industry or it may result more indirectly from the influence of consumer's organisations. The principle of 'Caveat emptor' relieved the seller of the obligation to make disclosure about the quality of the product. In addition, the personal relation between the buyer and seller was one of the major factors in their relations. But with the growth of trade and its globalisation, the rule no more holds true. It is now impossible for the buyer to examine the goods before hand and most of the transactions are concluded by correspondence. Further, on account of complex structure of the modern goods, it is only the producer/seller who can assure the quality of goods. With manufacturing activity becoming more organized, the producers/ sellers are becoming stronger and organized whereas the buyers are still weak and unorganized. In the age of revolutionized information technology, Internet and with the emergence of e-commerce and m-commerce related innovations the consumers are further deprived to a great extent. As a result buyer is being misled, duped and deceived day in and day out.

Mahatma Gandhi, the Father of Nation, very rightly held that "A Consumer is the most important visitor on our premises. He is not dependent on us we are on him. He is not an interruption to our work; he is the purpose of it. We are not doing a favour to a consumer by giving him an opportunity. He is doing us a favour by giving an opportunity to serve him." In spite of these views consumerism is still in its infancy in our country, thanks to the seller's market and the Government monopoly in most services. Consumer awareness is low due to the apathy and lack of education among the masses. No one has told them about their rights—to be informed about product quality, price, protection against unsafe products, access to variety of goods at competitive prices, consumer education etc. What consumers lack here are education and information resources, testing facilities, competent leadership, price control mechanism, and adequate quasi-judicial machinery. The providers of goods and services have been reluctant to give due consideration to consumer interest protection.

Some business in India have come together to adopt a code of conduct for regulating their own activities. Regulation of business through legislation is one of the important means of protecting the consumers. Consumerism has over the time developed into a sound force designed to aid and protect the consumer by exerting legal, moral and economic pressure on producers and providers in some of the developed countries. The success of consumerism lies in the realization of the business that there is no substitute for voluntary self-regulations. Little attention from the business will not only serve consumers interest but will also benefit them. The best possible solution is that the consumers must be aware of their rights, join voluntary consumer organizations, raise voice against exploitation and seck redress of their grievances in time.

Law can only protect all consumers through rules which are essentially national, and which can only be enforced within national frameworks. Consumer protection laws enable the correction of market failures and the redress of inequalities of information and power. Recent cases indicate that consumer protection laws, for a number of reasons, will be of little practical use to protect consumers in the global economy. Globalisation is almost inevitable but mostly desired at the same time from the consumer's point of view. In fact it enforces consumer's 'right to choice', as envisaged by UNO in its guidelines for consumer welfare, in more sensible manner by exposing him to varieties of availabilities.[3]

This is what all about existing Indian consumer, who is now heading opposite to its own philosophy of consumerism when we compare and contrast it with that of the Gandhiji's which says that "while there is enough on earth for every man's need there is not enough for everyone's greed" and that poverty is really the other face of the problem of possessiveness. "It is the consumerist mode of thinking."[4]

In the World Economic Forum 1999 meet, Nobel Laureate and UNDP Goodwill Ambassador, Nadine Gordimer, condemned the process of globalisation for increasing consumption unprecedentedly, jeopardising truly human prospects: "While those of us who have been the generations of big consumers need to consume less, for more than one billion of the world's poorest people increased consumption is a matter of life and death and a basic want—the right to freedom from want." She asserted that consumption is necessary for human development "when it enlarges the capabilities of and improves people's lives without adversely affecting the lives of others."[5]

Globalisation and Consumer Protection

Consumers have sought protection through legislation because the general laws and market forces have failed to provide it. Many consumer protection laws either relate to the terms and conditions of contracts that consumers make with suppliers for the supply of goods and services, or to conduct intended to encourage the making of such contracts (marketing, packaging, advertising and provision of information). Previous laws, especially the law of contracts, assumed that the parties to contracts are legally equal in terms of power and information. In substance, in real markets, almost invariably consumers have markedly less power and information than suppliers. The law deems the action of a consumer in buying a commodity to be the making of a contract—in theory a free, consensual act. In practice, the legal consequences are attributed to the action by the law without any consideration of what the consumer actually knows or wants. The common law of contracts simply cannot afford consumers the protection they probably would seek if they were rational, fully informed, and equal in economic power to the supplier. Because, contract law offers an inadequate basis for an equitable legal transaction, it must be modified by legislations in order to afford greater protection to consumers than they can negotiate individually for themselves.

About the Book

Globalisation is the process of integrating the world markets thereby benefiting the consumers in terms of better goods and services. Globalisation has changed the way consumers behave in the market. With the entry of a large number of multinational companies and the growth of e-commerce, the problems faced by the consumers are much more complex. The problems are mainly due to unfair business practices and the weakness of the consumer complaint redressal mechanism. As a result, the exploitation of the consumers is rampant. This is more rampant in the rural areas where due to illiteracy and ignorance it is easy to exploit the rural consumers. Low purchasing power due to poverty and availability of limited choice has added to consumer exploitation. The rural markets are full of spurious products which not only harm consumers financially but also are a health hazard. The problem is that our policies mainly address the concerns of the urban consumers and the rural consumers are taken as a homogeneous entity.

The book is an outcome of a National Seminar on "Globalisation Markets and the Rural Consumers" organised by the Centre for Consumer Studies, Indian Institute of Public Administration, New Delhi. The seminar was sponsored by the Department of Consumer Affairs, Government of India. The book contains twenty three chapters written by eminent experts working in the area of consumer protection and welfare. They focus on how globalisation has changed the Indian markets and its overall impact on the rural consumers. Various strategies and policy interventions have been suggested by the authors to address the problems faced by the rural consumers.

Notan Bhusan Kar in his chapter on "Globalisation and Its Impact on Rural Market, Consumers and Farmers in India" opines that globalisation, liberalisation and privatisation have brought many changes in the Indian economy. Since 1991, the New Economic Policy has been implemented in India and that policy is certainly associated with Globalisation. As a result, many multinational companies (MNCs) along with indigenous products have entered into Indian Market. The rural market is a biggest market in India as because two-third of Indian consumers live in rural areas. Most consumers of these regions around 70 per cent are engaged in agriculture and its allied works for their livelihood.

He asserts that over 70 per cent of sales are made to middle class households today and over 50 per cent of the middle class is in rural India. Thus, the rural market has been growing to the Fast Moving Consumer Goods (FMCG) and is now bigger than the urban market. According to a study by Chennai-based Francis Kanoi Marketing Planning Services Pvt. Ltd., today the rural market in India is worth Rs. 1,23,000 crore, among them Rs. 45,000 crore are agri-inputs' market. To capture this lucrative market everyday many producers including multinationals have been developing their marketing strategies. It is a fact that due to ignorance and low awareness, most of the rural consumers are helpless to the unethical marketing practices of the greedy marketers. This chapter aims to examine whether the purchasing power of the rural people has really changed after implementation of New Economic Policy in India? If it has then with increase which section of the rural population has been benefited. The chapter also suggests measures to protect the rural consumers.

Geetanjali Dash in her chapter on "Globalisation and Rural Women Consumers", asserts that globalisation has restructured the world. It signifies greater movement of people, goods, resources and ideas due to the increased economic integration, which in turn is propelled by increased trade and investment. It is like moving towards a borderless world. There has always been sharing of goods, services, knowledge and cultures between people and countries, but in recent years improved technologies and reduction of barriers means the speed of exchange is much faster. Unthinkable progress in modes of communications, transportations and computer technology has given every individual a new dimension and a new lease of life. Even people living in rural areas are affected by this process favourably, but sometimes they also becomes victims in the process of globalization due to their ignorance and lack of awareness.

According to her globalisation has many adverse effects on rural women consumers. As consumers, women are the targets of a host of dangerous products, regarding which they are unaware because of their ignorance and lack of awareness. Many products related to women's health have been found to be dangerous or giving rise to illnesses which in some cases have hazardous impacts and even led to deaths.

Most FMCG companies use rural markets as dumping grounds for low end products basically designed for urban markets. This creates health hazards for the rural women. Most disheartening fact is that some of the substances can trigger health complications and possible birth defects when used by expecting mothers. Dr. Geetanjali is of the view that globalisation has modernised the rural women consumers much more, though not in location, but in mind-set. As conscious consumers of the modern era, they should be made aware to guard their right to safety, right to choose and right to health. It is better to wake up to the gimmicks of business than to get lured by it.

Chitra Kasana in her chapter on "A Roadmap to Rural Market Penetration" opines that Indian rural market is the largest potential market in the world, with rural consumers buying healthy, hygienic, packed food products, consumer durables and personal grooming and household items mainly due to enhanced incomes. Yet, it is untapped by established companies. The current chapter identifies the reasons for this avoidance or the inhibiting factors that have left this sector of India still unorganised. It is apparent that the Indian rural structure is very heterogeneous; each area depicts new and different picture and each has its distinctive demand patterns. Consequently, any study at an all-India level is not only difficult but inappropriate as well.

It is essential to break-up the rural markets based on groups classified on area attributes; cultural diversity; language; distance from urban centres. On the basis of these differences, a profile of rural consumers can be drawn area-wise. The current chapter has profiled twenty villages in the States of Uttar Pradesh (Western) and Haryana chosen randomly, to study the characteristics of rural consumers and consumer behaviour based on income levels; literacy-level; size of household; distance from urban township etc. This Chapter draws a parallel at the all-India level based on secondary data and the 2011 Census Report to seek variations, if any. Based on the survey, a model has been developed with an example and case analysis of HUL's attempts to penetrate into rural markets. The chapter's objective is to suggest marketing techniques to be replicated by others and which can be exemplified for further research in other rural-regions of India.

Sourabh Munjal in his chapter on "Rural Marketing: Big Potential in Small Markets" is of the view that Indian rural market claims a huge customer base and over the past few years India has witnessed an increase in the purchasing power of rural consumers, accompanied by their desire to upgrade their standard of living. However, research shows that there is uneven growth in the rural markets but is proving vital for growth of most companies. Because of intense competition and near saturation of urban markets, companies are looking towards rural consumers with glittering eyes. Retail hubs like Godrej's Aadhaar, ITC's e-chaupal, HLL's project Shakti, Haryali Kisan Bazar (DMC), have changed the rules of the marketing game in rural India.

The chapter discusses the profile of the rural Indian consumers and analyses the characteristics of the diverse and scattered rural market. The chapter will explore the major opportunities existing in rural sector for major retail players and how they are implementing the innovative strategies to cash the present and future opportunities in the rural markets.

Pradip Kumar Parida and *Smita Raut* in their chapter "De-mystifying the Facts of Globalisation: Analysing the Institutional Support for Rural Consumers Awareness in India" examine the awareness and information level of rural consumers with specific reference to developing countries, i.e. India, due to the impact of globalization. While doing that, it also try to find out how to establish the linkage between citizens (consumers) welfare and the role of various stakeholders in this process, apart from 'state'. Though the classical notion of 'bounded state' is no more relevant and 'border-less state' has come into existence, today we witness a rapid expansion of market economy, with the onslaught of globalization process.

According to them, the question is how to establish the legitimation of the role of the State and to avoid 'crisis of legitimation'? Though the challenges are numerous, however, the role of institutions like, Panchayats, Media, schools, educational institutions, voluntary organizations are prominent in this context. How to strengthen their role in this background? The ongoing forces of Globalization along with the process of ongoing marketisation has led to a situation, where there are question marks regarding the governance in totality. What about the voiceless and the marginalized sections? What about the population of rural society who are otherwise, the largest consumers of various household items, consumer durables etc.? This chapter is an attempt to explore some possibilities to address those issues.

Samiulla in his chapter on 'Overemphasis on Marketing Opportunities and Its Impact on Rural Consumers: Some Reflections' opines that in India since last six decades, marketing has acquired a large urban base. Hence, there was no attempt on the part of marketers to know the rural consumer and satisfy their needs. After liberalisation and globalisation of Indian economy, the companies are looking for expanding their market from urban to rural area. The National Council of Applied Economic Research (NCAER) survey report says that there are 720 million consumers across the villages in rural India. Hence, the development of the nation largely depends upon the development of the rural population. In India, 70 per cent of consumers are rural consumers. If their right is not protected it is not only a shame to the marketing, but also to the nation.

In his view rural consumers are the most exploited segment among the consumers in our country due to a number of reasons such as low level of literacy, low per capita income, lack of communication, transportation problem, warehousing problem, scattered population and absence of strong consumer movement etc. Markets are becoming increasingly more competitive, and marketers are focusing on studying buyer behaviour with the intention of widening their market rather than satisfying the real needs and wants of rural consumers. Advertising agencies and their creative advertisement messages concentrate only on enhancing profit by way of giving misleading advertisement.

Samiulla advocates that protection of rural consumers is necessary because they are less powerful than the urban consumers. Rural consumers need to be protected from unfair trade practices and misleading promotion programmes. The Central Government, State governments and other local bodies should organise awareness programmes to empower the rural consumers regarding unfair trade practices and also protect their interest as they constitute the bulk of Indian consumer base. In the above backdrop, the present chapter intends to analyse the impact of overemphasis on widening marketing opportunities on the rural consumers and to suggest some possible remedies.

Snehalkumar H. Mistry in his chapter on "Consumer Empowerment and Marketing Strategies for Rural Markets in India" highlights that in recent years, rural markets have acquired significance, as the overall growth of the economy has resulted into substantial increase in the purchasing power of the rural communities. Fast pace of technological advancement has brought change in every sphere of political, social, economic and cultural life of people in the country. With such changes and developments, rural market is also witnessing winds of change. Earlier rural market used to demonstrate the features of traditional and agro foods only, but now rural market has created some distinguished demands of products which are now specialized categories for many of the company's marketing their products in India.

Due to wider penetration of media and allied services in rural areas, consumers now-a-days have become more knowledgeable or empowered, which not only gives opportunities for many firms to design and develop products which suit rural market requirements but also asking many corporate to work in conjunction with rural consumers' needs and preferences. His chapter attempts to identify the effects of rural empowerment on rural marketing strategies.

Vijay Kumar Singh in his chapter "Competition Law and Policy for Rural Consumers" argues that rural markets today comprise major markets in India. About 70 per cent of the population lives in villages/rural areas and are consumers of various products and services. With growing technological know-how and communication channels, the flow of goods and services from urban to rural areas has potentially increased. This has given birth to the concept of rural marketing. As 'market' is central to the concept of rural marketing, it is equally important when we look at it from the competition law perspective. The mandate of competition law extends to the whole of India except Jammu and Kashmir, which includes both urban and rural markets. The law does not make a distinction as to its applicability to urban or rural areas. The objectives of the law are: to prevent practices having adverse effect on competition, promote and sustain competition in markets, to protect the interest of consumers and to ensure freedom of trade carried on by other participants in markets. However, rural market may be classified as different market under the definition of 'relevant market'.

The present chapter examines the competition law provisions and its applicability specifically to rural markets and rural consumers. It may be noted that Eleventh Planning Commission has observed that in rural areas only 13 per cent of the population has heard about the Consumer Protection Act. In view of this, awareness about competition law may be gauged. The chapter would seek to bring out the areas of competition law relevant for rural markets and how this can be utilized for the benefit of rural areas to protect the interests of consumers and ensure freedom of trade.

K. Ganesan and *D. Dev Anand* in their chapter "Consumer Behaviour in Rural Marketing" are of the view that consumer behaviour in rural marketing is a behaviour which is exhibited by people in planning, purchasing and using of economic goods and services. The reason for the study of the consumer behaviour in rural marketing is to analyse the effectiveness in the various areas of consumer behaviour such as planning, organising, implementing and controlling the marketing process and strategies; to adopt the concept of marketing mix and its application in rural marketing; and to gain a better understanding of the factors of rural consumers, by maintaining satisfactory exchange relationship.

There are various types of theories of consumer behaviour in rural marketing such as the Economic Theory, Psychological Theory, Psycho-analytic Theory and Socio-Cultural Theory. Earlier theories suggest that the rural consumers gave much importance to the traditional taste with lower cost in the last century. Now-a-days, the consumers, taste and preference have changed their lifestyle. Rural consumer behaviour can be divided into four categories, namely, Innovators, Adaptors, Early Adaptors and Laggards. The chapter focuses on the consumer psychology, their social and economic characteristics which are to be analysed before marketing decisions are taken in rural marketing.

The Chapter "Spurious Products in Rural Market: Problems and Countering Strategies" authored by *Pushyamitra Joshi* and *Anurupa B. Singh* discusses about the issues related to selling of spurious products in Indian rural market with reference to Fast Moving Consumer Goods (FMCG) and also suggests possible practical solutions to fight against fake and spurious product manufacturers. It also discusses about the various factors influencing rural consumers in purchasing spurious products.

They are of the view that Indian rural market is one of the potential emerging markets in the world due to its mass market advantage and increase in the disposable income of rural consumers. One of the biggest challenges for genuine manufacturing and marketing companies in penetrating rural market is to differentiate and protect their brands from spurious and fake brands. According to the study done by AC Nielsen (2006) reveals that Indian FMCG market loses US$ 500 million every year due to spurious products. According to the report of Brand Protection Committee (BPC) formed by Federation of Indian Chambers of Commerce and Industry (FICCI) in 2006 10 per cent of the FMCG market is accounted for by fake products. 10 per cent-30 per cent of the cosmetics and toiletries and packaged food items were spurious. The estimated trade losses due to piracy in India in 2006 stood at US$ 1208 million. The main objective of their study is to identify the major problems due to spurious products, various factors influencing rural consumers in buying spurious products, to understand the spurious brand manufacturer marketing strategies and possible countering strategies to fight against spurious manufacturers.

Radhika Ganesan in her chapter on "Prevalence and Awareness of Food Adulterations and Misbranding in Rural Area of Kancheepuram District, Tamil Nadu" opines that frauds in various consumer sectors are now commonly practiced, particularly in developing countries including India. Foods are purposely contaminated with additives to increase bulk, attractiveness, disguise spoilage and increase profit. All food products targeted for adulteration are high commercial value products and/or produced in high tonnage around the world and have direct impact on national progress and production (GDP). As, there is a paucity of reliable data with regards to adulteration and misbranding in rural Tamil Nadu, the present cross-sectional study assesses the prevalence and awareness of food adulteration and misbranding among rural consumers in south India.

The study population comprised 75 households selected using systematic random sampling method from in and around Chunampet village clusters, Cheyyur Taluk, Kancheepuram district. Simple procedure was used to detect adulterants in fifteen commonly consumed food items in rural area. Commonly consumed food items were identified based on the household grocery list. The prevalence of food adulteration (in terms of purity) ranged from 75 per cent-10 per cent. Awareness level was highest for literates than illiterates. Further, awareness regarding rights and responsibilities related to food adulteration was found to bc poor among this population. Product, Nutrition and food label awareness level among the households was only 2 per cent. However, misleading statements in terms of (e.g. no added Mono sodium glutamate) was observed among 25 per cent of the branded products surveyed. Occupation, education and income have significant effect on awareness level. Thus, consumer movement in this direction has to be actively encouraged through awareness and education on food adulteration and misbranding among this population.

Suresh Chandra Ch. in his chapter on "Fake Branding in Pharmaceuticals—A Study of Select Rural Villages in Telangana Region" highlights the growth of Indian Pharmaceutical Industry in the past two decades resulting in record exports of Rs. 42,154 crore. The country has shown its worth by occupying the 3rd position in terms of volume and

14th in terms of value. The 2nd largest populated country has always shown its dependency on the pharmaceutical companies, but due to rising competition, the developing and small scale pharma companies have taken to fake branding as the source of survival in the rural market.

As 70 per cent of the Indians live in villages, for many companies which are producing counterfeits, the rural India remains an attractive destination. The fake brands have not only deceived consumers in terms of quality and usage but also in the price value. In view of this problem, the present research chapter focuses on the impact of fake pharmaceutical brands in rural market with special focus on three select districts of Telangana region. His study is based on field investigation. Further, the research provides the factors influencing the marketing of fake brands in pharmaceuticals and the remedial measures to be taken for effective control of fake brands in pharmaceuticals.

Zeeshan Amir and *Ali Ghufran* in their chapter on "Changing Lifestyle and Consumption Patterns of Indian Rural Households: An Analytical Study" discuss how an individual communicates about his/her activities, attitudes, interests, opinions, values, and allocation of income through his/her lifestyle. People's perception about their own image gets influenced by their changing motivation and needs. Indian market has seen a tremendous change in lifestyle of a common man. The remarkable change in urban lifestyle has trickled across the rural population too. Island of poverty still exists but most of the rural area has transformed beyond imagination. The changing economy has put unprecedented disposable income into the hands of rural consumers who are steadily moving forward towards better quality of life.

Their study takes into account the impact of changing lifestyle on consumption pattern in relation to selected demographic variables and socio-economic characteristics. The lifestyle has been explained with respect to food consumption, fashion trends, entertainment, and use of technology. The study is an endeavour to understand how the change in lifestyle of rural households is affecting their consumption patterns bringing a noticeable change in their living standard. The analysis of consumer lifestyles which reflects the psychographics is an important factor in determining how consumers make their purchase decisions and consume the lifestyle goods.

"Changing Tastes and Preferences of the Rural Consumers: Emerging Paradigm in Indian Market" is the chapter written by *P.N. Singh.* According to him, the rural consumers have become the prime target market for consumer durable and non-durable products. *'Go rural'* is the slogan of marketing *gurus* based on analysis of the socio-economic changes in villages. A number of renowned brands, like LG electronics, Coca Cola, Britannia, Philips, Colgate, Hindustan Unilever, ITC and LIC are among those organisations which have a very significant presence in Indian rural market.

Marketers trying to venture into the rural markets must understand the rural culture and treat it on priority if they want to tap the potential in this upcoming market of India. The key issues being referred in this chapter are: (i) Difference in rural customer taste and preferences from the urban customer; (ii) Factors that determine the buying decision-making of the rural customers; and (iii) Who makes the buying decisions? This empirical study is confined to the two villages in Mirzapur District of Uttar Pradesh State. Information has been collected by interviewing the customers through structured and unstructured questionnaires. Both group interviews and personal interviews have been conducted.

His chapter highlights some interesting dimensions of rural marketing. It deals with issues that how the marketer should approach the rural customer along with marketers' strategies to capture the attention of the rural customer by focusing around plugging the segments with the right product, using value for money pricing, selecting the most appropriate channel of distribution, building long-term relationships with the customers and finally, using the power of emotional branding.

Sanghamitra Choudhury and *Shailendra Kumar* in their chapter "Marketing Strategy in the Context of Changing Tastes and Demand of Modern Rural Consumers of India" assert that rural India is growing and this is evident from the increase and change in the consumption pattern of the rural people. Considering that rural India comprises 41 per cent of India's middle class and accounts for 58 per cent total disposable income accounting for consumption and with approximately 7 out of 10 consumers residing in rural India, the rural buyers are spurring growth and driving demands. The companies of late have started recognizing the potential of the rural market. They have started focusing on the changing tastes and demand of the new modern rural consumers.

According to them, the modern rural Indian consumers have also started making demands for those premium products which were earlier exquisitely meant to cater the demand of the niche urban market. Hence, a proper marketing strategy is the need of the hour. The chapter aims to study the potential of the rural market and the marketing strategy to be adopted for this market. Their chapter also explores why the rural market is different from the urban market and why the marketing thumb rules and strategies meant for the urban market may not work for the rural market.

Meenu Agrawal and *Nitish Aggarwala* in their chapter "Consumer Behaviour and Rural Marketing: A Case Study of Ghaziabad District of Western Uttar Pradesh" opine that the ultimate objective of any production is consumption to satisfy varied needs of man. A free market economy provides freedom to the consumers to buy and consume goods of their choice. In recent years, behaviour and lifestyle of the consumer has changed dramatically and the process of change is on. A few decades ago, rural consumer was a silent person who uncomplainingly purchased the goods. But this is not so today. Now, the consumer is choice empowered. This change is due to enhanced awareness, expansion of information technology and more importantly governmental intervention through legislations.

To understand the marketing behaviour of rural consumer they studied 16 villages of Ghaziabad district selecting 320 households. It was found that consumers in the area are not well aware about the mechanisms to properly safeguard their interest as buyers. Due to unawareness of the consumers, they are generally cheated by the traders in the market. It was found that the attitude of the consumers in the area, towards the products was not logical. They had no conviction and the decisions taken by them was not based on sound footings. In most of the cases, the consumers had no knowledge of the brands of the products. Lack of information was mainly responsible for their plight as consumers.

Basanta Kumar in his chapter "Awakening Rural Consumers Towards Sustainable Development: A Case Study" highlights that development in rural India consists of many contradictions. While the country has seen rapid growth, the rural people are still victims of poverty related problems due to corrupt practices. Though these developments have changed the rural lifestyle, poor knowledge about their rights, duties and responsibilities as consumers seem to be a major cause of concern. Rural consumers are still subjected to harassment and exploitation in the process of sustainable consumption. The awareness programmes implemented by the Government have not produced desired result. A more vibrant policy perspective is the need of the time.

Against this background, the chapter examines the magnitude of involvement of rural people in corrupt practices and the need to empower them as sensible consumer. The case study covers two villages of Angul district in Odisha—a remote village with more tribal population, road connectivity under PMGSY and power connection under RGGVY and another village with better infrastructure, education and awareness.

Respondents include members of village committees and self-help groups, school/college going students, and public servants looking after the developmental work in these villages. The study provides insights for policy-makers to reorient the awareness programmes suitable to local conditions.

The chapter on "Changing Tastes and Preferences of the Rural Consumers: Opportunities and Challenges ahead of Oil Marketing Companies (OMCs) in India" is written by Kaushal Kishore. According to him petro retailing is known as the face of Oil Marketing Companies (OMCs). In early days, petro-retailing business was confined to selling petroleum products to the consumers. In the recent years, customer expectations and preferences have changed. The growing per capita income and higher education of the rural consumers are creating more pressure on OMCs to supply right quality and quantity of fuel at the right time. The entry of private players like Reliance, Shell and Essar in petro-retailing business has changed the meaning of the business.

He opines that the past research on rural consumers claims that the rural consumers are price sensitive and less brand or service conscious. The current scenario looks a little different as rural consumers are equally good at many occasions in comparison with urban consumers. The rural consumers are well aware about the products and services they buy or consume. Thanks to the electronic media and several consumer forums for creating huge impact on consumer's perception. Of course, the rural consumers have to travel miles to protect their interest in the long-term. His chapter attempts to define the role of OMCs in empowering the rural consumers and helping them to meet the satisfaction level through the petro-retailing business. The chapter shall also try to highlight the overall initiative taken by the OMCs for the rural consumers in the last decade.

According to *Shrimant F. Tangade*, insurance in India is not a new thing. Since 1818, Insurance has firmly established in India. It has a deep rooted history. Through his chapter on "Protection of Consumer Interest in Insurance Sector: A Study of Belgaum District in Karnataka State", he argues that Insurance sector in India has gone through number of phases and heavy changes. After 1990, the Government of India opened up the insurance sector to allow the private insurance companies to solicit insurance. After this, the Indian insurance sector is considered as a booming market and varieties of global players have entered to grab a share of the pie in Indian Insurance sector. At present, India's largest insurance company is owned by the Government of India, i.e. LIC of India.

According to him today there are 24 General Insurance Companies and 23 Life Insurance Companies operating in India. The insurance sector is growing at a speedy rate of 15-20 per cent. Insurance sector is adding about 7 per cent to the country's GDP. A well developed and evolved insurance sector is a boom for economic development as it provides long-term funds for infrastructure development and also strengthening the risk taking in the country. Even after establishment of IRDA in 2000, so many dissatisfied life insurance policy-holders of different insurance companies have filed their complaints in different Consumer Forums and also in complaint cell of different insurance companies. Hence, the present study evaluates the extent of dissatisfaction of the insurance policy-holders in Belgaum district of Karnataka.

"Service Quality in Telecom Services in Rural Areas: A Study with Reference to BSNL in Chittoor District, Andhra Pradesh" is written by *K.S.S. Hari Prasad.* According to him in the 21st century, the world has become a global village and this is due to prompt, easy and accessible communication. Geographical distances seem to be shortened due to telecom revolution. Due to the enormous competition among different service providers in telecom industry in India, companies are investing seriously in this sector. Usually, any commercial organisation provides services where it expects huge customer base and in return profits. In India, rural telecom has been identified as one of the important areas in which Government has been giving continuous sustained emphasis. In spite of lot of incentives provided by the Government of India to the telecom service providers to bridge the gap between the rural areas in terms of access to telecom and allied services, not much is happening. As a result, India is lagging much behind the world statistical ratios in the rural telecom access.

Hari Prasad's study is based on an empirical survey in the rural areas of Chittoor District, Andhra Pradesh in respect of availability of telecom services of BSNL (being a Government PSU). The service quality and customer satisfaction of the rural customers are analysed. An attempt has been made to analyse the customer awareness in rural areas, in respect of the various benefits and concessions provided by the BSNL, to the rural customers and its impact on the BSNL in particular and industry in general. The theoretical findings are further supplemented by an empirical analysis emphasising internal service operation, the service quality, service recovery, and customer loyalty within different service branches. The empirical research reveals that service quality is the primary concern even in the rural areas.

Aravind Suhas Ingole in his chapter on "Banking and Insurance Services for the Rural Consumers: Special Reference to the State Bank of India (SBI) Village Chas, District Ahmednagar (Maharashtra)" examines how efficiently the services, marketing strategies, rural policies and the technology helps the State Bank of India Group to provide better quality and services to the rural customers. The Banking and Insurance industry is focusing on rural areas and the emerging rural markets.

According to him, banks need to upgrade technology to be customer friendly, efficient and competitive. They also need technology for providing new products and new forms of services in an increasingly dynamic and globalised environment to empower the rural customers. According to him, often rural marketing is confused with agricultural marketing. Particular emphasis is placed on the impact of the four As (Availability, Affordability, Acceptability and Awareness). There has been a positive effect on all these services through the creation of vast marketing opportunities. The driving force of this success is "market forces", generating virtuous cycles in the transition marketing.

R.K. Uppal and *Aditi Baghla* in their chapter on "E-Banking Service in Rural Punjab: Emerging Issues, Challenges and Potential Strategies to Create Awareness among Rural Masses" assesse the current status of developments in e-banking in rural areas of Punjab and explore how awareness can be created for e-banking to make the work easy and time savvy. The study focuses on perception, selection and motivational parameters. On the basis of empirical study conducted in Rural Punjab, it has been concluded that various factors play a vital role for enhancing e-banking services in rural Punjab. Perception factors include availability of more products and services, grievance redressal, high rate of interest on deposits, low penalty charges for not maintaining minimum balance in account and better customer relation management. Selection factors include convenient location of bank and security/less risk to use. Motivational factors include cost-effective services, time savvy and provide accurate information.

Their study concludes that availability of more products and services is an important factor in rural areas of Punjab. The chapter suggests that overall satisfaction of the rural customer towards e-banking service is good. All the banks need to concentrate more on responsiveness. The study also suggests strategies to overcome the problems of awareness.

Poojara Jayesh and *Christian Sejal* in their chapter on "Problems in the Banking Service Marketing in the Mofussil: With Special Reference to HDFC Bank of Anand District," are of the view that in India more than

70 per cent of households live in rural areas. Therefore, the rural bank marketing assumes a significant importance. A rural bank is one which serves a population of less than 10,000. The most notable transition in the post-nationalization period has been that of from class banking to mass banking. This means that lending to the select elite in the urban areas has given way to lending to the rural masses. This has recognised the potentiality of rural India which was earlier underestimated. The research chapter reflects the concept of Mofussil Bank Marketing identifies problems in the Banking Service Marketing and gives suggestions to overcome the problems faced by the consumers of service rendered by private banks.

NOTES

1. *Globalisation—Type, benefits, The controversy over globalisation* http://www.referenceforbusiness.com/small/Eq-Inc/Globalisation.html #ixzz1objihbb1
2. *Rural Landscape: Rural Communication:Audience* http://www.linterland.com/core/rurallandscape/19.htm
3. P. Hirst and G. Thompson, 1995, "Globalisation and the Future of the Nation-state," *24 Economy and Society.*
4. S.H.Venkatramani: "Wretched of the Earth", *The Times of India*, 22.8.1995.
5. "Globalisation with a human face: towards a value-added society", www.weforum.org/site/

SECTION I

Globalisation and Rural Consumers: Opportunities and Marketing Strategies

1

Globalisation and Its Impact on Rural Market, Consumers and Farmers in India

NOTAN BHUSAN KAR

Concept of Globalisation

Some people think that the concept of globalisation is the free movement of trade, investment, services and exchange of culture worldover. But according to some experts, globalisation is integration of nation's economic system with the international market forces. Ironically, some other describe globalization as a strategy of the imperialist forces to loot the 'Third World' countries. In fact to our concern, globalisation is the mobility of finance capital across the world, particularly of the poor countries. The unprecedented technological progress has enabled the easy flow of finance capital at the fastest speed to any country. In the process of globalisation, the three International Institutions, namely International Monetary Fund (IMF), World Bank (WB) and World Trade Organisation (WTO) play a major role. These three organisations in a close collaboration function as the "Intelligence Agencies" on the economic policies of the underdeveloped countries. Trade-Related Intellectual Property Rights System (TRIPS) appears to have the greatest impact. And lastly, some feel that Globalisation stands for the ultimate rights of multinational companies to allocate resources according to their own criteria.

Globalisation in India

Globalisation, liberalisation and privatisation started in India during 1991 when Government of India implemented the New Economic Policy under the directives of International Monetary Fund (IMF) and World Bank (WB). After that so many changes have been made in Indian economy. Government of India had opened Indian market for the multinational companies to carry on their trade, business with their Indian counterparts. Before starting globalisation in India, IMF and WB had imposed some vital conditions on Indian Government to follow. One of these was to withdraw subsidy from Indian agriculture. Thus, successive Indian Governments have been following the instructions of those agencies and subsequently withdrawing the subsidies from the agricultural sector. As a result, the cost of production and cultivation has increased manifolds, making traditional farming an unprofitable option for the Indian farmers. On the other hand, land acquisitions in the name of various developmental projects have rendered many peasants landless and jobless. Now-a-days, Indian farmers are in deep trouble. According to NSSO (59th round) Report which was held in 2003 revealed that 27 per cent of farmers did not like farming because it was not profitable and 40 per cent of the farmers have expressed their desire to quit farming and would take up some other profession. As a result, many marginal and poor peasants have been forced to migrate to urban areas for their livelihood. The report of National Commission for Enterprises in the Unorganised Sector says 77 per cent of Indian population live on rupees 20 or less per day. At this juncture, multinational companies and big Indian corporates have entered the Indian rural market which no doubt would have long lasting effect on the rural economy and the livelihood of the rural people.

Nature and Characteristics of Rural Market

(1) Large and Scattered Market

It consists of approximately 75 crore rural consumers who live in approximately 6,38,365 villages and the rural market is geographically scattered. About 1,45,098 villages or 23 per cent of the total number of villages in India have population less than 200 and another 21 per cent have population between 200 and 500 and on the other hand 13 per cent of the villages have 50 per cent rural population and they possess 60 per cent of the rural wealth.

(2) Heterogeneous Market

It shows linguistic, religious and cultural diversities and economic disparities. As many as 20,000 ethnic groups are present in rural India and this poses a formidable challenge to the marketer. There are 24 languages and 1,642 dialects (*boli*) which varies every 100 km or so and thus it is extremely difficult to develop a uniform promotional message.

(3) Income from Agriculture

Agriculture is the main source of income. Nearly 55 per cent of rural income comes from the agriculture and the income being seasonal in nature is fluctuating. The type of crop production method of agriculture and the amount of land directly influence this income.

(4) Standard of Living

Over 70 per cent of the rural population is employed in small scale agriculture and its related occupations. The rural market is undeveloped, as the people who constitute it still lack adequate purchasing power. It is largely agriculture-oriented, with poor standard of living, low per capita income.

(5) Infrastructural Facilities

The infrastructural facilities like roads, warehouses, communication system and financial facilities are inadequate in rural areas. Nearly 50 per cent of the rural villages in the country are not properly connected by roads. Over 50 per cent rural households have access to electricity as main source of lighting but 46 per cent use kerosene or other means for lighting.

Marketing System in Rural Areas

FMCG companies are trying to reach rural consumers through village markets (or *haats*), agricultural markets (*mandis*), rural fairs (*melas*) and many other ways. *Haat* is a public gathering of buyers and sellers of commodities, meeting at a customary location at regular intervals. Most of these periodic markets are held once a week. *Haats* function as physical markets for selling agricultural surplus as well as retail points for buying daily-use items and supplies for farming activities. *Mandis* or agricultural markets are set-up by the State Governments for facilitating exchange of agricultural produce and for the procurement of food grains by the Government agencies. Companies use *mandis* to promote their brands by setting-up "stalls" for carrying out sales promotion activities and for gathering market-research information. *Melas* or fairs are an integral part of human life. There are different types of fairs: commodity fairs, cattle fairs, and fairs in connection with religious festivals. Most of the fairs are held in connection with religious festivals and, have limited marketing value. But the remaining fairs are used by companies to promote their products and brands.

Rural Market in India

The globalisation of the Indian economy has given an added advantage to sophisticated production, proliferation and mass distribution of goods and services. With the rapid pace of technological improvement and increase in people's buying capacity, more and better goods and services now are in continuous demand. Rural India is the real India. The bulk of India's population lives in villages. Today rural market is the largest potential market in India. At present about 70 per cent of Indian population lives in rural areas and the rural market scenario is changing rapidly almost everyday. Now-a-days, rural consumers spend about US$ 9 billion per annum on 'FMCG' (Fast Moving Consumer Goods) and these consumption are growing much faster than urban areas. The reasons why companies are going rural are manifold. Higher rural incomes driven by agricultural growth, increasing enrollment in primary schools, high penetration of TV and other mass-media have increased the propensity to consume branded and value-added products in rural areas. Most Fast Moving Consumer Goods Companies (FMCG) in India are introducing customised products especially for rural areas. Thus, the sales of FMCG products in rural markets is growing at a fast pace. Marketers and manufacturers are increasingly aware of the purchasing powers, vast size and demand-base of the once neglected Indian hinterland. A survey by the National Council for Applied Economic Research revealed that the rural middle class is growing at 12 per cent against the 13 per cent growth of urban counterparts. Over 70 per cent sales of total products are made to middle-class households today and over 50 per cent of the middle class is in rural India.

Impact of Globalisation on Rural Market

The impact of globalisation has been felt by the Indian rural market as much as the urban counterpart. Hence, we can see that today changes are taking place rapidly in all walks of life and rural areas are no exception to this. Improved infrastructure facilities, economic liberalisation, renewed emphasis on agri-business and small industries, fast changing agricultural technology, scope for commercialisation of agriculture, greater budgetary provision for rural people are few reasons to mention. Moreover, various socio-cultural, psychological and political aspects of rural life are also changing. Rural people today are less fatalistic, less attached to religious beliefs, getting more individualistic, achievement-oriented and aspiring than before. All this has opened up new vistas for the marketers at least in the states, which are leading in per capita income with a sustained growth, like Punjab, Haryana, Maharashtra, Tamil Nadu, Karnataka, Gujarat, Delhi and Western Uttar Pradest etc. Many features of rural India have been analysed by *National Council for Applied Economic Research* (NCAER) and some of them are as follows:

1. Rural India constitutes 70 per cent of India's total population.
2. It accounts for 56 per cent of national income.
3. It contributes to one-third of India's total savings.
4. It accounts for 64 per cent of India's total expenditure.
5. Rural economy is estimated to reach a size of Rs.18 trillion by 2012-13 as against Rs. 12 trillion in 2007-08.
6. Rural consumer's share of total ownership of low cost items like bicycles, pressure cookers and watches during 2006-07 was 60 per cent.
7. The share of rural India in the FMCG market is around 53 per cent and is expected to reach 60 per cent in future. There are as many 'middle income and above' households in the rural areas as there are in the urban areas.
8. The data showing the consumers demand in rural India is shown in Tables 1.1 and 1.2.

Table 1.1 shows that the rural share in demand for cars/jeeps has increased from 2.1 per cent in 1995-96 to 10.9 per cent in 2009-10 and for scooters it has increased from 33.1 per cent to 39.9 per cent during the same period. Similarly, the share of fans, moped, motorcycle and other low cost items have also increased. However, the rural share in demand for television and other white goods have decreased from 54 per cent to 44.2 per cent and 23.8 per cent to 23.7 per cent respectively over the same period. But, here it needs to be mentioned that though the percentage of rural share in demand for television, automotive and other white goods have decreased but the numbers of demand for them have increased.

Table 1.1: Rural Share in Stock of Consumer Demands

Demand	*1995-96 (in '000)*	*Share in per cent*	*2001-02 (in '000)*	*Share in per cent*	*2009-10 (in '000)*	*Share in per cent*
Scooters	368	33.1	355	39.4	311	39.9
Motorcycles	359	47.3	1036	39.8	4045	48.3
Mopeds	286	52.7	235	58.2	141	57.7
Cars/Jeeps	6	2.1	63	8.0	376	10.9
Automotive	1016	37.9	1689	36.0	4873	37.9
Television	4852	54.0	6400	54.5	7712	44.2
Other white goods	819	23.8	1439	23.9	3120	23.7
All Fans	7050	50.0	14627	56.9	32561	56.7
Low cost items	29228	58.1	45139	60.1	88607	61.3

Source: The Great Indian Market, NCAER.

Table 1.2: Rural Urban Demand

Category		*2001-02 (figures in '000)*	*2009-10 (figures in '000)*	*Growth in percentage*
Edible oil	Urban	2328.0	3986.5	71.24
	Rural	4681.6	666.2	**42.3**
Health Beverages	Urban	96.5	223.4	131.5
	Rural	37.0	88.9	**140.2**
Packed Biscuits	Urban	550.4	1091.0	98.2
	Rural	294.4	521.6	**77.1**
Shampoos	Urban	13.6	31.4	130.8
	Rural	6.7	16.3	**143.2**
Toilet Soap	Urban	335.9	464.2	38.1
	Rural	469.4	657.7	**40.1**
Washing Cake	Urban	510.7	616.5	20.7
	Rural	1351.7	2104.5	**55.6**
Washing Powder	Urban	847.1	1485.4	75.3
	Rural	1005.2	1847.8	**83.8**

Source: The Great Indian Market, NCAER.

From Table 1.2 we can see that percentage increase in demand of edible oils and packed biscuits are more in urban areas as compared to rural areas. Whereas in all other items like health beverages, shampoos, toilet soaps, washing cakes and washing powder the increase in demand is more in rural areas in comparison with urban areas. Therefore, we can say that the consumption of such items in rural areas is increasing at a high pace, even higher than the growing demand in urban areas. Thus, after studying the rural share in respect of stock of consumer goods, consumer demands, demand for consumables and difference in rural-urban demand we can say that the rural markets are becoming more and more lucrative for the marketers, because of the growing demand in villages.

Companies' Role in Rural India

The Indian rural market is larger when it is compared to the urban counterparts in many respects. The rural areas earlier used to be dominated by so many factors like low per capita income, low level of infrastructure facilities, problem of metal-roads, low literacy level and slow progress of industrialisation etc. These factors were responsible for limiting the capacity for consumption of goods and services and the irony was that marketers were hardly interested in these markets. In recent times, however, the scene has changed in agriculture and allied activities like horticulture, animal husbandry and rural industrialisation etc. In rural areas, the scope for marketing of goods and services depends heavily on agriculture, as it is the main occupation of the rural people. Good monsoons leading to bumper harvests, increase in procurement price for agricultural items, a four-fold increase in the outlay for rural development from Ninth to the Twelfth Five Year Plan etc. have contributed to this rural boom. The market for agriculture inputs like fertilizers, tractors, irrigation equipments, and hybrid seeds has been in the growth phase for last few decades and hence contributing a major breakthrough in the earning capacity of the farmers.

It is thus obvious that rural India has become the hot target for FMCG companies. Indian rural market has been growing steadily over the years (53 per cent share of the total market) and is now bigger than the urban market for Fast Moving Consumer Goods. For these FMCG companies are formulating their rural marketing strategy to catch this potential market. Big industries Like Hindustan Lever Ltd., Colgate-Palmolive, Britannia, Marico, Tata Tea, Parle, P & G etc. are showing deep interest in rural India marketing. Recently, as a strategy Godrej Consumer Products Ltd., introduced smaller pack sizes of its soaps and put them on the market for Rs. 5 only. HLL has also launched a special type of Lifebuoy soap for targeting the village folks. HLL has established a single distribution channel by consolidating their products and this channel seeks to build a network to sub-stockist. Likewise, Coca Cola India has started out by drawing up a distribution channel to reach to rural villages. Chennai based Cavin Kare Ltd. which makes hair dyes, organizes live demonstrations in remote areas where villagers gets a free of cost slice hair dye packet for their uses. Brook Bond Lipton India distributes their tea packet to village folks free of cost. Reckitt and Colemen uses NGOs in rural areas to educate customers about their product benefits. LG India is targeting the rural and semi-urban markets and to keep foot consciously into the hinterland of rural India. These are some examples of the big FMCG companies' marketing strategies to target customers in rural India.

Unethical Marketing Practices

Rural population is about 74 per cent of the total population in India. The demand for products and services has increased a lot in rural areas. Green revolution in the North and white revolution in the West has brought about a new prosperity in the lives of rural people. Government's emphasis on rural development has caused significant changes in the rural sectors. Moreover, the special attention given for infrastructure development through the successive Five Year Plans has improved the buying and consumption pattern of rural folks.

But, it is a fact that due to lack of awareness, many rural consumers are vulnerable to the unscrupulous and unethical marketing practices of the greedy marketers. Sub-standard and spurious products are being passed on to the rural consumers under the brand name which are deceptively similar to the popular brand names. For example: 'Colgote' for 'Colgate'. Due to their lack of information, most of the rural consumers have less bargaining power. On the pack of the products the 'MRP' is printed but many rural consumers do not check it. They are being deceived by the spurious traders. There are also other unethical marketing practices like selling of prohibited drugs, misleading advertisement etc., and unscrupulous traders are openly flouting trade laws in rural areas.

Government Initiatives

To protect consumers from unethical and unscrupulous traders, Government of India and various State Governments have taken some preventive measures and enacted Acts. These are: (1) The Prevention of Black Marketing and Maintenance of Suppliers of Essential Commodities Act, 1980, (2) The Standards of Weights and Measures (Enforcement) Act, 1985, (3) The Bureau of Indian Standards Act, 1986,

(4) The Consumer Protection Act, 1986, (5) The Competition Act, 2002 etc. Recently, some awareness programmes have been taken up by the Department of Consumers Affairs and here are few examples:

(a) A campaign programme "*Jago Grahak Jago*" to focus on consumers' rights.
(b) The Scheme of Consumers Clubs in schools educates students about their rights as a consumer and to mobilize youngsters to strengthen the consumer movement in the country.
(c) The National Consumer Helpline has been launched by Department of Consumer Affairs to attend to consumer grievances from all-over India.

The Department of Consumer Affairs has engaged IIPA, New Delhi as the nodal agency of the Government of India, responsible to adopt consumer protection and welfare. However, traditional media can also create awareness of the rural consumers about the fake products and to protect them from unethical marketing.

Impact of Globalisation on Farmers

In India, roughly 90 per cent of the rural population is engaged in agriculture. In absolute terms they are nearly 600 million or 60 crore. Since 1990, when Globalisation was implemented in India many important changes have been made in cultivation (e.g. multi-cropping, the shift from rain-fed to irrigation dependent farming in many areas) and a certain degree of development of productive forces (in inputs like HYV seeds, machinery, techniques, skills) has taken place due to the opening of agriculture sector for the multinational companies and big corporations. Consequently, the cost of agricultural production has increased because cost of chemical fertilizers, pesticides, irrigation etc. has increased manifolds. The capital intensive and import based agricultural activity have naturally started displacing mostly poor, small and marginal peasants from land. Now, the estimated annual business from rural market of agri-inputs including tractors is worth Rs. 45,000 crore. Multinational agri-business companies like Cargill, Pepsico, Monsanto, ITC etc. are already in the field to monopolise this lucrative market. A new class has emerged in rural India during the period of globalisation that has been benefited by this process. These are mainly the rich and high middle class farmers. Many of the owners themselves do not till land, they supervise the agricultural activities and such supervising families are basically engaged in services in the Government or private sector or business especially related to agribusiness. In some places they also act as moneylenders and lend money to poor peasants at a high interest and control the local political power. Basically, these classes have more purchasing power and are the main customers for durable and other luxurious goods in rural India. The remaining poor and marginal peasants ironically who constitute the major portion in rural areas have been subjected to deep trouble in the era of globalisation and their purchasing power are too low and has been decreasing over the years. Small farmers in particular are least benefited by this globalisation whereas big farmers with their economic and political influence, are able to reap the benefits of globalisation as they can get best technologies, grow cash crops, negotiate agreements, and move their products. On the other hand, distressed peasants who are feeding the nation are mostly indebted. According to the National Crime Bureau record, in the ten years period between 1998 and 2008 as many as two lakh farmers have committed suicide in India.

Development Programmes by Governments

The five-year plans have witnessed massive investments in rural areas in terms of number of developmental programmes implemented by the Central and State Governments. These programmes have generated incomes to ruralites and helped them. Some of these programmes are:

- Intensive Agricultural District Programme (IADP-Package Programme)
- Intensive Agricultural Area Programme (IAAP)
- High Yielding Varieties Programme (HYVP-Green Revolution)
- Drought Prone Areas Programme (DPAP)
- Small Farmers Development Agency (SFDA)
- Hill Area Development Programme
- Operation Flood I, II and III (White Revolution)
- Fisheries Development (Blue Revolution)
- Integrated Rural Development Programme (IRDP)
- Jawahar Rojgar Yojana (JRY).

After the beginning of economic reforms in 1991, the Government has been giving special attention to the rural India by providing certain developmental schemes for these areas. Some announcements were made by the Finance Minister in the Union Budget to enrich the existing programmes and to initiate some new schemes for the rural areas like *Kisan Credit Cards*, *Micro Finance* and *Pardhan Mantri Gramodyog Yojana* etc. The latest budget is focused on agriculture and rural development.

Suggestions

A few initiatives of Government can ensure higher level of income of the farmers and these are:

Increase of Farm Income: If Government guarantee the farmers better prices for farm products and induces them to invest their surpluses in the purchase of modern inputs then the production and productivity may increase. This again results in an increase in the marketed surplus and income of the farmers. If the producer does not have an easy accessible market-outlet he would find it difficult to sell his surplus produce. This would have little incentive to produce more. The need for providing adequate incentives for increased production, is therefore, very important and this can be made possible only by the Government's help.

Protective Subsidies: Subsidies are given to farmers in industrial countries while other developing countries are discouraged. In some countries zero tariffs are imposed. United States gives over $18 billion a year in subsidies to its own farmers. This has affected prices of agri-products for farmers in other countries. Farmers in developing countries like India should be given subsidies by Governments. It will help farmers to create purchasing power in rural market.

Seed Saving: In India, peasants depend on farm-saved seeds as the primary seed source. Farmers who traditionally grew pulses, millets, and paddy have been lured by seed companies. Their native seeds have been displaced with new hybrids which cannot be saved and need to be purchased every season at a high cost. Hybrids are also very vulnerable to pest attacks. Spending on pesticides in some countries has increased to 2,000 per cent. Now farmers are consuming the same pesticides as a way of killing themselves so that they can escape permanently from unpaid debts. So, Government should take necessary steps immediately to provide alternative seeds to the farmers so that they are not forced to buy the genetically modified seeds.

Spread of Markets: Most of the farmers lack access to markets, where they can sell their products at profitable prices and purchase inputs and better technology. They also lack sufficient access to local markets and face unfair competition from subsidised imports. Inputs and outputs are controlled by multinational companies. Controlling both the inputs and the marketing of commodities jeopardises the farmers existence. In India trade regulations that govern international trade have affected the small farmers very much. A well-knit marketing system may widen the market for the products by taking them to remote corners both within and outside the country. The widening of the market helps in increasing the demand on a continuous basis and thereby guarantees a higher income to the producer.

Growth of Agro-based Industries: An improved and efficient system of agricultural marketing helps in the growth of agro-based industries and stimulates the overall development process of the economy. Many industries depend on agriculture for the supply of raw materials.

Strengthen Cooperatives: Cooperatives are expected to build up an organised system for underdeveloped agricultural growth in particular and rural development in general. Transfer of technology, fertiliser production and distribution, irrigation, processing of agricultural products, micro credits etc. are some of the roles which are played by the cooperative sector very effectively. The main advantage of cooperatives is that the farmer-members can sell their produce through co-operative marketing societies instead of commission agent or middlemen who usually adopt malpractices.

Inspection and Quality Control: To ensure the confidence of consumers, it is essential that grading is done in accordance with the standards that have been set. For this purpose, the inspection of the goods at regular intervals is essential. Inspection involves the testing of the graded goods to conform to the prescribed standards of quality.

Conclusion

Nearly 75 per cent of the total income in rural areas is related to agriculture and its related activities. So, now it can be said that growth in agriculture automatically leads to rural prosperity and in return provide a great potential for the marketers. So, it is the task of the marketers to decide as to which segment of rural consumers they want to cater. Today the rural market is a huge and untapped market, having a great potential. Development programmes in the field of agriculture and allied activities like health, education, communication, rural electrification etc. can improve the life of the rural populace and some market research agencies have forecast that the rural demand will supersede the urban demand in the coming future. So, there is a need to first understand the rural market not only in terms of households and population but also in terms of their occupational pattern, income generation, the process of rural and cottage industrialisation, rural buyer behavioural attitude and beliefs of rural people and their aspirations.

Agriculture is the centre of economic life in rural India. It provides employment to a majority of the working population of the village and gives them their primary identity. Globalisation demands export-oriented cash crop farming, free trade and discouragement of subsidies. Statistics show that the impact of globalisation has resulted in the decline of household subsistence production. Today, rural demographics is rapidly changing. So, it is an urgent and essential task for both the Central and the State Governments to protect the small, poor and marginal peasants and landless agricultural labourers who constitute the vast rural folk. In most of the villages, farmers are indebted to money-lenders, traders or landlords. They are often forced to enter into advance sale contracts or sell the produce to them at low prices. Hence, the Government task is to protect these farmers and provide them micro-loan by co-operatives or banks at low interest and provide marketing facilities and supply seeds, fertilizers, irrigation, electricity etc. for cultivation at cheaper price. These steps would then create the real demand for consumption in the rural market and result in the rural boom. Ultimately, this rural boom will help to strengthen the overall Indian economy.

REFERENCES

Acharya, S.S. & N.L. Agarwal, *Agricultural Marketing in India.*

Census of India, 2001.

Economic Review, 2011-12, Government of India.

Economictimes.indiantimes.com/news

EPW, *Review of Rural Affairs*, 2012.

Financialexpress.com/news

Gupta, S.L. *Rural Marketing Text and Cases.*

John Mano Raj, S., *Social Changes and the Growth of Indian Rural Market.*

Marketing: Thrust and Challenges, New Delhi: National Publishing House, 1997.

Pollack, Andrew. 2001 "The Green Revolution Yields to the Bottom Line." *New York Times*, May 15, 2001.

Shukla, R.K., "*New Perspective in Rural Marketing*".

Wath, M. and Preeti Agarwal, *Exploring Indian Rural Market: The Way Ahead.*

www.business-standard.com/india/news

www.rural.gov-ncaer.org

2

Globalisation and Rural Women Consumers

GEETANJALI DASH

Introduction

The human society around the world, over a period of time, has established greater contact, but the pace has increased rapidly since the mid-1980s. The term globalisation means international integration. It includes an array of social, political and economic changes. Unthinkable progress in modes of communications, transportation and computer technology have given the process a new lease of life. The world is more dependent now than ever before. Multinational companies manufacture products across many countries to sell consumers across the globe. Money, technology, and raw materials have broken international barriers. Not only products and finances, but also ideas and cultures have breached the national boundaries and have become international in character.

There is an emergence of a new cross-culture market as the world has become smaller and smaller due to the quickest and cheapest transport facilities and thereby a true global market place has developed, where growing global middle class consumers have emerged. This middle class consumer buys a lot of consumable goods without being judicious. A type of society has emerged where the manufacturers have organised on a global scale, and not the consumers. In this context, consumerism is fast developing, aimed at regulating the products or services, methods or standards of manufacturers, sellers or advertisers in the interest of buyers. This becomes a need of the hour as globalisation permeates the grassroots level of the society.

The term consumerism is used to refer to the consumerist movement or consumer activism, which seeks to protect and inform consumers by requiring such practices as honest packaging, product guarantees and improved safety standards. In this sense, it is a movement or a set of policies aimed at regulating the products, services methods and standards of manufactures, sellers and advertisers in the interests of the buyer, which can be termed as a step towards consumer protection.

Women Consumers

Women constitute nearly half of the world population. They are the largest consumers of a variety of products and services. The whole cosmetic and fashion industry runs on their goodwill as consumers. They buy variety of products daily and are most affected in terms of food adulteration, misleading advertisements, inferior quality of products and unfair trade practices. Perhaps they are the most exploited consumers in the market. The rural women consumers lack education and hence fall prey to the marketers. There are a number of studies conducted which reveals that housewives (home-makers) were the actual buyers for the food in the family. Home-makers took independent decision in all the areas of food buying except financial aspect. Studies have highlighted that "availability of money resource and availability of the product" in the market were the most important factors, whereas "food habit" and "nutritional requirements" were the least important factors while buying a product. On the other hand, low income group home-makers preferred rationing store, and independent store for the groceries and miscellaneous items. For the selection of stores low income group home-maker gave more importance to credit facilities, lowest price and location of the store. Majority of the housewives (home-makers) from low income group collected all information from friends and neighbours. Among housewives (home-makers) retail shops are more used than wholesale shops for purchasing grains, monthly purchasing was most common among the employed and unemployed home-makers for grains and grocery.

If we want this movement to grow, more women will have to come in. Consumer movement has to move towards pro-poor, pro-rural, pro-women. Although efforts have been made to detect the percentage of food adulteration in number of cities—big and small, none of the study deals with knowledge and awareness of women (home-maker) about food adulteration. That is why it is necessary to generate awareness among the housewives (home-makers) about the existing food adulteration practices of the retailers and manufacturers and equip them with simple household test for detecting adulteration.

It is highly unlikely that more legislations or increasing fines and jail terms alone will help reduce adulteration, particularly given the corruption that exists in the enforcement area and the low conviction rate. Greater consumer vigilance and action alone can help improve the situation. But such efforts are not fruitful unless consumers themselves are aware of their rights and responsibilities. Under these circumstances, consumer literacy is the need of the hour with special attention to low income groups particularly living in the rural areas who suffer the most.

International Development

History of consumer protection can be traced to the United States of America in the early part of the twentieth century which passed through the stages of its development in 40s, losing vigour in 50s and early 60s but taking a real shape thereafter with Ralph Nader's single handed crusade against the mighty automobile industry. On the 15th March, 1962 when the Bill for Consumer Rights was moved in the US Congress, President John F. Kennedy had remarked, "If a consumer is offered inferior products, if prices are exorbitant, if drugs are unsafe or worthless, if the consumer is unable to choose on an informed basis, when his dollar is wasted, his health and safety may be threatened, and national interest suffers." They equated the rights of the ordinary consumer with national interest. He gave four basic consumer rights:

1. *The Right to Safety*—to be protected against the marketing of goods which are hazardous to health and life.
2. *The Right to Choose*—to be assured, whenever possible access to a variety of products and services at competitive process and in those industries where competition is not workable and Government regulation is substituted, an assurance of satisfactory quality and services at fair prices.
3. *The Right to Information*—to be protected against fraudulent, deceitful or grossly misleading information, advertising, labelling or other practices is to be given the facts he/she needs to make an informed choice.
4. *The Right to be Heard*—to be assured that consumer interest will receive full and sympathetic consideration in the formulation of Government policy and fair and expeditious treatment in its

> administrative tribunal. Thirteen years later, the then American President General Ford had felt that the four rights constituted in Kennedy's Bill of Rights were inadequate for a situation where most consumers are not educated enough to make the right choices. So, he added the right to consumer education as an informed consumer cannot be exploited easily.

The Guidelines for Consumer Protection adopted by General Assembly of the United Nations on 9th April, 1985 provided further impetus to the protection of consumer interest. These guidelines provided a framework for the Government in enacting and amending their consumer protection laws. The main objectives were to:

(a) Assist countries in achieving or maintaining adequate protection for their population as consumer.
(b) Facilitate production and distribution pattern responsive to the needs and desire of consumers.
(c) Further, international cooperation in the field of consumer protection.
(d) Promote and protect the economic interest of the consumers and the interest of the consumers and the availability of effective consumer redress.
(e) Encourage high levels of ethical conduct of those engaged in the production and distribution of goods and services to the consumers.
(f) Assist countries in curbing abusive business practices by all entrepreneurs at national and international level which adversely affects consumers.
(g) Facilitate the development of independent consumer goods.
(h) Encourage market condition which provides consumer with greater choice at lower prices.

Consumer Protection in India

In India, as in other countries, the need for consumerism is a necessary step to be taken for the protection of the consumers. Though references are made even in Kautilya's *Arthashastra* to protect the consumers against the exploitation by the trade and industry, adulteration, and punishment for these offences, consumer movement found a clear conception during the freedom movement of 40s when Mahatma Gandhi took a lead in this direction. Gandhi has been defined as the greatest Consumer advocate the world has ever seen. Gandhi's concern for the consumer is reflected in the following statement "a customer is the most important visitor on our premise. He is not dependent on us. We are dependent on him. He is not an interruption in our work; rather he is the purpose of it. We are not doing him a favour by serving him. He is doing us a favour by giving us an opportunity to serve him. Year 1949 saw the first consumer organisation in India established by a Gandhian, R.P. Dalvai in Madras. Since then the consumer movement in India started taking shape and assumed the role of a pressure group, with few mass organisations. After 1986, India provided legal measures to consumers by promulgating the Consumer Protection Act, which came as a panacea for consumers all-over the country, providing swift and inexpensive justice right at the doorstep of the aggrieved consumers.

Ways and Means of Consumer Protection in India

Consumer Protection Act—Aims and Objectives

Consumer Protection Act, 1986, which shifted the emphasis from caveat emptor "Let the buyer be aware" to caveat venditor "let the seller be aware" was enacted with a view to provide quick, inexpensive, easy and time bound solution to consumer grievances. Explaining the objectives of the Act, the Apex Court has observed, "It attempts to remove the helplessness of a consumer which he faces against powerful business, described as a network of racketeers or a society in which procedures have secured powers "to rob the rest" and the might of public body which are degenerating into store house of inaction where chapters don't move from one desk to another as a matter of duty and responsibility but the extraneous consideration leaving the common man helpless, bewildered and shocked. The malady is so rampant, widespread and deep that the society instead of fighting against is accepting it as a part of life. The enactment in these unbelievable yet harsh realities appears to be silver lining which in course of home succeeds in checking the rot." [Ref: Lucknow Development Authority *Vs.* M.K. Gupta, 1993 CTJ 929 (SC) (CP)].

Rights of the Consumer

The Act seeks to promote and protect the various rights of the consumers, *viz.*

(a) The right to be protected against marketing of goods or services which are hazardous to life and property.
(b) The right to be informed about the quality, quantity, potency and purity, standard and price of goods or service to protect the consumers against unfair trade practices.
(c) The right to be assured, wherever possible, competitive prices.
(d) The right to seek redressal against unfair trade practices or unscrupulous exploitation of consumers.
(e) The right to be heard and to be assured that consumer interest will receive due consideration at appropriate forums.
(f) The right to consumer education.

Other Initiatives

Lok Adalats

The consumer can approach the *Adalat* with his grievance. The issue is discussed and decision is taken on the spot. This saves time and money. *Lok Adalat* has become a speedy, effective and economical redressal system. Indian Railways, Delhi Transport Corporation, Delhi Development Authority, Delhi Vidyut Board etc. hold *Lok Adalat* from time-to-time to sort out problems faced by users.

Publicity Measures

Every year 15th March is celebrated as World Consumer Rights Day all-over the World. In addition, the Ministry undertook a massive outdoor publicity programme such as displaying hoardings, banners, bus panels etc. Telecasting programme on consumer protection also done fortnightly.

Redressal Forums and Consumer Protection Councils

Under the Consumer Protection Act of 1986, a quasi-judicial machinery such as District Forums, State and National Commissions have been set-up to provide speedy, effective and economical redressal of consumer grievances and disputes within stipulated time.

Environment Friendly Products

The Ministry of Environment and Forests has introduced an "Eco-mark" scheme. It is a label that has a symbol of an earthen pitcher. If this label appears on a product, it means that the manufacturer has satisfied the conditions laid down, regarding the production, process and used environmental friendly materials. This scheme has been started with consumer items like soap, detergent, paints, food items, edible oil etc. This scheme is consumer oriented so that people manufacture, use and dispose of products which are least harmful to the environment.

Consumer Education in Schools/Colleges Syllabus

Many School Boards and Universities have formally introduced consumer education in their curriculum. In 1994, the Maharashtra Education Board introduced consumer education at the 9th Standard level, progressively covering students from the 4th standard. The CBSC has also introduced in its school curriculum and efforts are on to persuade other institutions also to incorporate a chapter on Consumer Protection to enhance awareness about consumer rights. Many Law Universites have also started courses in Consumer Welfare.

Consumer Clubs in Schools and Colleges

The government has funded the setting-up a large number of consumer clubs in schools and colleges. A variety of activites are carried out by these clubs to educate the students and the consumers. They have been found to be a very effective mechanism to reach the students and through them the community, particularly in the rural areas.

National Youth Award on Consumer Protection

To encourage young consumers to participate in the field of consumer protection, every year the Union Minister gives two national awards—National Award on Consumer Protection and National Youth Award on Consumer Protection. The Ministry also gives a National Woman Award to involve women outstanding work in the field of consumer protection. However, of late this is not being done.

Protecting Rural Consumer

If we observe the profile of India's consumers, we find that 73 per cent of the total population lives in rural area and the rural share of popular consumer goods and durables ranges from 30 per cent to 60 per cent. Though the rural consumer was not an important segment in the market due to the low purchasing power and the inaccessibility of the business agencies in rural areas, after 1991 onwards, the emergence of a liberalised and privatised economy has given rise to varied marketing policies which business agencies have adopted to attract rural consumers. In this age of a cut throat competition, the consumers are the centre of focus and when the urban market is saturated day by day, the rural consumer has become their target. So, there is a growing need to protect the interest of these rural consumers as they are more vulnerable to the market forces due to their ignorance. So, educating the rural consumers has become a necessity. To make consumer movement a nation-wide movement, it is of utmost importance. There are certain problems relating to rural consumers:

- Market structure is dichotomous, having rural and urban markets.
- Rural market is not developed, as the urban market. But the rural market is growing fast, has not reached the saturation point unlike urban market. It is more or less unexplored till now. The increase in literacy rate may be a factor, as compared to the other south Asian countries.
- Socio-economic changes in villages have led villages to think of material well-being.
- Change in the attitude of farmers is sweeping across the country. Expanding rural market is also important to the growth of economic development of India. Marketing focus is also changing towards villages "go rural" is the slogan of marketing *gurus*.
- Untapped rural consumers face a lot of problems such as they are not in a position to distinguish between the ordinary and fake brands.
- The main difference between urban and rural consumers is that the urban consumer will go to consumer court of there is any problem with the product he consumed, but the rural consumer does not know what to do with the product because of the lack of awareness in them.

Indian Rural Market—A Scenario

Rural market is one of the growing markets, the potentiality of the rural market is said to be like "awoken of sleeping giant". Countries like China and India shows the augmentation of rural markets. There are certain reasons for this like increase in the standard of living of the rural people and also Government provides a number of incentives and subsidies, development of transportation facilities and communication network.

Main Difficulties

- They don't have a stable or regular pattern of buying, as the rural market depends upon agricultural situation, and agriculture to a very large extent depends upon monsoon.
- Many rural areas are not connected by rail transport. Interior village roads become inaccessible during monsoon and other natural calamities, thereby disrupting the flow of consumer goods to various localities.
- Distribution—an effective distribution system requires village-level shopkeeper, Mandal/Taluka-Level wholesaler or preferred dealer, distributor or stockist at district level and company owned department or consignment distribution, at state level. The presence of too many tiers in the distribution system increases the cost of distribution.

Communication Problems

Facilities such as telephone, fax and telegram are rather poor in rural areas. Moreover, life in rural areas is still governed by customs and traditions and people don't easily adapt new practices. For example, even rich and educated class of farmers does not wear jeans or branded shoes. But this type of mind-set is changing very fast.

Media for Promotion

Television has made a great impact and large audience has been exposed to this medium. Radio reaches large population in rural areas at a relatively low cost. However, reach of formal media is low in rural households. Therefore, the market has to undertake specific sales promotion activities in rural areas like participating in *melas* or fairs. The major reason behind the type of change in rural scenario is our response to globalization. Over the last decade, Indian economy has transformed from sluggish and inward-looking into one of the fastest growing in the world which may be ascribed to the expansion of electronic media. In this backdrop, the desire of the multinationals to do business in the Indian market has resulted in the rapid spread of FMCG products like toilet soaps, shampoo, mobile phones etc. in both rural and urban India.

Most of the FMCG corporate treat rural markets as dumping grounds for low end-products. Added to it, India's 460 billion FMCG market remains highly fragmented with roughly half the market going to unbranded, unpackaged home-made products. Rural mass, especially women, are either illiterate or with little education. They also feel allured by the media and colourful advertisements in various forms. They are ignorant of the business mechanisms of the corporate; they identify a product by its size, price, visual and colour. Consequently, a large quantity of counterfeit products enters into the market. Women and young girls are very much influenced by the cosmetics, which come in tiny sachets. Different companies like Godrej and Coca Cola produce more product variants with attractive prices to attract rural women. Rural people have more cash in hand following monsoon and consumers are more inclined to spend a great deal more during this period.

Two fast-growing categories in the FMCG sector are food and personal beauty care products. These products have been spread among the rural women because of their cheap price, and they can not realise their impact on health. This creates health hazards for the rural women. Some of these substances can trigger complications in a woman's body. These also amount to serious violation of human rights of the consumers.

Most of these FMCG companies use rural markets as dumping grounds for low end-products which are basically designed for urban markets. There is a proliferation of spurious products these days. FMCG market in India remains fragmented with roughly half the market going to unbranded, unpackaged, home-made products. Rural masses are either illiterate, or with little education and ignorant and they identify a product by its packaging. When they go to the shop, they ask for "*panch rupiahwala sabun dena*". So, it becomes very easy to counterfeit products to eat into the market share of established and reputed brands. Retailers also get larger share of profit on selling the counterfeits, so they are biased in favour of these, instead of the genuine ones. Such products use low quality materials which has serious health impact in the long-run.

Impact of Cosmetics on Women's Health

India provides the 13th largest market in the world in case of cosmetics. Women in rural India use common cosmetics everyday to maintain their skin and beauty. Health conscious women today use many bio-products which are too costly. Rural middle class neither has the money to afford such products nor have the knowledge to know the utility of different herbal items. The reasons are obvious, due to the diversity and inequity. But recently, rural women have seen marked improvements in their living standards. This has resulted in the spread of cosmetics that the urban women use, without knowing the negative impact on health.

The cosmetics of relatively cheaper variety use lower quality ingredients. Many experts believe that foundations that come in liquid form contain mineral oil which has been classified as petrochemical pollutant by the US Government. These creams when used daily can prove to be carcinogenic. Choosing the wrong foundation can lead to premature skin ageing and hormonal imbalance. Many of these anti-wrinkle creams contain lanolin, dioxins, pesticides and some more animal by-products. Nail-polish is a favoured cosmetic among adolescent and young girls. Many popular nail-polishes contain toluene, phenol and xyline. Continued exposure to these products causes harm like fatigue, headaches and nausea. Nail-polish also contains formaldehyde which has been shown to cause discoloration of nails. Most women use acetone for removing nail polish. Acetone can cause rashes, and can also lead to adverse respiratory effects when inhaled. All these are serious health concerns and needs attention of policy-makers.

With the increasing use of cable and satellite television, the rural people have an increasing access to all these means of communication, which can be instrumental in consumer education. The role of electronic media has acquired a greater significance given the fact that majority of rural population is illiterate or semi-literate and hence, this media can be best used for a more effective dissemination of message and information of consumer interest. Instead of misleading the rural consumer, they should try to educate the consumers in a more constructive manner.

REFERENCES

Consumerism.answers.com.

Dixit, Kavadeep, *Rural Marketing Issues and Strategies, Marketing Mastermind*, Vol. VII, issue 8, Hyderabad: the ICFAI University Press, 29-36.

Dogra, Balram, Karnider Ghuman, 2008, *Rural Marketing Concepts and Practices*, New Delhi: Tata McGraw Hill Publishing House.

Meenu Agrawal, 2006, *Consumer Behaviour and Consumer Protection in India*, New Delhi: New Century Publications.

Ramaswamy V.S., S. Namakumari, 2004, *Marketing Management—Planning Implementation and Control,* New Delhi: MacMillan.

Veblen, Torstein, 1994 *The Theory of the Leisure Class: An Economic Study of Institutions,* New York: Dover Publications, Mineola.

3

A Roadmap to Rural Market Penetration

CHITRA KASANA

Introduction

For the first time since Independence, the absolute increase in population is more in urban areas than in rural areas. As per the data of 2011 Census, the Rural-Urban distribution is 68.84 per cent and 31.16 per cent respectively. Further, the improvement in literacy rate in rural area is two times that in urban areas; and rural urban literacy gap which was 21.2 percentage points in 2001, has come down to 16.1 percentage points in 2011.

Against this backdrop, the scope of rural demand for consumable and durable goods is far greater than the urban sector, especially in terms of quantum. It is a gold mine for marketers. Yet this sector remains untapped, neglected and undervalued by the Corporate. Current chapter adheres to identifying the existing characteristics of rural areas that discourage and frustrate the Corporate to cater to the vast market potential of rural India. And then recommend entry strategies that will lead to sustainable business prepositions. If the Corporates do not compete in the rural market they will keep themselves out of about half of the country's market.

Methodology

Dealing with a heterogeneous clusters each with different groups based on religion, caste, occupation, income, age, education, behaviours it was befitting to go for multifarious research methods to be able to understand the real scenario of rural markets in terms of changes in lifestyles due to rise in income and literacy; buying behaviour and factors influencing buying behaviour; socio-economic position and bearings; proximity to town and cities (urban-impact); occupational category; income flows and economic conditions. Therefore, a survey based on structured questions was conducted randomly for 20 villages of Haryana and Western Uttar Pradesh. The enumerators were trained to fill-in the schedule and gather "between-the-lines information" through observation and interview techniques. Each enumerator submitted their viewpoints which were incorporated along with Expert opinion from the industry. A "partial Delphi method approach", was adopted to verify results, and variations if any.

The Rural Environment

The rural environment can be bifurcated into 'structural' and 'behavioural'. From a marketing perspective the peculiar characteristics of rural areas in this part of India have been observed as:

Structural	*Behavioural*
• Large and scattered market. • Major income from agriculture (irregular and seasonal). • Low standard of living. • Diverse socio-economic backwardness. • Inadequate infrastructure facilities. • Lack of proper physical communication facilities. • Dispersed markets. • Low per capita income. • Low purchasing power. • Low levels of literacy. • Prevalence of spurious brands and seasonal demand. • Small and marginal farmers. • Agricultural labourers and artisans constitute the largest segment. • Computer education at the bare minimum.	• Traditional outlook. • Many languages and dialects. • Different way of thinking. • Joint-family decision-making functioning. • Semi-literate culture and behaviours. • Festivals are important aspect of life. • Marriages still dominated by dowry system and spend thrift demonstration effects. • Risk averts. • Value conscious. • Suspicious and apprehensive towards new experiments. • Lack of confidence in using technology, especially computers and internet. • Deflecting male/female behaviours. • Enlarged media reach through T.V. channels.

There are different groups based on religion, caste, occupation, income, age, education and politics and each group exerts influence on the behaviour of people in villages. Considering the environment in which rural markets operate and other related problems it is imperative to evolve effective strategies. Based on the characteristics, an appropriate segmentation of a highly heterogeneous rural market can be realized with following combinations:

1. Landholding size and Income levels.
2. Educational levels and Progressiveness.
3. Occupational category and Mix of Enterprises.
4. Proximity to towns and cities and people in jobs in nearby cities.

Marketing Mix

Based on our survey findings, we advocate the following approaches:

Product Strategies

Innovative products, differentiated packaging, value-for-money offerings, utility-based solutions are required to get to the goldmine named Rural Marketing.

(i) Small units and low-priced packing.
(ii) Rural oriented names and brands which are eye-catching for illiterate and semi-literate folks.
(iii) Product design keeping their lifestyle in mind.
(iv) Sturdy Products—the product meant for rural areas should be sturdy enough to stand rough handling and unmannerly storage.
(v) Colours Usage—bright colour combinations red, yellow, blue, green, gaudy pink (but avoid Black as they opine it as bad).

Pricing Strategies

Since, the rural consumers are price and value sensitive, utility conscious, their demand is highly elastic. A small increase in rural income will result in an exponential increase in buying power, and likewise a marginal decrease in prices would increase demand. The biggest challenge in rural markets is to create a brand loyalty among the consumers. An unorganized low price products retail sector gives a fierce competition to retail biggies, as it is difficult for the retail companies to cut down on costs as compared to their local counterparts and maintain the same brand loyalty. A large segment of rural India in this region has exhibited preference to low priced products.

(i) Low cost/cheap products.
(ii) Avoid sophisticated packing; loose packs that can be touched and felt by the buyer is preferred.
(iii) Give preference to re-fill packs in small and medium size/reusable packaging.
(iv) Match value with affordable levels of income and purchase.
(v) Price reduction by passing overhead expenditure to suit rural income, and still maintaining marginal profits.
(vi) Do not compromise with utility and sturdiness of the product.

Distribution Strategies

Cost and logistics are the challenge but need to be addressed today or tomorrow because large potential customers are residing in rural areas of our country and their income and purchasing power are increasing, along with product awareness through T.V. Channels. The survey indicated that T.V. advertisements with jingles were more effective. Use of village background was also more effectual as they could associate themselves with the advertisers/artists on the screen. Effective distribution is directly proportional to cost, and hence, an effective distribution system requires village-level shopkeeper, Taluka level wholesalers/dealers, distributors or stockist at district or block level and company-owned depot. There is a belief among rural people that experience is more important than formal education. Therefore, it is desirable that sales persons, especially those who have been brought up in cities are given thorough training consisting of both theory and practical aspects of village life.

A better alternative is to breed rural managers. We often hear of young people leaving agriculture and moving to the city in search of opportunities and jobs. The key to rural upliftment and rural access lies in action-plan jointly by industry and Government to enhance rural capacity in rural areas. Using the "Sons of the Soil", is more effective, as they are more adaptive and groomed with local sentiments, dialects, local life-styles and expectations. Internally backed human resources can create everlasting relationship, and because loyalty depends on relationship, brand awareness and brand loyalty can be generated through local participation.

People in the rural areas mostly do not prefer places which look costly or have a rich ambience. Therefore, a Mall Culture may not be appropriate. Outlets should be developed in such a way that they are simple in appearance and not too costly, which would otherwise create hesitation and doubt in the simple-minded rural folks. Few approaches that will assist in rural penetration:

(i) Supplies based on characteristics of the product, its shelf life and demand pattern.
(ii) Use the existing co-operative society's distribution network.
(iii) Horizontal Marketing System—where two or more companies can join hands to use collective facilities or club their products for twin sales.
(iv) Multi-purpose distribution centres.
(v) Bulk distribution to feeder markets/*mandies*/*hats*/*melas*.
(vi) Tie-up with agriculture input dealers.
(vii) Rural skills development programme initiative for educated rural unemployed youth, as part of CSR and building sales teams.

Promotional Strategies

Rural market is comparatively easy to understand, as the purchase trends can be mapped over a period of a year. Most of the patterns are seasonal in trend. Cash-Flows depend on harvesting periods and expenditures on Festivals and marriage occasions. Marriage seasons are dependent on Horoscope periods in a year. Mapping the time trend and demand patterns will decide the marketing communication and timing of sales promotion.

Life in rural areas is wrapped by customs and traditions and people are disinclined to try new products and practices. It is hard to convince them and this is one of the main barriers to introducing new products.

(i) Communication in vernacular language is an important aspect.
(ii) Logos and symbols to be folklore oriented.
(iii) Brands to be promoted with the help of celebratory endorsement, with whom they can associate with faith and trust.
(iv) Start small but think big, back it up with lots of planning and realism.
(v) Word of mouth is more germane than mere billboard appearance.
(vi) Creating First Time Users—Free small size samples as combo

packs attached with the main purchase will give them a chance to use the product and build positive impression for recurrent purchase. (As per the survey—this would be a substitute of the 'lubhave' concept used by village *baniyas* to attract the customers to his shop. And as endorsed by the households about their trust on local shopkeeper.)

Cracking a Tough Market

Companies like Hindustan Unilever Ltd., Dabur, P&G, Ghari generate more than half of their revenues from rural India. Products of Colgate Palmolive India and Marico drive nearly 40 per cent of their revenue from rural markets. The companies are adopting innovative techniques to attract rural consumers. HUL launched a unique combo pack of Clinic shampoo bottle, fair & lovely and pond's dream flower talc for rural markets. Coca cola attracted rural consumers by reducing the price of its 200 ml bottle to INR 5 as rural consumers are very keen to buy products at discounted rate.

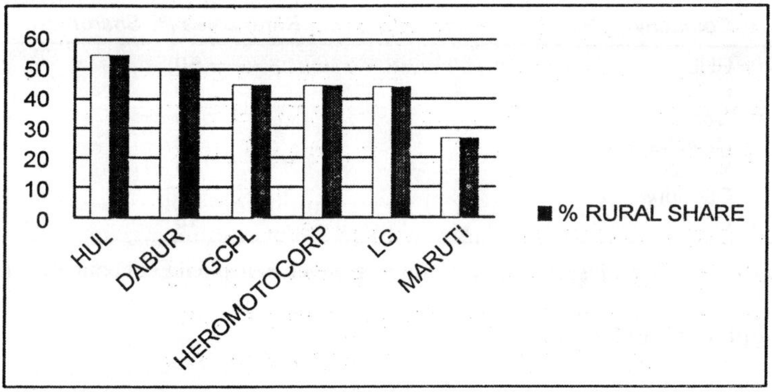

Fig. 3.1: Rural Market Share 2013-14

Source: MART Knowledge centre.

FMCG products which hold great potential in rural and semi-urban markets include soaps, detergents, cold drinds, consumer durables, toothpastes, batteries, biscuits, namkeens, mosquito, repellents, refined oil, and hair oil (Table 3.1).

Table 3.1: Top FMCG Companies of Rural Markets of India

Companies	FY12	FY13	FY14
ITC	267	309	355
HUL	229	261	298
Nestle	76	94	117
Dabur	51	59	69
Marico	39	45	53
GCPL	45	55	64
Britannia Ind	53	63	74

Source: The Great Indian Market National Council of applied Economic Research.

Regular Rural Demand

As per our Survey there is an increasing demand for the following products in the rural areas.

Many companies have already taken to the rural markets in a big way.

Table 3.2: Company Sales of Rural Areas in Percentage

Company	Rural Sales (% Share)
HUL	50
Colgate	50
Godrej	30
Cavinkare	33
Marico	25
Cadbury	25
Cipla	18

Source: The Great Indian Market National Council of applied Economic Research.

Regular Rural Demand

As per our survey there is an increasing demand for the following products in the rural areas:

- Pressure Cooker
- Cooking utensils
- Batteries (Torch)
- Agriculture related tools
- Diesel pump
- Pressure pumps
- Cycles, bikes, scooters

- Radio/Tape recorders
- Pesticides
- Tea
- Toothbrush/paste
- Sewing machines
- Artificial jewellery/Bangles
- Cheap cosmetics
- Medicines (OTC) (analgesic)(Paracetamol)(Balm)
- Tobacco and products
- Bathing soaps, washing cakes, washing powder
- Cell Phones
- Fans and coolers
- T.V.
- Wrist watches
- Clothes/readymade children wear.

Who Buys the High-Priced Durables in Rural Areas?

NCAER (National Council for Applied Economic Research) classified durables into 3 categories:—

- Low priced durables—watches, radios, irons, fans etc.
- Relatively higher priced durables—TV, sewing machines, mixer 2-in-1, music system.
- High aspiration and high priced—colour TV, refrigerators, motorised two-wheelers.

Our survey showed that high priced goods were only purchased for weddings as dowry display. People purchase these goods as demo effect and social compulsion to maintain harmony. There was a two-way flow concept that was observed and also admitted by households—"While we give away dowry, likewise we also receive the expensive durable goods in return as dowry."

Conclusion

Rural India is a major part of India's domestic consumption story today. Our survey was 'hard-won information', shedding new lights on rural-consumer behaviour; perception and decision-making behaviours of the sample villages taken into consideration. The companies eyeing the rural areas of India can utilize the base information while in the process to plunge into unknown areas. There has to be a collective, concentrated approach to build priority infrastructure through Government intervention, which either removes impediments to rural market entry, or creates opportunities for growth. If full potential of rural demand is met out we can expect an exponential growth in employment. The dependency on primary sector will be substituted by secondary sector contribution to GDP. Consumption patterns will change with ever-rising incomes. In fact, if we profile the creamy layer of the rural households which are in the top quintile (20%) in terms of income, we find that 39 per cent are land-owning farmers, 31 per cent are regular salary/wage earners and another 18 per cent are self-employed in non-agricultural activities. The point to be considered when examining all rural data is that even a small percentage of rural population is relatively large count in terms of number. Let the Corporate play on this number game.

Acknowledgements: The Author acknowledges the support and contribution of the group of enumerators, especially, Arush Singh Rathour, Deepak Singh and Kumar Harsh, who are undergraduate students and voluntary agreed to do the survey. The author is indebted to the expert opinions of Dr. V.K. Pandey, Abhishek Srivastava and Mr. Shrirang Altekar.

4

Rural Marketing

Big Potential in Small Markets

SOURABH MUNJAL

Introduction

It is widely acclaimed that India is one of the largest consumer market in the world. Estimation signs that the Indian consumer market is likely to grow four times by 2025 (McKinsey Report—"The Rise of Indian Consumer Market"). India's overall retail sector is expected to rise to US$ 833 billion by 2013 and to US$ 1.3 trillion by 2018, at a Compound Annual Growth Rate (CAGR) of 10 per cent. As a democratic country with high growth rates, consumer spending has risen sharply as the youth population (more than 33 per cent of the country is below the age of 15) has seen a significant increase in its disposable income. Consumer spending rose an impressive 75 per cent in the past four years alone. But the consumer in India shows wide variation in size and potential of various consumer market segments. These differences can be seen in terms of geographical differences, urban-rural consumer (there style of living, consumption pattern etc.), age and family life cycle, income level, education level, linguistic and religion diversity, food habit, festival etc. Marketers are trying to determine the underlying need and motive of consumer as well as various factors which influence the formation of these needs and satisfaction of these needs in every sector.

India's Rural Scenario

India lives in villages, close to 72 per cent of Indian population lives in rural area. In the country we have 6.45 lakh villages out of which only 13 per cent villages have population above 2000. However, percentage of rural population has fallen in 2011 as compared to 2001 but there is significant growth in total number of population in rural India (Table 4.1 and Figure 4.1). The rural economy contributes nearly half of the country's GDP which is mainly agriculture driven and monsoon dependent. More than 50 per cent of the sales of FMCG and Durable companies come from the rural areas. The McKinsey Report on "the Rise on Consumer Market in India" predicts that in twenty years the rural Indian market will be larger than the total consumer markets in countries such as South Korea or Canada today, and almost four times the size of today's urban Indian market and estimated the size of the rural market at $577 billion.

Table 4.1: Population of India (in millions)

	Total	*Urban*	*Rural*	*% Rural*
2011	1,210.19	377.10	833.08	68.84
2001	1,028.74	286.25	742.49	72.79
1991	846.42	215.74	630.68	74.51
1981	683.33	157.68	525.65	76.92

Source: Census, 2011.

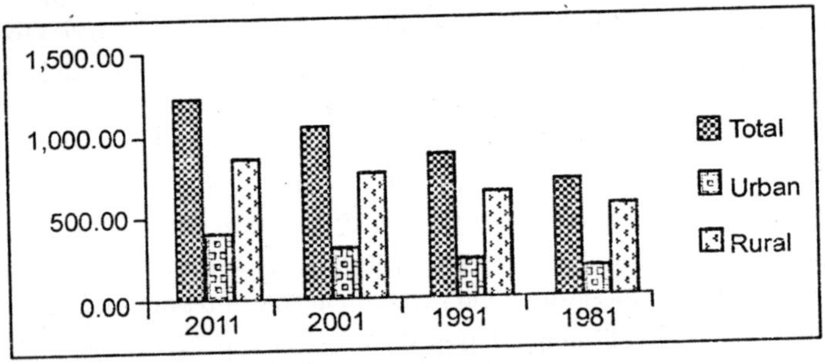

Figure 4.1: Population of India.

Households in the rural India have increased from 138 million to 167 million in last ten years from 2001 to 2011, which is much higher than urban households. Total household income is also projected to increase Rs. 1,56,000 cr. in 2015 according to NCAER-CMCR study. Between, 1981 and 2011, there has been tremendous improvement in the literacy levels, poverty and rural housing in the villages of the country. Rural literacy levels have improved from 36 per cent to 69 per cent. With increase in literacy levels today's rural consumer is more aware and demanding more in terms of quality and rights.

Table 4.2: No. of Households in India (in millions)

Year	*Total*	*Urban*	*Rural*
2011	246	78	167
2001	193	55	138
1991	152	40	112

Source: Census, 2011.

Table 4.3: Household Income 2015 (Rs. in crores)

	Rural	*Urban*
2009-10	1,23,000	2,50,000
2015-16	1,56,000	3,50,000

Source: NCAER-CMCR.

Table 4.4: Literacy Rate in Rural (%)

1981	*1991*	*2001*	*2011*
36%	45%	59%	69%

Source: Census, 2011.

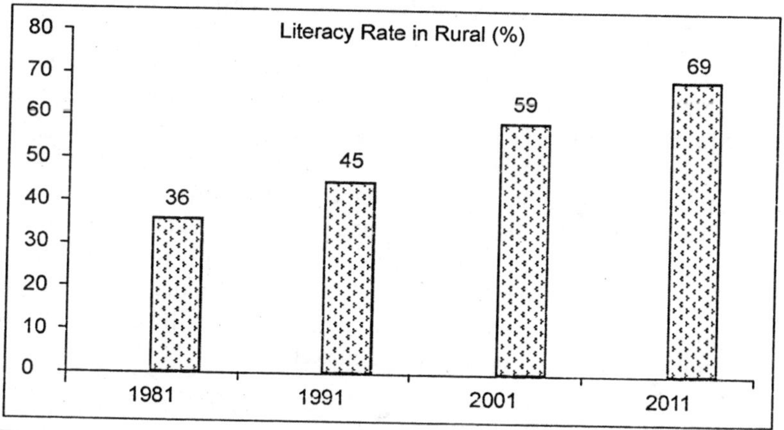

Figure 4.2: Literacy Rate in Rural.

Difference Between Urban and Rural Consumer

Urban and rural consumers differ in many ways. An urban consumer is in touch with his social group on a frequent basis, though not in a face-to-face manner. Compared to urban social occasions of parties, social gatherings, the rural community is more close knit with its *choupal*, community meetings, where people interact with each other on a daily basis. Urban consumer prefer more luxury as compared to rural, their purchasing decision rely more on utilization and basic needs. For example, car for urban users gets replaced by a more tractor for rural audiences. Moreover, there is significant difference between purchasing decisions; urban consumer is more independent in decision-making as compared to rural which is more influenced by family members.

Indian Rural Market

While urban areas will constitute the fastest-growing part of the Indian market, rural areas currently hold more than 70 per cent of India's population and have historically accounted for more than half of Indian consumption. Presently, the rural market accounts for a hefty share in most market segments—55 per cent of LIC policies, 70 per cent of toilet soaps, 50 per cent of TV, fans, bicycles, tea and wrist watches. With urban markets getting saturated, most companies are looking at huge potential in rural markets. Major corporations have seen great success with innovative strategies such as smaller packaging. Fast Moving Consumer Goods (FMCG) companies have creams and soaps priced at Rs. 5, hair oil and shampoo sachets at Rs. 2 and small Coke at Rs. 8. Companies have developed special products for the rural market, like Chic Shampoo sachets priced at Re 1, Parle G Tikki Packs at Rs. 2, customised televisions by LG, Shanti Amla oil by Marico. Even with increasing urbanisation and migration, 63 per cent of India's population will still live in rural areas in 2025. Thus, the rural market has been, and will remain, vitally important to the Indian economy. Rural consumption will have nearly tripled by 2025, creating a large potential market worth over 26 trillion Indian rupees ($577 billion). In the next 20 years the rural Indian market will be almost four times the size of today's urban Indian market.

Expanding Size

Consumption in rural India is growing faster than in urban India for the first time in last two decades, according to report of Crisil Ltd. (a credit rating agency). Between 2009-10 and 2011-12, additional spending by rural India was Rs. 3,750 billion, significantly higher than Rs. 2,994 billion by residents of urban areas. The growth in rural consumption is fuelled by a rise in household incomes due to greater non-farm job opportunities and Government initiated employment generation schemes. The Indian rural market has gained significance in the recent times as the overall economic growth of the country has led to an improvement in the living standards of the rural people. The boon of the Green Revolution combined with Government initiatives such as subsidies, loan waivers, and minimum support prices (MSP) and employment schemes (MNREGA) have caused an increase in purchasing power.

Table 4.5: Incremental Consumption Expenditure in 2011-12 over 2009-10 (in billion)

Urban	*Rural*
2994	3750

Source: NSSO and CRISIL.

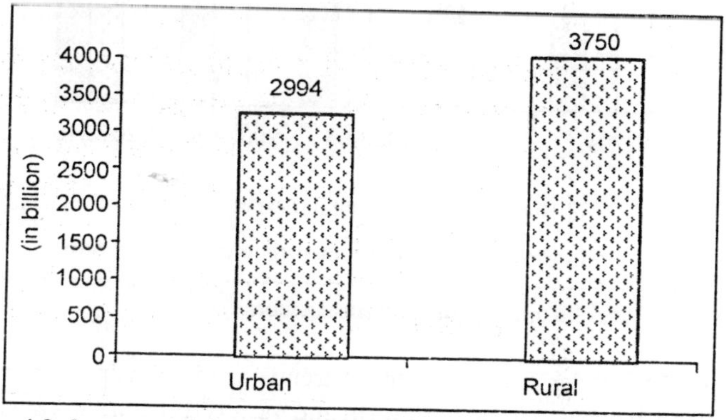

Figure 4.3: Incremental Consumption Expenditure in 2011-12 over 2009-10.

Purchasing power of rural consumer increased in the last few decades with increase in farm and non-farm income. Initially, the impact of green revolution could be seen only in the prosperous agricultural states of the country but now slowly its influence has spread across the country with the increase in irrigation (Bhalla and Singh, 2001). Though the income levels overall are still very low there are many pockets of prosperity which have come up in the rural areas in the country.

Table 4.6: Rural Income (% of total rural income)

	Farm	*Non-Farm*
1970s	74	26
1980s	66	34
1993-94	58	42
2007-08	40	60
2015-16 (Projected)	32	68

Source: NCAER-CMCR.

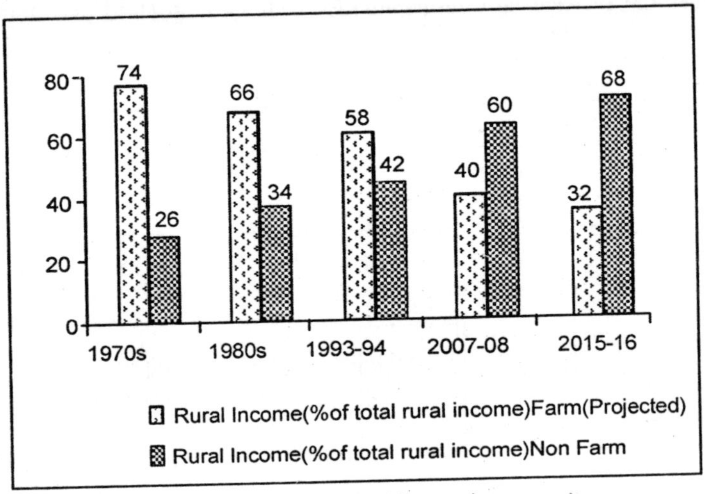

Figure 4.4: Rural Income (% of total rural income).

Rural lifestyles and behavioural trends are increasingly coming to resemble urban patterns, in both form and variety. Like urban consumers, the rural middle class is buying more fairness creams, many of the rural poor are keen to invest in a mobile phone connection. Growing aspirations are as much a factor in rural markets as price sensitivity and an acute sense of value for money. Fast Moving Consumer Goods (FMCG) will be witnessing more than 50 per cent of growth in its Rural and Semi-Urban Segments by 2012 which in totality is projected to grow at an CAGR of 10 per cent to carry forward its market size to over Rs.1,06,300 crore from present level of Rs. 87,900 crore, according to an analysis carried out by the Associated Chambers of Commerce and Industry of India (ASSOCHAM).

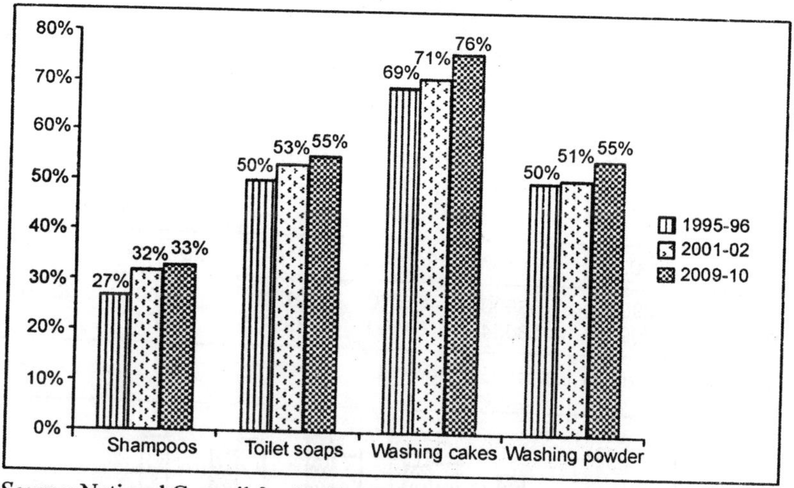

Source: National Council for Applied Economic Research (NCAER).

Figure 4.5: FMCG—Rural Market Share.

Rural households are purchasing a wide range of products—cars, flat-screen televisions, microwaves. Some industrial sectors have seen surprising growth coming from rural consumers. Fifty per cent of revenues from the fast moving consumer goods (FMCG) sector now come from rural sales. The automobile sector also shows the growth over years in rural areas and look for new unexploited markets. Rural India has emerged as an answer, owing to lack of strong presence by brands in most sectors as well as a high growth potential.

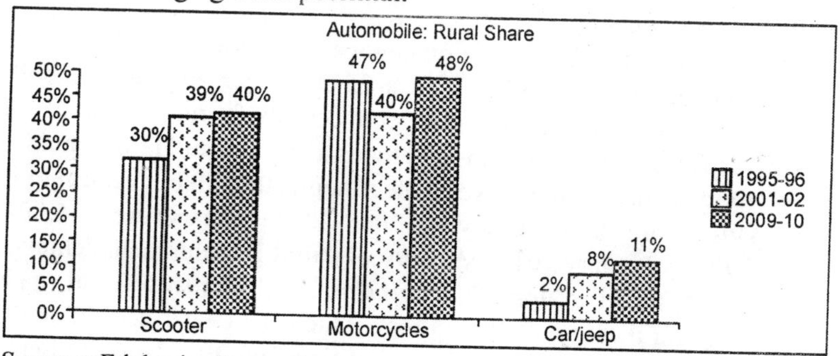

Scource: Edelweiss Research.

Figure 4.6: Automobile: Rural Share.

Further, improvement in infrastructure prompted by Government initiatives seems to have lowered entry barriers for many companies.

Government has approximately tripled the budget for rural development in last few years, which has opened the door of rural markets. Also, rural India is insulated against global economic downturns, which adds to its attractiveness.

Table 4.7: Outlay for Ministry of Rural Development for Eleventh Plan and 2012-13

(*Rs. in crores*)

	2007-08	*2008-09*	*2009-10*	*2010-11*	*2011-12*	*2012-13*
B.E.	29000	33900	65070	68760	76800	76376
R.E.	29900	58654	64180	78997.5	69564	—

Source: Ministry of Rural Development.

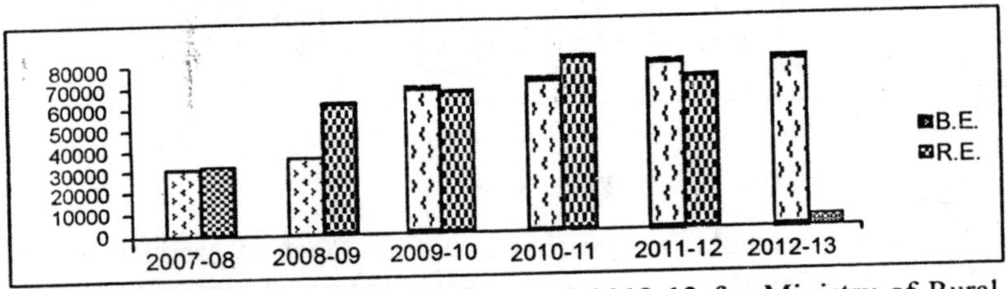

Figure 4.7: Outlay for Eleventh Plan and 2012-13 for Ministry of Rural Development.

Developments in recent times have got pace in rural areas, providing a strong platform to build strong marketplace. Household income is expected to be Rs. 1,56,000 crore in 2015. Developments like roads, IT, infrastructure, education level, organized trade have boosted the rural market attractiveness.

In order to give a boost to rural connectivity, Pradhan Mantri Gram Sadak Yojana (PMGSY) was launched on 25 December, 2000 as a Centrally Sponsored Scheme to provide road connectivity in rural areas of the country. Upgradation of selected rural roads to provide full farm to market connectivity is also an objective of the scheme, though not central to it. New roads in rural area in past years 2005-2012 (January) are 1,36,804. Since, 2005 to January 2012, Ministry of Rural Development achieved more than its target in upgradation and renewal of roads. Total roads upgraded in rural area is 2,30,575 k.m. which is 119 per cent of actual target. Indian villages are now also benefiting from the IT revolution in India. 'e-Panchayats' and 'e-medicine' are slowly taking over rural India. A study by Internet research firm Juxt Consult revealed that one out of every seven regular Internet users is from the rural belt, which gives a very positive signal for e-trading and e-business.

Big Players in Small Markets

India's rural markets present opportunities that companies seeking to become high performance businesses cannot afford to ignore. But the size and scale of those markets have been offset by concerns about the profitability of these markets and the durability of rural demand. Investors have always been fascinated by rural India, but there is a lack of executors focusing on the rural market. In the last few years some big companies have shown their presence in rural markets to get advantage of big opportunity in small markets. ITC, Godrej, Tata etc. have initiated organized retail sector in rural areas.

ITC e-Choupals

The e-Choupal—Choupal Saagar have connected rural local economies to a new level of productivity and consumption. e-Choupal is transforming the traditional, low value agricultural marketplace into an open arena—enabling more people to participate and succeed in the rural economy. The network of 6,500 e-Choupal centres spread across 40,000 villages has emerged as the gateway of an expanding spectrum of commodities leaving farms—wheat, rice, pulses, soya, maize, spices, coffee, aqua-products. The reverse flow carries FMCG, durables, automotive and banking services back to villages.

Aadhaar

Aadhaar, a joint venture between The Future Group and Godrej Agrovet Ltd. focuses on retail distribution of agricultural and consumer products for personal and household use in rural and semi-urban India. Aadhaar is positioned as a rural supermarket and currently has 40 stores spread over 1,00,000 sq. ft. across 3 States: Gujarat, Punjab and Haryana. Aadhaar also operates Cash and Carry store by the name Aadhaar Wholesale Market. Aadhaar stores empower the farmers by providing all solutions to them under one roof. Agri-business activities are supported by a strong specialized team at each store. Team members go to the farmers' field, discuss the problems of farmers, advise them, support them and provide consultancy to them on issues regarding farming. In this way, Aadhaar has moved beyond agriculture to meet the other needs of farmers as customers.

Hariyali Kisan Bazaar

Hariyali, a venture of DCM Shriram Consolidated Ltd. (DSCL) has been in operation for the last 9 years in rural India. Hariyali Kisan Bazaar has 300 plus outlets spread over Uttar Pradesh, Haryana, Punjab, Rajasthan, Chhattisgarh, Madhya Pradesh, Maharashtra and Andhra Pradesh. The company owns 85 of them, while the remaining are franchisees. Hariyali stores sell agri-products like fertilizers, pesticides, farm implements as well as FMCG items in rural areas.

Tata Kisan Sansar

TATA operates franchisee run centres called Tata Kisan Sansar Kendras (TSK). There are nearly 600 TSKs reaching about 4 million farmers across 22,000 villages in northern and eastern India. Each centre acts as a one-stop shop that offers a wide range of agricultural supplies such as fertilizers, seeds and pesticides, as well as services such as soil testing, crop advisory and foliar applications. The company maintains the PC terminals and provides software and connectivity upgrades across this extensive network. Today, the organization is exploring the option of using hand held devices that can be directly connected to a centralized server; the devices could provide online inventory accounting at every retailing point, print invoices, and give support for accounting and tax-related information.

Hindustan Unilever

Hindustan Unilever (HUL) is one of India's largest FMCG companies. About 30 per cent of its revenues come from rural sales. HUL makes its strong presence in rural India by innovation in fourth "P" of marketing i.e. Promotion. The company decided to increase penetration by extending its reach to villages with populations of 1,000, using new marketing options alongside the traditional distribution model.

"Project Shakti", a key element of HUL's alternate distribution strategy, launched in year 2001, involved working with self-help groups (SHGs) to educate and train rural women to become micro-distributors. A typical Shakti distributor sells INR 10,000-15,000 (US$ 208 to US$ 312) worth of products each month, earning INR 700-1,000 (US$ 15 to US$ 20) a month. The Shakti members, in turn, become consumers of higher value items such as consumer durables. Shakti distributors now account for 15 per cent of HUL's sales in rural India. Initially, run as a pilot in 50 villages of the Nalgonda district in Andhra Pradesh, the unexpected success of this project has encouraged HUL to expand it to 15 states, creating 37,000 women distributors covering 1,00,000 villages. Other initiatives like "Shakti-vani" and "i-shakti" provide a strong and smooth communication network.

Way to Success—Innovative Retailing

India's vast rural market offers a huge potential for a marketer facing stiff competition in the urban markets. The rural market environment is very different from the familiar surroundings of the urban market. Rural consumers have customs and behaviours that the marketers may find difficult to contend with. Marketers have to choose a variety of strategies to influence the rural customers and to get benefits from a large sized untapped market. The marketers have to providing products or brands to the customers when they are in a celeberation mood, which typically occurs during good harvests, festivals and marriages, when there is cash in hand to boost the sale in rural areas.

Haat—the Weekly Supermarket

Marketing has a crucial role in development of rural non-farm sector and rural *haats* are an integral part of the rural market system. Rural *haat* enables small farmers/rural artisans/producers/traders to sell their agri-produces, handicrafts and other products. The word *Haat* refers to a weekly market in rural, semi-urban and sometimes even urban India. *Haat* encourages face-to-face contact between sellers and buyers, thereby eliminating the middleman. It supports individual entrepreneurship and yet it is collective in nature. More than 42,000 *haats* are located in different parts of the country. Sellers at *haats* are typically mobile. They sell in one *haat* on one day and move to another on the next day. 81 per cent of visitors to *haats* said that they did not make purchases from their respective villages and regularly visited *haats* for their requirements. 58 per cent said that they specifically come to buy a particular product and that the purpose of visiting the *haat* is to complete their "shopping list". These rural super markets are much larger than all the world's K-marts and Walmarts put together (MART Study). There are approximately 47,000 *haats* and 25,000 *melas*, which function as the economic, social and cultural nerve centres of rural India. Each *haat* caters to the needs of a minimum of 10 to maximum of 50 villages from where an average of 4000 persons come to buy a range of daily necessity and services.

Table 4.8: Total No. of *Haats*

Before Independence	70%
After Indepandance	30%

Source: RMAI.

Table 4.9: Location of *Haats*

Market Place	52%
Bus Stop	35%
Temple	5%
Others	8%

Source: RMAI.

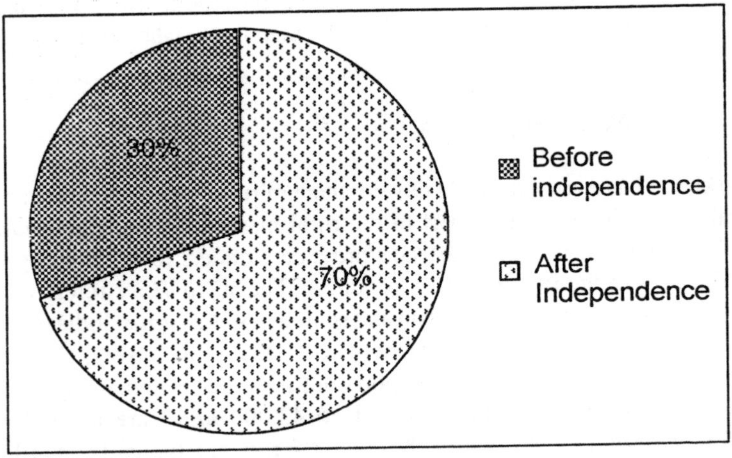

Figure 4.8: Total Number of *Haats*.

Melas

Everyday is known for celebration in India. India is a country of *melas*. Over 25,000 *melas* are held every year all-over the country. It is seen that 5,000 of these are commercial *melas*, 2,000 are cultural *melas*, while the majority of 18,000 are held with religious significance. Exposure of a company's product at the 500 "big" *melas* should be sufficient enough to generate product awareness in the rural market. Statistics reveal that the number of visitors per *mela* is approximately 7.5 lakh. On average, 850 outlets are set-up in every *mela*. In fact, the *Vali Yatra mela* is held from the time of the '*Ramayan*' and has over 3,000 stalls. Sales at the Sonepur *mela* of Uttar Pradesh average ₹ 40 crores. Haryana's Surajkund Craft mela and Rajasthan's Pushkar Fair witness the popularity of Indian rural *melas* not only in the country but all-over the world. The average sale per day at a *mela* is ₹ 25 lakhs. The efficiency of this system of distribution is evident from the fact that *melas* have been used for over 1,300 years and have continued to remain popular in spite of India going through so many rulers, invasions and conflicts. This speaks volumes of the rigidity and strength of this rural marketing system.

Strategies to Dig Deeper in Rural Markets

Creation and development of markets in the rural area demands consumer understanding, product customisation, relevant pricing, value engineering, and innovative modes of advertising and promotion—all designed to increase consumption and open up new markets. Companies have to choose some innovative strategies that can penetrate the rural markets.

Producing New Categories

Businesses may need to develop new products tailored to the unique needs and circumstances of rural consumers. BP Energy India saw an opportunity to offer a cleaner fuel alternative for the traditional charcoal- and wood-fired stoves used in the countryside—a move that the company believed could convert 3.6 billion potential consumers to more environment-friendly energy solutions.

Customising Products

Rural consumers typically seek product or service in terms of its durability, affordability, and fit for multiple uses. Understanding this attribute, many mobile manufacturing companies added some unique features like torch, FM radio and also put price range less than INR 2000 to suit the requirements of the rural folk.

Generating Awareness and Promoting Products through the Right Media

Non-conventional and interactive media such as puppet shows, and live demonstrations in *haats* and rural fairs have proven effective. Hindustan Lever ran a brand awareness exercise called "Operation Harvest" that used the audio-visual media and delivery vans to provide "mobile entertainment" in the form of songs and film sequences, interspersed with the company's advertrements.

Direct Consumer-Manufacturer-Producer Relations

This involves replacing middlemen enabled ITC to eliminate brokerage costs, better controlling and supplies, and developing its producer base for the long-term. The e-*choupal* network relies on self-driven computer kiosks with VSAT connections, manned by a *sanchalak*, or conductor. Farmers can use this channel to quote their prices directly to ITC and to close deals promptly, leading to greater transparency and creating a level playing field for all producers.

Mobile Retailing and Distribution Options

Delivery vans and sales vehicles can reach the rural interior. Nokia makes contact with its customers in remote villages through its "Care-on-Wheels" programme, providing after-sales service, building loyalty and supplementing the company's rapidly growing distribution network in rural India.

Infrastructure-sharing among Non-competing Companies

By collaborating with companies that already have a well-entrenched reach, new entrants can quickly scale up and expect quicker returns. The infrastructure provider gains a steady source of revenue at no additional cost. For instance, Samsung has partnered with the Indian Farmers Fertilizer Cooperative (IFFCO) to market its handsets using IFFCO's broad presence in rural markets.

Engage in Local Community and Add Reciprocity

Reciprocity is considered an ethical concept. It means giving and receiving in equal proportions. It is an idea that is handed down from one generation to another as children grow up and learn about life. The relationship between rural businesses and their customers is important. To succeed in rural markets, it is important for companies to engage local communities as partners. If companies are to build and retain public trust and confidence, particularly in rural regions, they must consistently demonstrate that they are genuinely interested in helping solve some of the major issues affecting socio-economic development. Rural market leaders such as HUL, ITC and Hero have moved beyond traditional vendor roles to partner with local communities; today, they regularly work to develop skills and to generate employment locally.

Conclusion

Indian rural retail has the tremendous potential and retail companies are getting only a piece of apple, to get the full advantage of rural market we have to go beyond the traditional methods. There is need of "Business Mind with Social Heart" (Pradeep Kashyap). Success in rural marketing depends upon Availability, Affordability, Acceptability and Awareness. Firms need to frame their business models in terms of brand marketing and distribution to remain relevant to the Indian rural market. Today small town population wants to shop like the metros. Evolved FMCG categories such as pre-post wash, hair conditioners, air fresheners and cheese appear to have topped consumer demand in small towns. Marketers who have recognized the potential and invested in these regions a few years ago are reaping rich dividends today. "Retailers and other players need to understand that the big hypermarkets and large malls will not work in a small town. Also, they should focus on issues relating to the needs and importance of consumers, the manner in which demand is picking up and the importance of marketing strategies that respond to the changing and dynamic consumer demands unique to India.

REFERENCES

Amarnath B. and G. Vijayudu, 2011 "Rural Consumers—Attitude Towards Branded Packaged Food Products", *Asia Pasific Journal of Social Sciences,* Vol. (III), Jan-June 2011, pp. 147-159.

Annual Report 2010-11, National Council of Applied Economics Research. http://www.ncaer.org/downloads/annualreports/NCAER_Annual_Report_2011.pdf

Annual Report 2011-12, Ministry of Rural Development.

Census of India 2011, 2001, 1991.

Consumption in Rural India Booming, http://www.moneycontrol.com/smementor/news/indianmarkets/consumptionrural-india-booming-says-report-755759.html/

Cooking to End Fuel Poverty, http://optimistworld.com/PFV.aspx?id=Cooking-to-end-fuel-poverty/

Economic Survey 2008-09.

Economic Survey 2011-12.

Hindustan Unilever Celebrates 75 Years in India, http://www.hul.co.in/mediacentre/pressreleases/2007/HUCelebrates75YrsInIndia.aspx

India's Rural Market—"The Fortune at the Bottom of the Pyramid", http://blogs.rediff.com/shinyvikas/2010/02/22/indias-rural-market-the-fortune-at-the-bottom-of-the-pyramid/

Indian Retail Industry, http://www.iseindia.com/ResearchPDF/Retail_Update1.pdf

Kashyap, P. and S. Raut, 2008, *The Rural Marketing Book*, 2006, New Delhi: Biztantra.

Masters of Rural Markets: *The Hallmarks of High Performance*, Accenture Research Report, 2010.

Mathur, U.C., 2008, *Rural Marketing: Text and Cases*, Excel Books.

Mckinsey Report, *The 'Bird of Gold': The Rise of India's Consumer Market*, May 2007.

Rafiuddin and Ahmed, Dr. Badiuddin, 2011 "Understanding the Potential of Rural Marketing in India—An Analytical Study", *Zenith International Journal of Business Economics and Management Research*, Vol. 1, Issue 2, Nov. 2011, pp. 126-139.

Singh, Jagwinder, 2012, "Influences on Rural and Urban Consumer Buying", *Global Journal of Management and Business Research*, Volume 12, Issue 7, Version 1.0, April 2012, pp. 35-42.

Srivastava, Deepti, 2010 "Marketing To Rural India: A Changing Paradigm", *APJRBM*, December, Volume 1, Issue 3, pp. 77-86.

Tata Farm Centers, http://www.tatachemicals.com/farm_centre/overview.htm

The "Bird of Gold": Rise of India's Consumer Market, http://www.mckinsey.com/locations/india/mckinseyonindia/pdf/India_Consumer_Market.pdf

The Financial Express, June 12, 2011, p. 9.

5

De-mystifying the Facts of Globalisation

Analysing the Institutional Support for Rural Consumers Awareness in India

PRADIP KUMAR PARIDA AND SMITA RAUT

Introduction

Globalization has led to opening of the economy to market oriented, in the process of LPG—"Liberalisation, Globalisation and Privatisation". The world is visualised as a global village today, where technology driven products with its linkages to day-to-day life of an ordinary individual is being witnessed across all the corners of the globe. The market driven economy is leading towards expansion of market—rapidly or in a slow pace depending upon the product as well as people's needs in such a way that, everyday something or the other—new product is coming to the market. As technology is changing in a rapid way, so also along with the application of technology, i.e. products, those are becoming the centre of transaction in our contemporary market economy. This resulted in a situation that, whether a particular product is necessary or not, that is not much important. What matters is technological advancement, new shape, size, colour—the product has more attraction for the consumers, due to the impact of variety of advertisement, be it electronic or print media. Some of the latest technological advancements and products have become the necessity of day-to-day life, i.e.—mobile in communication. All the sections of our society are affected by it. Today, it is not uncommon to find an auto driver or vegetable vender to communicate with his clients through mobile, which was not possible 10 years ago. Similarly, laptop or computers for technical and higher education. Students are more interested for e-learning, where the interest for regular book reading is somewhat decreasing day-by-day.

If we will look into the discourse on globalisation at a macro level, theoretically, much of the discussion on globalisation issues have focused on the need to address a range of issues including the following:

1. The relationship between Government and market.
2. The relationship between Government and citizens.
3. Relationship between Government and civil society including voluntary sector.

All the stakeholders are playing equally important role today in the governance sphere; State is responsible for creating a conducive atmosphere (socio-political-economic-legal) for the citizens of the country. Market is responsible for creating opportunities as well increasing efficiency on the principle of 'cost-benefit analysis'. The civil society is acting as a channel of expression of people's grievances as well as forum for people's participation. However, this has led to somewhat minimalist role of the state. The state is no more '*mai-baap*'.

Issues Related to Market Governance

As a matter of fact, the ongoing process of marketisation is not confined to the 1st world or developed countries. Even the so-called developing countries are not far behind it. There is considerable amount of market penetration to the rural parts of our country. This is partly due to increase in purchasing capacity of the people in some parts of the country and partly aggressive marketing strategy adopted by various companies keeping in mind the size of the rural market of our country which has led to the easy availability of various products in rural part of the country—even in small size, i.e. detergent powder, tooth paste, tea packets etc. in small size. These are created keeping to the targeted customers' need as well as their purchasing capacity. This is not only confined to the booming economy of urban sector. Even it has trickled down to the rural areas of the country. Even the economically so-called backward parts of the country are also getting affected by it. For example, in a block/panchayat headquarters of Kalahandi of Odisha or Bastar of Chhattisgarh, one can find various products of eatable items or cold drinks are available, though these parts are most backward and poverty-stricken areas of the country.

The above analysis shows that the rural market of the country has been growing in such a manner that, it is ever increasing. However, the lack of awareness, education and proper information creates lot of problems for the rural consumers anywhere, more particularly in India. As there are equally visible duplicates also available in our country, which is as much lucrative as the original one, which the rural consumers are not able to distinguish. There is a lack of proper grievance mechanism to address their problems. Particularly, in the sector of micro-finance and chit fund system, everyday we will find somebody has been cheated or some fraud has occurred etc. Even in the belt of acute poverty, there are cases of farmer's suicide because of money-lending system, crop failure due to duplicate seeds or fertilizers, private lenders exploitative approach etc. This is a common phenomenon in rural India today. That is one of the main reasons for mass migration and increasing number of informal economy based labour sector today. If we will microscopically examine the rural market and its consumers in India, we can notice the gravity of the situation and the numerous problems encountered by the innocent customers there. Above all it is their hard earned money, which they save and spend for some purpose. That is why there is growing demand for proper market governance. Somehow or the other the rules, regulations and principles of market has to be controlled or at least to be regulated.

There are number of factors responsible for this pathetic condition of rural consumers in India, i.e.

- Lack of proper education;
- Lack of proper information/awareness;
- Lack of grievances mechanism;
- The role of middleman/unscrupulous element; and
- Lack of governmental machinery to cater to the problems of rural consumers.

Institutionalising their Grievances

As a matter of fact there is urgent need to address the genuine grievances of the consumers from rural hinterland, as there is a lack of proper mechanism to cater to their grievances. Though there are number of Acts of Government of India in existence, it does not have any meaning for those sections of society. Reason being they are not aware about those specific provisions, nor are they capable of coming to a consumer forum to get justice out of it. The establishment of consumer fora at National,

State and District levels have not been able to address these problems to maximum extent possible. Forget about rural consumers even an urban educated consumer may not be able to know everything about the various issues related to Consumers Protection Act. Though in urban areas the issues are somewhat different due to various socio-economic-political-cultural factors and the level of education and awareness as well as accessibility to the forums to address grievances. Even the presence of vigilant and alert 'media' sometimes makes it difficult for the fake products as well as the producers, though it is striving in its own way. However, the situation is completely different at rural areas, more particularly if it is a tribal belt, if it is remote areas, or where education and awareness is low. Particularly in the context of medicine and life saving drugs, the rural India market is witnessing the exploration of duplicate, spurious drugs in a rampant manner. In spite of number of governmental provisions, we have not been able to stop them. This is a serious problem for the whole country.

Role of Institutions

The role of institutions which are serving or associated with the people from rural parts of the country is very much important in this context. For example *panchayats*, colleges, schools, cooperative societies, youth clubs, *mahila mandals* can come forward to curb such irregularities in terms of increasing awareness and education about consumer activities. Consumer forum at local level—at least *Panchayat* level can also cater to address certain problems in this sector. Every shop must be registered with a *panchayat*. If a shopkeeper is selling a duplicate product/spurious drugs, they must be heavily penalised along with the sponsored company. The local school and college through their consumer club can create awareness by spreading the message to parents and the community through students, as they are the unofficial ambassadors. Similarly, local cooperative, SHGs and *Mahila Mandals* can play active role in this context by spreading the awareness among its members regarding not to be involved with any dealings with such unscrupulous elements. But, the problem is, how these institutions of social change will carry forward these activities. Until and unless they are educated and sensitized enough in this regard they may not be so much proactive. Hence, it has to begin with them. Simply enacting rules, regulations or creating consumers forum is not enough or giving a special advertisement. Here and there in electronic or print media won't solve the problem. It has to be carried out in a mission mode. The Government will create a platform with the help of above-mentioned agencies/institutions. But active involvement of all the stakeholders including the common citizens—consumer is most important in this context.

The Government Today

As a matter of fact 'Government' is one of the most powerful institutions in our society in any system of governance. But free market, privatization, structural adjustment, deregulation and decentralization, the traditional role of 'Government', has changed a lot. The actors of governance, Corporate Sectors/M.N.Cs/TNCs in 'market economy' and NGOs in 'development sectors' are playing important role in this scenario. Hence, naturally the question comes to us, is governance 'good' with the minimum role of Government in policy matters.

Historically, capitalism has taken a new shape in 1980s. The idea of free private enterprise can bring economic prosperity—nationally and globally—championed by Milton Friedman, from Chicago University. It was politically implemented by Ms. Thatcher of UK in her regime as the Prime Minister and Mr. Reagan of USA during his tenure at USA as the President of the country, in 1980s. Subsequently, it was implemented in many countries across the globe. The advocates of 'neo-liberal' paradigm, supported the idea that, governmental interference leads to slow growth and productivity in economic sphere. Hence, they argued for 'less government', for the sake of 'good governance'. The arguments are flawed because capitalism as such has not triumphed as such across the globe. Even in the so-called champions of capitalism, particularly European countries and the countries from the West are facing a lot of problems in their social sector, employment scenario and social welfare measures.

In other words, the collapse of communism does not necessarily mean the triumph of capitalism. What really caused the collapse of communism was the systematic suppression of the civil society in the so-called communist systems. We have witnessed all these in recent past. Even there was specific role assigned to the state as well as market in that system.

Critics

The proponents of neo-liberal favours minimalist role of government and prefers market can do everything on the basis of principle of market economy. The most important point is people in a democracy are not merely 'customers' or 'clients', of the government, rather they are also 'subjects' and 'citizens', are also bounded by mutual obligations and are entitled to enjoy public infrastructure provided by the government, such as roads, ports, communications, court of law, monetary system, public sanitation etc.

In this context, it is argued by many that the pure private sector management model cannot cater to the needs of the citizens. As a matter of fact private goods are necessary. But they are worthless without public goods—such as policing and economic policies, meant to protect citizens. For example, media, it must not be fully under government control nor it should be entirely in private hands. However, the objective of democratic government is to create a conducive environment and protect free people, not free private groups, and institutions supporting them.

Government Today: A Macro Analysis

Government is a product of historical evolution. From Hobbes to Locket through Mill to Rawls, the fundamental message of political philosophy is that government as an instrument of governance is indispensable. Whatever may the ideological orientation or theoretical underpinning, all types of states—Marxist, liberalist or minimalist state, all of them believe that 'state' came into existence due to certain rationality. Accordingly, they defined the origin, nature and function of the state. Hence, the 'state' has certain activities for the citizens like protection of life, liberty and creating a conducive atmosphere for their development and maintenance of law and order.

In contemporary times, it is believed that the government must be re-invented to meet certain social needs and deserves to be reinvented once again when the number and nature of social needs undergo a radical change. With the on-going process of globalization, the functions and activities of the state are also undergoing a radical change over a period of time. To reinvent government is the slogan of successive government across all the corners of the globe, in all the states. Despite Thatcherism and Reaganism, the welfare state still exists. The important issue is whether some activities of government can be better in non-governmental ways as governments are frequently found unable to perform those activities effectively. Certainly 'more' and not 'less' government will be necessary to administer foreign policies and defence matters. What is demanded is that government which can work and can deliver services to its citizens with reasonable cost.

Conclusion

Good governance would mean nothing in these countries unless its goal is fixed to promote an egalitarian and equitable social and economic order. That goal would require government to be fully transparent and accountable to the people who would have a substantive role to participate in the decision-making process as well as implementation. It must address the problems of the marginalized, voiceless, the sub-alterns. It must promote growth with social justice. It must try for development with distributive justice. It must aspire for growth and development with human face.

In this era of globalisation, if we will minutely examine the nature and function of the state, the role of state in economic sphere is gradually diminishing due to the impact of liberalisation and privatisation. It is giving more space to market by accepting free market economy as its '*mantra*' in economic sphere. Hence in that context, I can argue that the role of the state is diminishing day-by-day. In political sphere, it is gradually strengthening itself at the cost of the liberty of citizens, for example the enactment and implementation of certain draconian legislative provisions, i.e. MCOCA, POTA and other similar provisions are making it amply clear that the state is becoming stronger day-by-day at the cost of civil rights of its citizens. In this context, it is pertinent to find the due space for the citizens—the legitimate entitlement of a citizen from the state' legitimate. Hence, to protect the rights of individuals, the citizens along with civil society, media, academia and judiciary must play active role in this context.

REFERENCES

Annual Report of National Consumers Dispute Redressal Commission on various Issues.

Bagchi, A.K., 1999, "Globalization, Liberalization, and Vulnerability: India and the Third World", *Economic & Political Weekly*, 34(45): 3219.

Basu, Kaushik, 2007, *The Retreat of Democracy*, Permanent Black, Ranikhet.

Bhaduri, Amit and Deepak Nayar, 1996, *The Intelligent Persons' Guide to Liberalization*, New Delhi: Penguin Books.

Bhagwati Jagdish, 2004, *In Defence of Globalization*, OUP, New Delhi.

Dasgupta, Samir. (ed.) (2004), *The Changing Face of Globalization*, New Delhi: Sage Publications.

David Held, *et al.* (1995), *Global Transformation: Politics, Economics and Culture*. Cambridge: Polity Press.

George, Soros, 2004, *On Globalization*, New Delhi: Viva Books Private Limited.

Harsh Mandr (ed.) *Good Governance*, Bangalore: Books for Change.

Jenkins, Robert, 1999, *Democratic Politics and Economic Reform in India*, Cambridge University Press.

Mathur, Kuldeep, 2008, *From Government to Governance*, New Delhi: NBT India.

Sen, Amartya, 2009, *The Idea of Justice*, London: Allen Lane (an imprint of Penguin Books).

Thomas Henk (ed.) (1995), *Globalisation and Third World Trade Unions: The Challenge of Rapid Economic Change*. India: Madhyam Books.

6

Overemphasis on Marketing Opportunities and Its Impact on Rural Consumers

Some Reflections

SAMIULLA

Introduction

In the present business world everything is considered to have a marketing dimension, businesses are largely concerned with marketing. According to Philip Kotler, "Marketing is a societal process by which individuals and groups obtain what they need and want through creating, offering, and freely exchanging products and services of value with others." In other words Marketing is a human activity directed at satisfying needs and wants through exchange process. Marketing management is the process of planning and executing the conception, pricing, promotion, and distribution of ideas, goods, services to create exchanges that satisfy individual and organisational goals. Whatever may be the definition, most of the marketers are concentrating on only creating a demand for their products. The present marketing strategy is not broad-based and enables an organisation only to develop its product to enhance their market share rather than satisfying the real needs of consumer. This is true especially in the case of rural consumers, even though they are a very significant part of the consumer segment. However, in recent years marketing has assumed greater importance. This is mainly due to the increasing production of wide range of consumer goods and services. The rural market has opened up a lot of opportunities for the marketers. The growing rural demand for goods and services has forced the companies to focus on rural consumers.

Distinction Between Rural and Urban Market

Earlier Marketers believed that rural consumers were similar to urban consumers. This led marketers to adopt similar strategies to attract the rural consumers. Understanding the distinctive features of rural markets in comparison to urban market will help the marketing firms to evolve appropriate strategies, and delivered goods and services as per the needs and aspirations of the rural consumers. Table 6.1 shows the difference between the rural and urban markets:

Table 6.1: Differences between Rural and Urban Market

Features	*Rural Market*	*Urban Market*
Demand	Seasonal	Constant
Structure of the Market	Scattered Population	Concentrated Population
Literacy Level	Low	High
Communication	Poor	Good
Product Knowledge	Unaware	Aware
Communication	Word of Mouth	Any Media
Consumer Protection	Rarely Available	Easily Available
Guidance	Very much needed	Not Necessary

There is no doubt that the rural people differ from their urban counterparts on a large number of important attributes, thus, their behaviour is also bound to differ having important implications for the markets. Most of the companies are now eager to enter the rural market and lure the rural consumers with a variety of goods and services. However, this urgency also enabled them to draw some wrong inferences that the rural consumers do not buy branded products, costlier products and are not fashion consciousness etc. Marketers must adopt appropriate strategy as rural markets have certain peculiar features as large portion of rural income comes from agriculture which is seasonal, habitually affecting the consumption pattern.

Marketing Managers and Rural Consumers: Roles and Responsibilities

Marketing managers have a diverse and varied job, and promotion should just be one element of the responsibility. Championing a marketing focused business structure will provide a greater chance of success in today's challenging business environment and lead to a more sustainable future. In the words of Henry Ford, management must provide those goods and services which the society needs at a price which the society can afford to pay. Management is supposed to provide good quality products to the rural consumers at reasonable prices because they are integral part of society. It should develop a liberal and fair attitude towards the rural consumers and maintain a regular supply of high quality products and services to the rural consumers. Managers must cater to the needs, tastes and preferences of the rural consumers. A businessman should act as a friend and guide to the rural consumer. It is his duty to protect rural consumers' interest at any cost. He must guard against adulteration, poor quality of services, misleading and dishonest advertisement, under-weighing and supply of inferior quality of goods. He must handle the complaints of the consumers more carefully and efficiently. The businessman should recognise that he is the trustee of the wealth that he has collected from the members of the society. Therefore, he must strike a balance between profit and social good. Broadly speaking, business has to have two major objectives, i.e. economic and social.

Areas Overemphasised by the Marketers

After liberalisation and globalisation of Indian economy, the companies are expanding their market from urban to rural areas. In recent time, marketing has undergone sea-changes as markets are becoming increasingly more competitive. Marketers are focusing on studying buyer behaviour of the consumers with the intention of widening their market share rather than satisfying the needs and wants of rural consumers. Advertising agencies with their creative messages concentrate only on enhancing their profit by way of giving misleading advertisements. As per the present marketing scenario most of the marketers concentrate on the following points:

- *Higher Production with Low Cost:* Every marketer's intention is to maximise their production with minimum cost. This leads to neglect of consumer expectation and quality of the product. The rural consumers fall victims to such practices as such substandard products are sold to rural consumers without much difficulty.
- *Most Profitable Price Fixing Strategy:* Pricing the product or service is a crucial issue. Price is the only part of the marketing mix that generates revenue. In the rural market pricing strategies are based on competitors' price or based on demand in the market rather than cost.

- *Overstress on Advertisement Budget and Attractive Copy*: The largest share of promotion expenditure is spent on advertisement; hence, marketer's interest is on returns. Ultimately, whatever may be the costs of advertisement every marketer's intention is to attract the general public towards their products. The advertising company mainly concentrates on AIDA effect on the public. This Attention, Interest, Desire, and Action (AIDA) effect may motivate people to buy products and services but it does not educate them or promote awareness of rural consumers. Such advertisements only create impulse in the minds of the rural consumers to buy things which are not necessary to them.
- *Search of Media to Communicate:* Media effect is measured in terms of sales and not consumer satisfaction. Every company is in search of media to promote their product rather than satisfy the needs and aspirations of the rural consumers.
- *Training the Sales Force to Increase the Sale:* Personal selling is a marketing process where consumers are personally persuaded to buy and get services. Every marketer trains the sales force to successfully draw the attention of rural consumer create interest in their minds and ultimately purchase the products. In most cases, the marketers do not undertake activities to know the extent of customer satisfaction.
- *Search of Channels of Distribution*: The rural market in India is a large scattered segment. The cost of distribution is much higher as compared to urban markets. Instead of understanding the problems faced by the rural consumers, the marketers are worried about the distribution of their goods with less cost to the scattered rural consumers.
- *Gathering Information of Rivals:* After the introduction of liberalisation, privatisation and globalisation business has become more competitive and complex in nature. Every marketer's intention is to overtake his rivals by framing effective strategy to face the competition. Generally, marketers concentrate on gathering the information related to the competitors rather than the needs of the rural consumers.

Challenges Faced by the Rural Consumers

Problems of rural consumers arise out of peculiar dynamics of the rural people coupled with the marketing strategies of marketers. In reality, rural market is characterized by special problems like low literacy level, scattered population, low income, lack of transportation, warehousing and seasonal requirements. Based on these problems, the marketers have categorised the rural consumers into the following:

- *High Price*: Rural consumer has to pay higher prices as compared to urban consumer. Many shopkeepers charge higher prices than MRP by putting their own price tags or increase the price by adding local taxes. If rural consumers protest they are denied the goods.
- *No Free Home Delivery:* The concept of free home delivery does not exist in the rural areas in spite of the claims of the marketers in their advertisements. However, after the purchases are made they are reluctant to deliver at home thereby charging extra for home delivery resulting into financial loss to the rural consumers.
- *Poor After Sale Service:* Rural consumer products are normally manufactured in urban centres and the service centres are generally located in large towns and cities which are not easily accessible to rural consumers. Therefore, the problem of after sales service remains critical to the rural consumer.
- *Inadequate Supply:* In rural markets the distribution network is not very good, therefore, the supply of goods and services remains erratic and may result in short supply. The marketer may supply goods through his own or hired vehicles to remote locations. This mobile distribution strategy affects the rural consumers by limiting their right to choice.
- *Artificial Scarcity*: The marketers of rural areas are known for creating artificial scarcity of essential commodities with the intention of earning higher profit resulting in the exploitation of the rural consumers who have no other alternative.
- *Adulteration:* Adulteration of goods is one of the major problems faced by the rural consumers in day-to-day purchases. The rural consumer does not get pure commodities even though he is willing to pay higher prices. Some commodities are sold in the market with a guarantee of purity but are found to be adulterated when used and are injurious to health. Rural consumers lack the capacity to judge the purity of commodities used by them.
- *Incorrect Measurement:* Unfair measurement is another problem faced by the rural consumers. Often standard weights and

measurements are not used in the rural markets. Especially in village fairs/*haats* most of the sellers are not using proper weighing machines.

- *Misleading Advertisements:* These days, everyday new products are launched. The manufacturer resorts to advertisements to promote the sale of their products. Normally, the manufacturer gives an exaggerated account of his products. Such advertisements trap the innocent rural consumer to buy these products. After the purchase, the rural consumer realises that it does not match with what has been claimed in the advertisement. Such misleading advertisements cheat the innocent rural consumers to a larger extent.
- *Misleading and Incomplete Labels*: The labels on products provide information about the products to the consumers. The consumer can decide judiciously after comparing the quality and price of the product on the label. Often the manufacturers try to cheat the consumer by manipulating the information on the label.
- *Sale of Substandard Goods:* Sometimes, substandard goods are sold at higher price in place of standard goods. For example, selling furniture made of inferior quality wood after polishing, using substandard sheets in steel cupboard and furniture, selling substandard cloth by claiming it of a superior quality and inflating its price, etc. The rural consumer is unaware of the quality of the products he is purchasing as they do not have any standard markings,
- *Sale of Inferior Goods:* The marketers do not hesitate to market inferior goods. In order to earn more profit spurious medicines, cosmetics, oil, ghee etc. are sold in original packing. The rural consumers are unaware about such issues. If rural consumers are not vigilant while purchasing goods they suffer a lot.
- *Malpractices Adopted by the Manufacturers or Sellers*: Manufacturers or sellers trap the rural consumer to buy their products by adopting misleading schemes like ‘free gifts’ or ‘heavy discounts’ which attract the consumer easily. In reality, there is no change in the price. Sometimes, the producer imitates the colour, shape, and name of popular brand available in the market. Thus, the consumer is cheated and he purchases an inferior good in place of standard ones.

Remedial Measures to Address the Challenge

One of the most effective strategies to solve the problems of the rural consumers is by improving the quality of service provided by the marketers, consumer forums, Government and local bodies. If the problems of the rural consumers are addressed in the right spirit they can be solved. However, some steps that can be taken to address the problems of the rural consumers are as follows:

- *Use Local Language in Communication*: Communication should bridge the gap between sender and the receiver. Communication is undertaken to pass on the message of a product to the ultimate consumers. Literacy levels in rural India are low, due to which rural consumers often find it difficult to understand other than local language.
- *Send Well Experienced Sales Force*: Sales force of rural markets basically aim at selling a product to the rural consumers, hence, they need to know the dynamics of the rural market. Marketers should send well experienced salesmen who understand the needs and wants of rural consumers and not treat them as commodity to be exploited.
- *Understand Local Culture*: Culture is a way of life and social heritage. It consists of unique set of attitudes, beliefs, customs, traditions, dress and philosophy. The culture of a region provides clear picture of their needs. Rural consumers are fundamentally different from urban, hence marketers should appreciate local custom and culture to serve rural consumers better.
- *Know Religion and Caste*: Religion and caste play a vital role in influencing the social, political and cultural behaviour of certain communities, mainly in rural areas. Buying behaviour of rural consumers is influenced by their religion and caste, which are stronger in rural markets than in urban markets.
- *Educate People about the Consumption Procedure*: Marketers should educate rural consumers about how to use their product and what are the benefits they get.
- *Segmenting Rural Consumer*: No market is entirely homogenous and we accept multidimensional approach to buyer behaviour—economic, demographic, social, cultural and psychological. Rural marketers must segment their consumers into similar cluster in order to market specialised products

and services to each group. Rural consumers can be segmented according to Demographic factors, Geographic factors, Psychographic factors and Behavioural factors.

- *Organising Consumer Awareness Programmes in Schools and Colleges:* Schools are the right place through which awareness can be given to students by way of conducting seminars, debates and other programmes with the help of some visual aids. Consumer awareness programmes to the students will develop critical awareness and living skills which are oriented towards building a better future for our society.
- *Consumer Forum at the Village Level:* For better protection of rural consumers' interests, the government may establish a village forum to provide effective safeguards to rural consumers against defective goods, unsatisfactory services, unfair trade practices and other forms of exploitation. This forum should take special care of illiterate rural consumers and redress their grievances without delay.
- *Strong Consumer Movement*: The consumer movement in rural area is not very effective. The government, media, trade associations, Chamber of Commerce and consumer voluntary organisations should realise their responsibility and make the consumer movement more effective.
- *Consumer, Seller and Local Leaders Meet:* Every village Panchayat should organise consumer, seller and local political leaders meet twice in a year headed by the panchayat president. They should discuss about the problems of rural consumers and find appropriate solution to their problem. Further, if any consumer has any problem he can raise the issue in the meeting and get it redressed. This kind of meet will bring different stakeholders on a common platform to understand each other better.
- *Special Regulation to Health and Beauty Care Products*: In the rural market the manufacturing, sale and distribution of drugs and cosmetic items must be regulated. Its main aim being to protect the rural consumer from substandard drugs and cosmetics. If local government is not satisfied about the quality of drugs, then it should be banned. The drugs which do not cause any risk on human health should only be permitted to be sold in the rural areas.

Conclusion

Today, India is one of the largest growing economies in the world. As a result of globalisation, Indian economy has become a vibrant, rapid growing consumer market. After the introduction of organised manufacturing activity, the sellers have become stronger and better organised, while the consumers of rural area continue to be unorganised and exploited. In a country like India, where a considerable number of the rural people are living below the poverty line, having high level of unemployment and poor literacy level; consumer awareness continues to remain low. Rural consumers are the most exploited segment of consumers in our country due to low level of literacy, low per capita income, lack of communication, transportation problem, warehousing problem, scattered population and absence of strong consumer movement etc. Markets are becoming increasingly more competitive, and marketers are focusing on studying buyer behaviour with the intention of widening their market rather than satisfying real needs and wants of rural consumers. The Central Government, State Governments and other local bodies should organise awareness programmes for the benefit of rural consumers. The rural marketers have to be sensitive to the needs of rural consumers and must design products that cater to rural condition. The rural marketing process needs to be evolutionary and not revolutionary. It has to be considered as an investment today for better future tomorrow. Companies should focus on nurturing the rural markets and have consumer's perspectives rather than concentrate on the achievement of short-term commercial gains.

REFERENCES

Agarwal, P.K., 2003, *Marketing Management—An Indian Perspective,* Meerut: Pragati Prakashan.

Behavioural Economics and Customer Complaints in Communication Market, a Report prepared for the Australian Communications and Media Authority (ACMA) in connection with the public inquiry "Reconnecting the Customer".

Gupta, C.B. and N. Rajan Nair, 2006: *Marketing Management,* New Delhi. Sultan Chand & Sons.

Kashyap, Pradeep and Siddhartha Kaput, 2008, New Delhi, *Bizantantra,* 2, 3,18, 25, 210, 284.

Muliyil, Hemachand, *Marketing Management*, Mangalore: United Publishers, pp. 133,136.

Philip, Kotler, 2002, *Marketing Management*, New Delhi: Prentice Hall of India Private limited, pp. 2-5.

Ramaswamy, V.S. and S. Namakumari, 2004, *Marketing Management,* New Delhi: MacMillan.

Shanbhag, Santhosh and P.G. Aquinas, 2007, *Marketing Management,* Mangalore: Sita Publishing House, pp. 2, 3,188,198, 211-219.

Teachers' Reference Book, Government of Tamil Nadu: Civil Supplies and Consumer Protection Department.

SECTION II

Rural Consumers: Opportunities and Marketing Strategies

7

Consumer Empowerment and Marketing Strategies for Rural Market in India

SNEHALKUMAR H. MISTRY

Introduction

Consumer empowerment is not a new, but least attended concept, because many marketers feel that by empowering the consumer, they are shifting control from former to later. Therefore, many marketers shy away from this approach. But with advancement of technology and change in market composition of rural markets many organisations are feeling the need of employing consumer empowerment as tool for penetration of their product into the market and modifying or developing the product or service according to the market as well as competitive requirement. Marketers need to fine-tune and re-evaluate their consumer expectations and their own marketing orientations so that they can take decisions to improve the quality of their offers to consumers. The purpose and effect of such marketing orientations are to increase consumers' purchasing satisfactions so that consumer empowerment has a beneficial effect in the short and long-term leading to improved business results. Therefore, in India also, many companies are opting for consumer empowerment, specifically of the rural market segment to reach out with their products.

Rural Market in India—An Insight

In recent years, rural markets have acquired significance, as the overall growth of the economy has resulted into substantial increase in the purchasing power of the rural communities. More than 70 per cent of India's population lives in villages and constitutes a big market for industry because of increasing disposal incomes and rising aspirations. Companies are realising slowly but surely that the key to gain true market leadership lies in tapping the rural potential. However, the rural sector in India suffers from different kinds of problems.

What Makes Rural Markets Attractive?

Rural market has the following facts to substantiate this:

- According to a study by research firm Nielson, the Fast Moving Consumer Goods market (FMCG) in rural India is tipped to touch US$ 100 billion by 2025 on the back of "unrelenting" demand driven by rising income levels. According to the study, rural India now accounts for more than half of sales in some of the largest FMCG categories.
- Rural purchasing power has grown faster than urban in the last six quarters.
- Faster growth in rural areas is not limited to penetration; today the rural consumer's frequency of consumption is growing faster as well, demonstrating their entrenchment in these categories.
- Seemingly 'urbane' brands in categories like deodorant and fabric softener are growing much faster in rural India than urban.

Literature Review

In the marketing literature, consumer empowerment is defined primarily in two ways. First, consumer empowerment can be defined as giving consumers power through resources such as greater information or greater understanding (e.g., Brennan and Ritters, 2003; Cutler and Nye, 2000; Rust and Oliver, 1994). Second, consumer empowerment is defined as a subjective state, caused by perceptions of increasing control (Wathieu *et al.*, 2002). We define consumer empowerment using the definition of Wathieu, *et al.* (2002) as well as a definition of personal control reported by Skinner (1996). Empowerment is a consumer's subjective experience that they have greater ability than before to intentionally produce desired outcomes and prevent undesired ones and that they are benefiting from the increased ability. Thus, consumer empowerment is a positive subjective state which results from a mental comparison of a consumer's abilities relative to existing or previous abilities. As such, it is only the perception of increasing control which evokes empowerment and empowerment may be experienced whether control actually increases or not.

Waterson (2004) considers consumer empowerment to be the availability of the means to more effective purchase of goods and services, with the increase of empowerment resulting in the lowering of search or switching costs. Nardo *et al.* (2011) identify the following as important elements for defining empowerment: consumers should be aware of their decisions when buying (e.g. terms and conditions, comparing prices, products' labels); consumers should be able to get information on their rights; and, consumers should have access to advocacy and redress mechanisms.

Denegri-Knott, Zwick and Schroeder (2006) map the research on consumer empowerment presenting three dominant explanatory models:

1. *Consumer Sovereignty:* A consumer is empowered when he or she is free to act as rational and self-interested agent. Consumers combine resources and skills to make producers do what they would not do otherwise and as such consumers' choices are positive instruments in directing and correcting the market. This results in more efficient production, better and cheaper products, and increased consumer welfare.
2. *Cultural Power:* This model argues that consumers are caught in political and cultural forces beyond their control, where the market is a place of conflict between consumers and producers, where the latter try to condition and control consumers' choices. Consumer empowerment here implies a strategic behaviour, tactics to react to buyers' actions and motivations and processes whereby communities of various forms invent tactics that counteract the strategic manoeuvres of powerful companies [De Certeau (1984, 1986) (Kozinets 2002, p. 23, but also Kozinets, *et al.*, 2004 references cited in Denegri-Knott, Zwick and Schroeder, 2006].
3. *Discursive Power:* This approach attempts to reconcile the above two approaches to consumer power by focusing on how consumers co-create markets, power, and knowledge. The discursive model takes power to be a (co)creative force that structures the possible field of (inter)action and exchange of free agents, recognising a positive role to the interaction between consumers, producers and marketers.

Consumer empowerment as traditionally understood can be considered as both a function of the skills, knowledge and assertiveness of consumers themselves, and the protection, rules and institutions designed to support them as they play their part (EC, 2011). It depends not only on good cognitive skills but also, on knowledge of consumer rights and information, well known and effective consumer organisations and public authorities, an active media and simple and accessible means of redress. The concept of consumer empowerment is, therefore, both about consumers themselves and the strength of the infrastructural framework and regulation within which they operate and which can facilitate empowerment. There are instances, however, where in tandem the outcome is vulnerable rather than empowered consumers.

Effects of Empowerment on Business Growth

The empowered consumer is a consumer with accurate information and the confidence that comes from effective protection and solid rights. This enables the consumer to make real and meaningful choices in the market (based on informed and accurate comparison of market offerings). Clear articulation and signalling of consumer needs and preferences to businesses improves competition and drives competitive markets. Consumer behaviour provides an incentive for businesses to improve, and to offer even better deals to their customers. Increasingly, however, consumers need (support) to be empowered to make the best choices because:

- products and markets are becoming increasingly complex;
- an ageing population finds itself unfamiliar and challenged to keep pace with new products; and
- consumers receive increasing amounts of information which is difficult to process.

At the core of consumer empowerment is the idea that consumers should have the tools to secure the best outcomes for themselves. An empowered consumer should be confident, knowledgeable and feel protected, and therefore, tends to make optimal decisions by understanding their own preferences, the choices available to them and their rights and the means of complaining and seeking redress if their rights are breached. The empowered consumer articulates preferences more clearly, allowing businesses to better understand the products required and better able to compete by differentiating themselves in the market. This leads to better offers, which results in increased consumer welfare because of better and cheaper products supplied more efficiently because of strengthened competition.

More commonly (and in essence), consumers might be empowered through the enhanced ability to search (overcoming imperfect information) or the ability to act on choice (switching) which heightens competition between suppliers, acts as a spur to suppliers to seek new or more efficient ways of supplying customers and generally supports supply-side competition. This might include, for example, new forms of collective consumption and collaborative purchasing which utilise the combined power of consumers.

Figure 7.1 provides a simplified representation between empowered consumers and businesses. It highlights the factors that are important for empowered consumers to incentivise businesses to compete in the market. The relationship between supply side responses and economic growth can only be inferred, however, in terms of how enhanced competition may drive structural economic change.

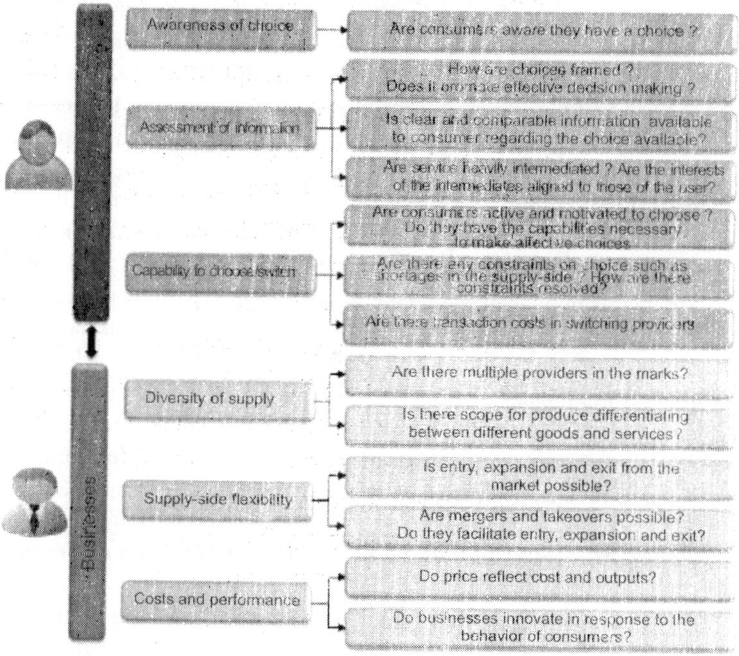

Source: Office of Fair Trading (2010).

Fig. 7.1: Empowered Consumers and Drivers for Growth.

Consumer Empowerment and Rural Markets

Consumers do not act in a vacuum—they need the right environment in order to flourish. This implies the requirement for Government to provide stimuli for consumers to become active and to protect consumers, particularly if vulnerable, such that they have confidence and make informed judgments. Only then can consumers be fully empowered. Markets are increasingly influenced by technology, globalisation, exploitative business practices and innovative products and services. In Indian context, there are various forms of empowerment techniques used by Government, companies and other stakeholders on addressing different objectives. Some of the techniques are as follows:

1. Educating Consumers about their Rights

In India, population growth rate is very high and till today majority of population lives in rural side. Majority of rural population is jeopardizing due to illiteracy, hence sometimes they are easily carried away by false claim and some malpractices practiced by vendors and retailers. Therefore, in order to empower the consumer, Government of India has started "JAGO GRAHAK JAGO" campaign through which by supplying the legal and true information, Government is attempting to empower the consumers and helping them to make wise decision while purchasing some of the products or services. For example, the campaign includes the advertisement on bargaining on Maximum Retail Price (MRP) or how proper weighing scale are required to be used.

Another example is financial literacy movement started by ICICI Bank relating to banking services and facilities. The ICICI group has spread this activity to stock trading and insurance services also, where they provide information to consumers of services regarding the possible threat of cheating and what are the possible remedies for the same, hence, the investor can be empowered with information and such information can help them to take right decision about using particular services.

2. Creating Awareness among Consumers about Product or Service

In India, Lifebuoy has started campaign regarding washing of hands for children below poverty line and spread message of healthier India, with liquid handwash brand of Lifebuoy. The consumption of electronic products is growing at a very fast pace. The challenge that will be seen in the coming years will be the need to create products that take into account the requirements of the common man in India at a cost that is affordable. These will include creating products that will work well despite the inherent limitations of infrastructure in the country. Some of the key limitations in India are the availability of power and network bandwidth. In addition, user interfaces need to become more intelligent to cater to the needs of the diverse population in India. All these challenges work as an opportunity for the formation and development of companies that will specifically focus on developing electronic products tuned to the Indian market. For example, Nokia has come out with very sturdy mobile which can be used by non-conventional user of mobile with robustness, on the other hand looking to the infrastructure challenges Samsung has launched its phone with solar charging function in that.

3. Collective Buying

In India, particularly in rural side, there are many cooperative bodies which are registered under Society Act of respective states; they are playing an important role in empowering consumer by indulging in the activity of group buying or collective buying. In such cooperative societies, there are people from village who are members and to protect the interest of their members, such societies are entering in negotiation with many companies and dealers regarding the purchase of their products. In this they may ask companies to produce several products on customised basis also. Because of collective buying the common interest of all buyers *via* cooperative societies is protected and they can have enough say in buying process also.

4. Empowering Business with Social Responsibility

With the belief that the private sector can help create solutions to social challenges through innovative strategies that meet both business and social objectives, Hindustan Unilever has developed project *Shakti* (meaning empowerment or strength), a direct-to-consumer sales distribution network that relies on over 45,000 female micro-entrepreneurs from 15 Indian States to tap into remote, rural markets in India. The initiative has proved a resounding success. Using an innovative distribution channel, *Shakti* has helped further rural development and has brought new business by opening previously unexplored markets. By packaging products into very small amounts and selling them at prices that are affordable to the rural poor, the company is helping improve hygiene and well-being in rural India. With the help of 45,000 female micro-entrepreneurs, Company has tapped into 3 million homes across 1,35,000 villages in remote, rural markets in India. The programme has brought competitive advantage and increased profits for the company while positively impacting local communities by increasing women's incomes.

5. Prosumption

'Prosumption' refers to the breaking down of the barriers between production and consumption, so that consumers can be directly and personally involved in the production of the goods they are purchasing (Lent, A. and Lockwood, M., 2010). In India many FMCG manufacturing companies interact with consumer groups while designing and developing their products, sometimes companies ask consumer to participate in designing of company logo or tagline *via* competition routes. Recently, launched campaign by Maggi noodles featuring Amitabh Bachchan in advertisement focusing on rural markets with smaller packets of Maggi noodles where they are asking the consumers to share their experiences and win prizes also, such an activity not only help the company to restructure the product but also to know hidden customer needs and ways to meet them.

Rural Markets: Marketing Strategies

Product Strategy

Our country's rural market is relatively special, which has different consumer community in the different physiographic region and the different consumer community has the different consumer demand. Therefore, when the enterprise launches product in the rural market, they should pay great attention to meet the consumer's need, emphasising different research. At the same time, product packing and brand also should conform to consumer psychology and the consumer custom. Here, what needs to be emphasised is that the enterprise must base on the enhancement of product's basic function and the reduction of unpractical accessional function, *via* consumer empowerment techniques.

Price Strategy

While purchasing the product, the product price is the most important factor for consideration to the rural consumer. Therefore, while entering the market, the enterprise should consider adopting low price. They must consider the rural consumer characteristic and measures the enterprise's own benefit, competitor and market demand and so on, and finally fix the most reasonable product price. Pricing strategies are very much linked to product strategies. Some of these strategies are: (i) Low cost/cheap products, (ii) Avoid sophisticated packing, (iii) Re-fill packs/reusable packaging, and (iv) Application of value engineering.

Channel Strategy

When choosing marketing channel, we should fully consider the differences between the rural market and the city market. Because the rural market's region is broad, the consumption is separate; the enterprise can utilize the unique superiority of Supply and Marketing Cooperative Society, such as—massive sales points and broad distribution, to expand the sales network. Rural markets have the practice of fixing specific days in a week as Market Days called "*Haats*", where exchange of goods and services are carried out. This is another potential low cost distribution channel available to the marketers. Also, every region consisting of several villages is generally served by one satellite town termed as "*Mandis*" where people prefer to go to buy their durable commodities. If marketing managers use these feeder towns, they will easily be able to cover a large section of the rural population.

Promotion Strategy

Promotion for rural market is going to be different from the urban areas, because the usage pattern is different and need preferences are different too. Therefore, planning promotion of product or services in rural market should have local flavour not only that it should focus on features attracting the consumers. According to recent research, as many people are watching the television and movie, there is large demand of products which are used by television or Bollywood celebrities in daily shows or movies. Hence, companies involved in rural promotion should consider latent as well as traditional medium of communication as tool for rural market.

Concluding Remarks

There are a substantial range of activities to support consumer empowerment. These, in turn, can help consumers to reduce market failures by their ability to improve producer understanding of consumer needs and to encourage business models that challenge existing structures that give rise to market failure and encourage innovation.

Three particular pathways or routes from consumer empowerment have been identified:

- *Empowered Consumers from all Activities*—leading to improved access to better quality information, reducing market asymmetry leading to improved articulation of preferences and more efficient and competitive markets and the release of resources as the basis of growth;
- *Empowered Consumers from Targeted Activities* (for example, switching, collaborative purchasing/consumption and specific sector interventions to improve competition in the supply chain)—leading to particular pressure points (for example, a cost saving and efficiency driver) and subsequent competitive responses by firms; and
- *Empowered Consumers as part of new (co) production Models* (and the emergence of new commercial opportunities that place 'empowered consumers' at the heart of business models)—leading to efficiencies, value creation, productivity impacts associated with innovation.

Consumer Empowerment activities have much impact on business activities. Efficiency savings are most obviously evident through data release and information activities which facilitate consumers to utilise comparison tools to seek the most cost-effective product or service in the market. Parallel savings to the consumer can be enhanced further in collective purchasing schemes which deliver access to economies of scale through bulk buying for consumers. Competitive markets, more broadly, are supported through consumer education and regulation providing pressures on businesses to be more productive, quality-driven and/or innovative.

REFERENCES

Carol, Brennan and Katrina Ritters (2004), "Consumer Education in the UK" *New Consumer Studies*, 28 (March), 97-107.

Carol Brennan, Katrina Ritters. (2003). Consumer education in the UK: new developments in policy, strategy and implementation, *International Journal of Consumer Studies*, Volumes 27, Issue 3, pp. 223-224.

Cutler, Tony J. and David A. Nye (2000). "Anything but 'Empowerment'? Smokers Tar and Nicotine Data and Cigarette Design". *Health, Risk, and Society*, 2 (1).

Denegri-Knott, J., Zwick, D. and Schroeder, J.E., 2006. "Mapping Consumer Power: An Integrative Framework for Marketing and Consumer Research". *European Journal of Marketing*, 40 (9/10), pp. 950-971.

"Developments in Policy, Strategy, and Implementation", *International Journal of. EC*, 2011, *Consumer Empowerment in the EU*: Commission Staff Working Paper, pp. 1 and 2.

European Commission, (2011). Consumer Empowerment in the EU: Commission Staff Working Paper, Brussels, http:// ec.europa.eu/consumers/consumer empowerment/docs/swd consumer empowerment eu en. pdf

http://pslforum.worldbankgroup.org/casestudies/unilever

Lent, A. and Lockwood, M. 2010, "Creative Destruction: Placing Innovation at the Heart of Progressive Economics", *IPPR*, London, December.

Nardo, M. Loi, M., Rosata, R., Manca, A., 2011, *The Consumer Empowerment Index: A Measure of Skills, Awareness and Engagement of European Consumers.*

Rust, Roland T. and Richard W. Oliver, 1994, "Video Dial Tone: The New World of Services Marketing", *Journal of Services Marketing*, 8 (3), 5-16.

Skinner, Ellen A. (1996), "A Guide to Constructs of Control", *Journal of Personality and Social Psychology*, 71 (3), 549-570.

Waterson M., 2004, *Consumer Empowerment and Links with Competition and Productivity.*

Wathieu, Luc, Lyle Brenner, Ziv Carmon, Amitava Chattopadhyaya, Klaus Wetenbroch, Aimee Drolet, John Gourville, A.V. Muthukrishnan, Nathan Novemsky, Rebecca K. Ratner, and George Wu (2002), "Consumer Control and Empowerment: A Primer", *Marketing Letters*, 13 (3), 297-305.

8

Competition Law and Policy for Rural Consumers

VIJAY KUMAR SINGH

Introduction

Rural India is a powerhouse propelling the economy's growth. Home to two-thirds of the country's one billion consumers, it is the zone where almost half of the national income is generated. Marketers are focusing on the Indian hinterlands to achieve their revenue targets by increasing their presence into the rural markets. Being an agricultural economy, a large part of its consumer comprise farmers, who belong to rural India (IBEF August, 2012). The reforms and developments in the last two decades have led to the emergence of rural markets as powerful economic engine. As per CRISIL Research, rural spending has outpaced urban consumption. Between 2009-10 and 2011-12, additional spending by rural India was Rs. 3,750 billion, significantly higher than Rs. 2,994 billion by urbanites.

It is pertinent to note that businesses have started reposing confidence in the rural opportunities. Now, as a strategy, business houses are devoting their resources in analysing how to leverage their position in rural markets. The spending patterns of the rural consumers have changed. A motorcycle, scooter, DTH connection, or for that matter a SUV is not a new thing for a rural inhabitant. More often rural population is shifting towards FMCG goods and packed food items similar to their urban counterparts. This change is attributed to several factors—increased level of income, improved access to finance, advertisement and media, migrant rural population and Government policies like NREGS (National Rural Employment Guarantee Scheme) are to name a few.

Rural Markets—the Concept

'Rural Markets' have emerged as a new concept. The National Sample Survey Organization (NSSO) defines rural markets as those areas with fewer than 5,000 residents, a population density less than 400 people per square kilometre and at least 75 per cent of the male working population employed as agriculturists. Thus, the rural markets focus upon the agriculture as the base, naturally the market is contemplated to constitute the agricultural produce, its production, distribution and sale. However, due to the increasing occupational migrant rural population (for instance, majority of population in rural Bihar has occupationally migrated from their villages to cities like Delhi, Mumbai, Kolkata, Bangalore etc.), the income remittance is not from the farm activities.

The rural markets thus can be discussed under two heads that is A. (i) Rural markets relating to farm activities; and (ii) Rural markets which deal mostly with non-farm activities like trading and agro-processing. This classification is from the supply side of the rural producers, i.e. where the farmers are the producers and approach the markets with their produce. Here, the market comprises purchasers who are monoposnists (monopoly buyer like APMCs) or the Government procurement agencies like FCI, who have the sole authority under law to deal with these markets/ consumers. The competition is between the seller, i.e. the producer of farm products to get a competitive price (which he does not get due to the fixed MSP or lack of competition among the buyers).

B. Another area of emerging rural markets is that of rural consumers who are increasingly consuming products and services specially their buying preferences having changed with the migrant income from urban areas. Moreover, the consumer behaviour has changed due to this migration, as these migrants stay for a significant period of time in cities and carry along with them the urban consumer behaviour along with the money to sustain the same. This market is of significant interest to the business houses. From a competition law and policy perspective, both the markets are important. The major issue arises in the former market of farm produces as may be noted from the discussion in the following pages.

Rural Consumers

Rural consumers are fundamentally different from their urban counterparts. The lower levels of literacy and limited exposure to products and services are well-known, but there are also differences in occupation options, with a direct impact on income levels and income flows, and a high level of interdependency affecting the dynamics of rural community behaviour. All contribute to make rural consumer behaviour starkly distinct from the urban (Rural Market Research). There are several factors which contribute to influencing buying behaviour in rural India, like environment of the consumer, geographic influences, family, economic factors, creative use of the products etc.

Information asymmetry is the biggest problem with rural consumers. The rural people, comprising poor farmers, who purchase for their farms and households may not be much aware of the malpractices going on in the market due to their ignorance and high level of illiteracy (Singh and Sangwan, 1994). Further, rural consumers are widely scattered and unorganised (Sayulu and Reddy, 1998), may be due to the nature of the rural markets which covers a large area and less population density as per definition. These factors have led to the need for identifying rural consumers as a separate class and protect their consumer rights under both consumer law and competition law. However, over time, the lifestyle of rural consumers has moderately changed in India due to many reasons and factors—(a) Government policies like 100 days' work; (b) free education for poor children at school and colleges; (c) every corner of the village is now connected with nearby towns, i.e. frequent visits to towns of rural people; and (d) rural people's connectivity with electronic media (Amarnath, 2011), but still the rural consumer behaviour is distinct and demands a separate treatment.

Relation between Competition Law and Consumer Law

Before the discussion on the competition law and policy for rural consumers, it is important to understand the relationship between the Competition Law and Consumer Law in brief. The Planning Commission notes that promotion of consumer welfare is the common goal of consumer protection and competition policy. At the root of both is the recognition of an unequal relationship between consumers and producers. There is strong commonality between competition policy and law on the one hand and consumer protection policy and law on the other hand (Planning Commission, 2007). However, the relationship between competition law and consumer welfare is not always as clear cut as it may seem (Buttigieg, 2009).

An analysis of laws in the US and EU shows that the goal of

competition law is to protect the freedom of individuals to compete. The goal of competition law is not to promote consumer welfare directly. Rather this is brought about indirectly by protecting the freedom of actors to compete in markets. The reason for this is that freedom to compete generally leads to competition, and competition leads to an efficient allocation of resources and thus to consumer welfare. Therefore, the goal is to safeguard the competitive process and neither the competitors nor the consumers (Singh, 2011).

Competition Law

India came up with its modern competition law by repealing the erstwhile MRTP Act of 1969 in 2002. However, it took almost 9 years to get its all provisions notified. Competition Act, 2002 basically deals with three areas: (i) prohibition of anti-competitive agreements including cartels; (ii) prohibition of abuse of dominant position; and (iii) regulation of combinations. Other than these, the Act also provides for an advocacy mandate wherein the Commission shall take suitable measures for the promotion of competition advocacy, relating awareness and imparting training about competition issues. Competition Act gives a specific mandate to the Competition Commission of India which is highlighted in the Preamble, further echoed under Section 18 of the Act. The duty of the Commission is "to prevent practices having adverse effect on competition, to promote and sustain competition in markets, to protect the interests of consumers and to ensure freedom of trade carried on by other participants in markets."

Thus, protecting the interests of consumers is one of the duties of the Commission. However, the philosophy of modern competition law differentiates "competition law" from special consumer protection measures, like the Consumer Protection Act. The decisive adjudication principle is undue competition restriction and not consumer welfare. Thus, it is argued that the expression "to protect the interest of consumers" in the Act, must be interpreted broadly in deciding disputes of individual consumers. One should not lose sight of the fact that as a specialised body, the CCI may not have been created to do the same job for which there is a body already in existence in the form of a Consumer Forum/ Commission. The challenge before the CCI is to balance the expectations of consumers in the short-term and focus upon prohibiting anti-competitive conduct and abuse of dominance, regulating mergers and forestalling market failures, ultimately protecting the interest of consumers (Singh, 2011).

'Consumer' has been defined under the Competition Act, and the definition is broader than the "consumer law" such that it even includes the purchase of goods or hiring of services even for commercial purpose which is not the case with Consumer Protection Act. Further, the Act defines the 'enterprise' to include government departments within its purview, except sovereign function of the Government. The competition law basically is concerned about the fair and free competition in the markets and steps into action whenever there seems to be an "appreciable adverse effect on competition" (AAEC) in markets in India. What amounts to AAEC has to be determined keeping into view the factors mentioned in Section 19(3) of the Act. There are six factors—three are negative (creation of barriers to new entrants in the market, driving existing competitors out of the market, foreclosure of competition by hindering entry into the market) and three are positive (accrual of benefits to consumers, improvements in production or distribution of goods or provision of services, promotion of technical, scientific and economic development by means of production or distribution of goods or provision of services).

Relevant Market

Determination of "relevant market" is an important step in competition law analysis, especially when one does an abuse of dominance analysis as well as while analysing vertical agreements and combinations. For determining whether a market constitutes a "relevant market" for the purposes of the competition law, the Commission shall have due regard to "relevant geographic market" and "relevant product market". Here, just like consumer law, competition law does not have any special provision in relation to rural markets or rural consumers. However, while determining the relevant market, the Commission may have due regard to the special circumstances applicable to rural markets which differentiates it from urban or other markets analysing the factors mentioned in Section 19(5), (6) and (7).

While determining the "relevant geographic market", the following factors needs to be considered—(a) regulatory trade barriers—for example Agricultural Produce Marketing Committees (APMCs) licence is required for establishment of structured retail chain in order to have the permission to procure, store, transport and market the agricultural products; (b) local specification requirements; (c) national procurement policies—specifically in relation to agricultural markets, the government minimum support price (MSP) and the sole nodal procuring agency, i.e. the Food Corporation of India (FCI); (d) adequate distribution facilities—

distance to markets and lack of roads is a major concern for rural consumers/producers; (e) transportation costs—to approach competitive markets, the transportation costs are high and a major concern; (f) language—the rural consumers/producers are not conversant with the language of the market, say a farm producer coming from a remote place in Haryana may not be conversant with the language in the *mandi* at Delhi, more so the language of the trade; (g) consumer preferences; and (h) need for secure or regular supplies or rapid after-sales service. Thus, considering the aforesaid factors, rural markets may be identified as a separate market and the rural consumers can accordingly be given the benefit of competition through the enforcement of competition law, as and when the cases arise.

Further, while determining the 'relevant product market', the factors to be considered are: (a) physical characteristics or end-use of goods; (b) price of goods or service; (c) consumer preferences; (d) exclusion of in-house production; (e) existence of specialised producers; and (f) classification of industrial products. It may be noted that the consumer preferences play an important role in determining the relevant geographic as well as relevant product market. Rural consumers' preferences may vary from that of urban consumers. Thus, the competition law provides for a greater scope to differentiate the rural consumers from that of urban consumers and accordingly provide a suitable remedy for them while enforcing the competition law.

Competition Law and Policy for Rural Consumers

"Access to market" and "market development" are key areas of concern for rural consumers. As noted above the rural consumers as per the competition law comprise the following classes:

(A) rural consumers relating to farm activities—here the rural population becomes consumer as a producer in relation to access to markets, wherein the APMCs act as service providers providing the platform for trading. Further, the procurement agencies like FCI also act as service providers to procure the agricultural produce. This leg of the market is very important to the rural consumers/producers. It has been pointed out by many that the issues that arise in relation to the functioning of APMCs is that they are adopting policies and practices that (i) limit the market for the farmers; (ii) prevent purchasers from accessing the markets directly from the farmer or at the level of initial wholesale market; (iii) prevent development of infrastructure to support marketing of agricultural produce; and (iv) prevent development of markets (Gujral *et al.*, 2011). In the farm market, another special market may be identified as inputs to the farm activities, i.e. the markets for fertilizers, seeds, insecticides and agricultural implements.

(B) Rural consumers in the markets of consumer goods and services. Here, the rural population is a consumer of the agricultural produce (they are also the producer of the same) as well as the other products and services by different players in the market. This is the market in comparison to the urban markets, specifically in the current scenario sectors like telecom, FMCG, automotive, electronics, and other non-farm goods. According to industry experts, this market is poised to grow ten-fold by 2025 to become a US$100 billion proposition for retailers. A report by Boston Consulting Group (BCG) and CII projects that small town and rural customers would be single largest market segment constituting 36 per cent of households by 2020.

In the categories 'A' and 'B' discussed above, there are own problems relating to competition law and policy. In the category 'A', the biggest issue is that of the policy at the State level. As agriculture is the state subject, the State governments have the authority to notify areas within which the purchase and sale of agricultural produce, livestock or products of livestock can occur. These areas are basically under the control of APMC which have the power and functions that have been statutorily vested which includes both the creation of markets as well as they participate in such markets for agricultural produce. From a competition law point of view, APMC qualifies as an 'enterprise' and thus subject to the provisions. As of now, no case has been brought before CCI against the APMCs for alleged abuse of dominant position or entering into anti-competitive agreements, however, with the allowance of FDI in retail, issues may crop up when there would be conflict of interest due to competition in procurement by the FDI investors in retail chain as well as the APMCs/FCI/Government Agencies. This is a grey area to be watched for. At present, for the farmers as producers (consumers of APMC market platform) there is a structural constrain in the form of asymmetry of market relations, as there is reliance on monopsonistic traders, agro-processors, or the market boards (APMC) whose market power allows excess profit shares. This is coupled with other problems like poor roads, high transport costs, perishable goods, lack of understanding of how markets operate, lack of information and lack of relevant skills (IDAF, 2001).

In category 'B', there are issues like cost of entry is high in rural markets which acts as a potential entry barrier and thus, if a firm establishes its position in rural market, it would be difficult for a new firm to enter, more so when the dominant firm undertakes abusive practices mentioned in the Act. Further, the competitors in the rural market may enter into cartels or may enter into exclusive supply or distribution agreements, tie-in arrangements leading to denial of market access or a consolidation between two competitive firms in rural markets may lead to potential abuse. These potential competition law violations in rural markets may be discussed as follows:

Anti-Competitive Agreements (Section 3)—An agreement is said to be anti-competitive, if it causes or is likely to cause an appreciable adverse effect on competition within India. Such agreements are void as per law. Anti-competitive agreements are of two kinds—Horizontal Agreements, wherein the AAEC is presumed when the agreements relate to (a) direct or indirect determination of purchase or sale price; (b) limiting or controlling of production, supply, markets, technical development, investment or provision of services; (c) sharing of market by way of allocation of geographic area of market or type of goods or number of customers or in a similar way; and (d) bid rigging or collusive bidding. Horizontal agreements are entered into between the enterprises at the same level of production chain and includes 'cartel'. Vertical Agreement is an agreement between the enterprises at different stages or levels of the production chain in different markets. Here the AAEC needs to be proved. With reference to rural markets, all the aforesaid violations are possible and there is a requirement to deal with them with special reference to the rural parameters as discussed above.

Abuse of Dominant Position (Section 4)—Competition law does not prohibit a firm from acquiring dominant position in the market, what it looks at is the abuse by such firm. In an analysis of abuse of dominant position, the first step is the determination of relevant market, and then the alleged firm's dominant position is ascertained. A firm may be said to be dominant if it has 'market power', that is it has a position of strength which enables it to operate independent of competitive forces prevailing in the relevant market or affect its competitors or consumers or relevant market in its favour. A dominant firm may abuse its dominance by (a) directly or indirectly imposing unfair purchase or selling prices including predatory prices; (b) limiting production, markets or technical development to the prejudice of the consumers; (c) indulging in action resulting in the denial of market access; (d) making contracts with obligations which have no connection with the subject of the contract; or (e) using dominance in one market to move into or protect other markets.

With reference to rural markets, potential abuse of dominant position may be high because of the entry barriers due to local laws promoting APMCs, illiteracy of the consumers, and other factors discussed above. An Enterprise which may have entered the rural market may gain the market power and use the same in imposing unfair purchase (from farmers) or selling prices (to the rural consumers). The choice may be limited by limiting production or technical development or event there can be denial of market access to upstream players by a dominant enterprise.

Regulation of Combinations (Sections 5 and 6)—Combination has been defined to include acquisition, change in control, mergers and amalgamations. The provisions relating to combinations require a compulsory filing before the Commission if the combining firms meet the statutory thresholds with respect to asset or turnover prescribed under the law. While dealing with these findings, the Commission looks at the potential anti-competitive affect or AAEC in the relevant market by the combined entity. Accordingly, the combination is approved or disproved.

Conclusion

Competition law and policy is a very important tool in the hands of rural consumers to protect themselves from the anti-competitive agreements and abusive practices of a dominant enterprise. It is important to note here that Competition Commission has a duty not only to prevent practices having adverse effect on competition but also to promote and sustain competition in markets. Thus, the role of the competition agency is not only passive as regards enforcement, but also an active towards promotion of competition in markets. Now, where three-fourth of the country's population (approx. 1.1 billion) is residing in villages, the promotion and sustenance of competition in rural markets is more so important. As regards rural markets, it seems the development of rural markets for the benefits of consumers may be one of the goals of competition law and policy in the country. This aspect is further made clear in the draft national competition policy, as one of its avowed objectives is to promote, build, and sustain a strong competition culture within the country through creating awareness, imparting training and capacity-building of stakeholders including public officials, business, trade associations, consumer associations, civil society organisations etc. Commission has a mandate to do these under Section 49 of the Act.

Overall, the competition authorities carry out their enforcement duties on the presumption that ensuring the maintenance of competition on markets will ultimately benefit consumer welfare. Competition law seeks to protect the process of free market competition in order to ensure efficient allocation of scarce economic resources. The idea is to create benefits for consumers by maximising the efficiency including improvements and innovations in lower costs and prices, choice and services. Eventually, this would benefit the consumers, rural consumers in this case.

To use any tool or law, one must know about the tool or the law. Education and awareness about these legislations is important. It is sad to find that the report of a study on the Consumer Protection Act commissioned by CAG of India in July 2005 brought out that 66 per cent consumers were not aware of consumer rights and 82 per cent were not even aware about the Consumer Protection Act. In rural areas, only 13 per cent had heard of the Consumer Protection Act. If this is the situation with a basic legislation of consumer protection enacted way back in 1986 and having direct application to consumer grievances; then one can ascertain the situation of Competition Law which is of recent origin and indirectly benefits the consumers. There is a need to create more and more awareness by advocacy measures. Unless the rural consumers know about their rights, they would not understand what they are entitled to and what is anti-competitive.

It may be pointed out here that out of approximately 300 cases before the Commission, there has been no significant case relating to rural markets or involving rural consumers. The cases have dealt mostly with urban markets and urban consumers; most of the times the dispute between to business enterprise involving a competition issue affect the market as a whole. Here, the NGOs have to play a significant role in studying the rural markets and try to bring up information before the Commission wherein there is alleged violation of competition law or where competition in market is jeopardised by the conduct of enterprises, especially in distant rural markets affecting rural consumers.

REFERENCES

Amarnath, B. and Vijayudu, G., 2011, "Rural Consumers' Attitude towards Branded Packaged Food Products", *Asia Pacific Journal of Social Sciences*, Vol. III (1) January-June 2011, pp. 147-159.

Buttigieg, Eugene, 2009, *Competition Law: Safeguarding the Consumer Interest*, Volters Kluwer.

CRISIL, *Annual Report*, 2012.

Gujral, Jyoti, IDFC; Piyush Joshi and Anuradha, R.V., 2011, Clarus Law

Associates, Facilitating Legislative and Administrative Reforms in Agriculture Marketing by Leveraging the Competition Commission of India, *NCAER*, February 2011.

IFAD (International Fund for Agricultural Development), 2001, *Rural Poverty Report Markets for the Rural Poor.*

Masters of Rural Markets: The Hallmarks of High Performance, Accenture Research Report, 2010, available at http://www.accenture.com/SiteCollectionDocuments/PDF/Accenture_Masters_of_Rural_Markets.pdf accessed on October 3, 2012

Ramachandra, V.A., Kulkarni and Handigol, 2011, "Awareness of Consumer Rights and Responsibilities among Farmers in Karnataka", *Agricultural Situation in India*, September 2011, pp. 273-277.

Report of Eleventh Five Year Plan: Inclusive Growth, Planning Commission (2007-12), Para 11.1, http://planningcommission.gov.in/plans/planrel/fiveyr/11th/11_v1/11v1_ch11.pdf (Last visited September 10, 2011)

Rural Indians outpace urbanites in spending growth: Rural wages rise faster than inflation, aiding consumption, CRISIL Research (August 2012) available at http://crisil.com/Ratings/Brochureware/News/CRISIL-Research-rural-indians-pr_290812.pdf

Rural Market Research: *A Different Ballgame,* http://www.martrural.com/docs/kn-series/Rural%20Market%20Research.pdf

Rural Market, India Brand Equity Foundation (IBEF) http://www.ibef.org/industry/consumermarket/ruralmarket.aspx accessed on October 3, 2012.

Sayulu, K. and Reddy, V.V.R., 1998, "Socio-economic Influences of Rural Consumer Behaviour—An Empirical Study", *Khadigramodyog*, 44: 431-44.

Singh, K. and Sangwan, I.V. (1994), "A Comparative Study to Assess the Problems of Rural and Urban Consumers", *Consumer Confrontation*, 14: 44-45.

Singh, Vijay Kumar, "Competition Law and Policy in India: The Journey in a Decade", 4 NUJS L. Rev. 523 (2011).

9

Consumer Behaviour in Rural Marketing

K. GANESAN AND D. DEV ANAND

Introduction

In the competitive world, business concerns adopt various effective marketing strategies to attain first position and also make a name in the global market. More or less the urban areas are covered by all business organisations, therefore, the face of business has changed towards the rural markets and they are studying the behaviour of rural consumers in order to survive in the markets as a result of tough competition and technological upgradations. Today, every aspect of business is focused on business development/promotion activities to cover consumers and also retain the consumers especially in the rural areas. Organisations have introduced subscription-based membership programmes to win customer loyalty and commitment and are using rural markets as a medium to earn profits. It is imperative for business concerns to generate ideas and continue to retain the most valued rural customers for business sustainability. An effective consumer acquisition and retention programme in rural marketing has the power to increase business development in the current scenario. Consumer loyalty, customer lifetime value and developing long lasting customer relationship have become the need of the hour. With a well planned consumer acquisition and retention programme in the rural market, the business concerns can develop the consumer relationship in a healthy manner by collecting critical data on their consumers to better understand their needs relationships and maximize profits for better business performance in rural marketing.

Consumer Behaviour

To survive in the competitive world the business enterprise should know about the consumer acquisition and retention strategies in rural marketing. This can be done by analysing the various strategies of consumer acquisition and retention in rural marketing. To identify the factors influencing consumer behaviour in rural marketing is of prime importance for modern business so as to formulate effective strategies of consumer acquisition and retention in rural marketing.

"A consumer is an ultimate buyer". Consumers are households who buy and use products and services in order to satisfy their personal needs and wants. For a marketer, the attitude of the consumer decides as to how existing goods and services will be sold. Therefore, consumer behaviour relates to the activity and the action of people for purchase and use of economic goods and services including his influence on those activities and actions. In a broader sense consumer behaviour includes all the psychological and physiological reasons of individual consumer's response to marketing activities. Consumer psychology is based on the consumer's knowledge, attitude, intention and motive. Physiology is based on purchases and uses of goods and services. In nutshell consumer behaviour in rural marketing is behaviour exhibited by people in planning, purchasing and using of economic goods and services in rural marketing.

Dr. Sarvepalli Radhakrishnan, the then President of India said, "India is a great country with rich resources but with poor people". India's resources are rich but then resources are not reaching the poor, particular the rural masses. Of course, there are few rich people in rural areas but majority of them are poor. But this situation is fast changing in India especially in rural India due to the impact of globalisation, liberalisation and expansion of information technology.

Government of India's "The New Trade Policy of 1991—Liberalisation, Privatisation, and Globalisation (LPG)"—had far reaching consequences on the Indian economy which accelerated the pace of development in the new millennium. On the marketing side with particular reference to rural marketing, the information revolution added by the green revolution (agriculture), the white revolution (dairy farms—milk) has benefited the rural consumers thereby improving the economic climate of the rural consumers. In the industrial side, also though the urban and semi-urban areas have benefited by way of employment opportunities, the people in the rural areas are not left behind to a large extent, as people employed in semi-urban areas are pumping money in the rural areas by way of housing, transportation and other activities in the rural areas.

Consumer Acquisition and Retention in Rural Marketing

Consumer acquisition and retention in rural marketing are two important components. Customer acquisition is the process of attracting customers for the first time through first purchase. Customer retention is most likely to be the purchase of a similar product or service for a second time and may be for a number of times on a regular basis. How to attract consumers in rural areas is a challenging and interesting task. One of the most common and easy ways to attract rural consumers is by providing small gifts and offering discounts to the consumers. Rural consumers give importance to low price products because of their income and lifestyle. If business concerns want to attract the rural customers, low price and small size product should be sold. Changes and challenges occurring in the rural environment must be taken as opportunities. To survive, the companies must have the capacity and capability to meet the challenges of taste and preferences in the rural areas.

Factors Influencing Customer Retention in Rural Marketing

Due to low income, seasonal and weekly wages payment, credit sales facilities influence and retain the customers in rural areas. More or less rural workers are paid daily wages but the payment is made on weekly basis. So, rural people normally purchase on credit and pay for their purchase only on the days of wages (probably on Monday). Therefore, introduction of variety of products can somewhat retain the customers in rural areas as they do not pay and buy but do so on credit. For example in a provisional store fancy items can be sold. This needs some planning to be done to attract the rural consumer like:

- What consumers are planning to buy?
- When they are going to buy?
- Where they are going to buy?
- How often they are going to use?

On the basis of the above information, the business concern should introduce the product into the rural marketing. Moreover, the marketer should also know the consumer taste; it may be different from area to area, consumer to consumer. On the basis of the taste of consumer new products should be introduced in the rural market. There are various theories to understand consumer behaviour. A few are analysed below to help the readers understand better.

Theories of Consumer Behaviour in Rural Marketing

Economic Theory: This theory was developed by the classical economists. According to them, a consumer will continue to buy such products that are, and will deliver him the most utility or maximum satisfaction at relative prices. The income and the savings theory is based on the fact that purchasing power is the real determinant of buying, purchasing power on the other hand is dependent on the disposable income.

Psychological Theory: The essence of this theory lays in the fact that consumer learn from experience and the results of future occasions.

Psycho-analytical Theory: It follows that the consumer behaviour is a function of the interaction of these three systems. It is a free mechanism that leads to the strong derives—such drives are not influenced by morality or ethics. Ego refers to the act of weighing consequences and tries to reconcile with reality. The ego weighs the consequences of an act rather than rushing blindly into the activity.

Socio-cultural Theory: This theory was formulated by "Thorsten Veblen" and he asserted that man is primarily a social animal and his works and behaviour are largely influenced by the group of which he is a member.

The trend in rural marketing not only relates to products but services like rural banking, rural finance, rural health, rural farming etc. Much importance is now being given to improve rural economy and tap the rural consumers due to rise in rural prosperity. India's vast population lives in rural and remote areas and various kinds of products have to reach the rural areas for consumption. Marketers hitherto were familiar with urban markets which were more familiar to them. The importance of "rural marketing" is gaining momentum due to the change in the rural environment and development of infrastructure. Therefore, there is a large scope for "Rural Marketing" and this can be better achieved by appropriate marketing strategies including use of media to educate the rural consumers.

The trend in the corporate world is to target the rural consumers as the income level of the villagers in rural areas are raising, their habits, tastes, preferences, attitudes are fast changing. Therefore, there is an urgent need to build-up expertise in rural marketing. The challenges faced in building up efficient rural marketing are:

- Reaching the markets in rural India—Transportation facilities.
- Educating the rural consumers as to understand the utility of the products and service due to low literacy rate among them.
- Influencing the consumers as to maintain 'Brand Loyalty' is difficult, because the villagers are more concerned about the utility rather than 'Brand name'. There is a lot of potential in rural markets as the economy of the people in rural areas has improved due to rise in their income. Rural penetration and awareness remain low and much need to be done to tap the potential in rural marketing.

Conclusion

The development of the rural areas began with the First Five Year Plan but the New Economic Policy introduced in 1991 has changed the face of rural India to a large extent. Rural India, being the heart of India, plays a vital role in contributing to the total national income. The per capita income (PCI) of the rural population is also slowly increasing and their purchasing power has steadily increased over the years. Rural economy includes improvement in rural marketing, rural services including rural housing, rural health etc. for which the States and Central Government have introduced a large number of schemes. Improving infrastructure facilities by way of transportation, power, communication etc. to rural areas are essential not only to promote rural marketing but also to provide better quality of products and services to the rural consumers.

There is, therefore, a large scope for "Rural marketing" in India and this can be better through appropriate marketing strategies. The importance of consumer behaviour in rural marketing has increased mainly on account of its ability in promoting sales and preparing the ground for more expansion in rural marketing. However, marketers should also be careful that the rural consumers will not stick to the products and services, if they are exploited. There is also a need to build institutions to protect the rural consumer so that the marketers do not take the rural consumers for a rise in the name of marketing.

REFERENCES

Balakrishna, M., 1977, *Rural Market,* End of Lane Road for the Consumer Marketers.

Chatterjee, Adite, 1992, *Brand Equity,* Marketers Hit the Rural Dirt Trucks, October 24.

Cook, V.I. and Schutte, T.F., 1967, *Brand Policy Discrimination,* Boston: Allyn and Bacon.

Drucker, Peter F., 1954, *The Practice of Management,* New York.

Holmes, P.M. and Bartel, R., 1963, *Readings in Marketing,* Columbus, Ohio: Charles E. Merill Book. Inc.

Kotler. P.,1972 *Marketing Management.*

Little Field, J.F. and Kirk, Patrick, 1971, *Advertising Mass Communication in Marketing.*

Pradeep Kashyap and Siddhartha, 2007, *The Rural Marketing Book,* Biztantra Publishers.

Stanton, J.W., 1983, *Fundamentals of Marketing.*

10

Spurious Products in Rural Market

Problems and Countering Strategies

PUSHYAMITRA JOSHI AND ANURUPA B. SINGH

Introduction

The recent Government initiatives and the resulting good financial health of the rural market have resulted in increase in the purchasing power of rural consumers. Latest National Sample Survey Organization (NSSO) data show that during 2009-10 and 2011-12 rural consumption per person grew annually at 19 per cent; which is 2 per cent more than its urban counterparts. In the urban market, the companies are facing severe competition due to saturation. The focus of the companies have now shifted to the rural market which consists of two-third of the total 1.21 billion population of India residing in 6,40,867 villages.

According to the National Council for Applied Economic Research, the Rural market stands at an estimated size of Rs. 1,23,000 crore out of which FMCG accounts for Rs. 65,000 crore, Durables at Rs. 5,000 crore and Agri-inputs at Rs. 45,000 crore. Although there exists a conducive condition and statistics, the FMCG companies, face a colossal problem. The payback which would otherwise have benefited the companies is being gradually eroded by the sale of spurious products in rural market. FMCG companies like HUL, ITC, Dabur, Emami, Parle-G and many others successfully penetrated rural market since last 10 years. They also have been afflicted by the quandary due to emergence of fake product manufacturers who are using the look alike packaging scheme, spell alike names and even copied the same name, packaging and address of the original FMCG brand.

The study conducted by ASSOCHAM (The Associated Chambers of Commerce and Industry of India) in the year 2007, estimated the loss at Rs. 300 billion. One of the biggest losers was the FMCG sector losing Rs. 17 billion every year due to counterfeit products. The emergence of spurious or fake product manufacturers is a matter of concern for branded FMCG companies in rural market because it is mostly found in rural areas due to lack of awareness in rural people. Spurious or fake or counterfeit products are also affecting the business of branded companies by hurting their brand image and value. Spurious products are broadly divided into four categories:

1. *Fake or Duplicate Products*: Manufacturer of fake or duplicate products use the identical name of the product, packaging, colour scheme, logo and even the same name and address as the genuine manufacturer.
2. *Look Alike Products*: Look alike products are those products where manufacturer other than original producer cleverly uses the similar looking packaging or colour or design or logo scheme to deceive the customers.
3. *Spell Alike Products*: Spell alike products use names which are similar sounding or similar in spelling (for example "Viks" or "Vix" for "Vicks", "Fire and Lovely" for "Fair and Lovely", "Nilima" for "Nirma", "Daily Milk" for "Dairy Milk").
4. *Brand Deceiving Product:* On the basis of interview of Mr. Pawandeep Singh (Former Head, Rural Distribution, Philips); it is a new category found in the spurious product category where fake manufacturer is using the name, logo or goodwill of the original manufacturer in the related product category which is actually not produced by the original manufacturer. It is found that in rural areas fake manufacturers are selling electrical switches with name and logo of Philips. Philips is a well-known company in electrical and electronic product category but does not involved in manufacturing of electrical switches.

Review of Literature

In this study literature relating to spurious and fake products has been discussed focusing on various strategies adopted by companies and also strategies suggested by few experts/researchers to counter the menace of spurious products.

Rana Sharma Gunjan[1] studied four sectors—FMCG, consumer durables, pharmaceutical and rural and came to know about that counterfeit defeat branded companies business. Research discussed about the Trademark Act, 1999, BPC's (Brand Protection Committee) fourfold strategy and example of Mumbai based PRS Permacel Private Ltd. company's solution named "*Kavach*" to counter the fake products. Research also suggested conducting seminars and workshops, advertisements to educate customers and give customers incentive who detect fake products in the market. Chapter is conceptual in nature and based on secondary data.

Kanan, K.V.[2] suggested few strategies for chocolate companies to kill the fake products in Indian rural market. Chapter discusses about the segmentation of rural market into three segments; rural rich consumers, rural consumers above poverty line and consumers below poverty line. It further discusses about the laws governing in India which protects the rights of original manufacturers. Finally, it suggested strategies with reference to 4 Ps of marketing: without compromising the quality of product, follow penetration pricing, increase retailers' margin, create awareness about the fake products through advertisement campaigns and appoint sales professionals from local region.

Sridhar, G[3] discussed considerably about the good and the ugly aspects of counterfeiting. Further, it discusses about the different strategies like generic strategies, proactive strategies (government lobbying, proactive changes in marketing mix and labelling), and reactive strategies (warning and legal action). Study provides a conceptual model and strategies to counter fake products. Simi, T.B.[4] found in his study that Fast Moving Consumer Goods (FMCG) sector in India is the biggest loser with loss of Rs. 17 billion of revenue annually due to counterfeits. Research further discussed about the impact of counterfeiting on the consumer, economy, manufacturers and Government as a whole. Chapter further discusses law enforcement in India and few cases where companies won the cases and protect their brands, trademark rights and business from counterfeiting. Research also discusses international cases related to copyright and trademark infringement laws. Joshi, P., Sabharwal P.C. and M. Vishnoei[5] have discussed AALAP (Analyse, Awareness, Legal Action and Protection) strategy model in their chapter "Strategies to Counter Spurious Products with Reference to FMCG in Rural Market", to counter fake and spurious product companies with special focus on the rural market.

The broad objectives of the study are:

- To provide strategy with conceptual model to FMCG companies against spurious product manufacturers.
- To discuss the major factors behind sale of spurious products in rural market.

Research Methodology

This is a conceptual research based on the extensive study of the secondary data available on internet, journals, magazines, newspapers, books and interview schedule of industry experts.

Problems due to Spurious Products

Selling of spurious products has a threefold negative impact on the consumers, company and government. Spurious product manufacturers produce imitated products of original manufacturers which not only has a negative impact on the business of original branded manufacturer but it also has negative impact on the health of consumers. It also results in loss of taxes for the government. It is a way of cheating the rural consumers who are purchasing these products keeping in the mind that they are purchasing original branded products. In a study done by A.C. Nielsen, it was found that eight out of ten customers who purchased pass-off products realized after the purchase that they were cheated. Spurious and Pass-off products are negatively affecting the Industrial growth and economy of India. Manufacturers of spurious products do not pay duties and taxes, and ultimately the government revenue suffers. In order to increase the revenue collection the government in turn increases the taxes and duties, which negatively impact the consumer's demand because of increase in price. According to an estimate of ASSOCHAM products across different sectors like electronics, automobile sector, consumer durables, pharma, herbal medicine and cosmetic will capture a market size of Rs. 55,000 crore through illegal channels by 2013. According to the General Secretary of ASSOCHAM, FMCG companies are losing up to 45 per cent and an average loss around 25 per cent of their market share in the well-known category of products.

Loss to the Company: Due to sale of spurious and fake products in the rural markets, the business of the companies is get affected in two ways—one in terms of loss of sales and second in terms of loss of goodwill.

Loss to the Consumers: Due to sale of spurious products in the rural markets consumers are cheated by purchasing cheap and low quality products and it may also have a negative impact on their health. Use of spurious medicines may even result in the death of the consumer.

Loss to the Government: It is affecting the revenue of government in terms of taxes and also by infringing the law set by government to protect the trademark and copyrights of the owner.

Table 10.1: Comparative Table of Different Categories of Spurious Products

Features	*Duplicates*	*Spell Likes*	*Look Alikes*
Brand Name	Original	Misspelt	Different
Pack Appearance	Replica	Identical	Similar
Manufacturer's address	Original	Incomplete	Own Name
Price	M.R.P.	40 per cent low	10-15 per cent low
Margins	200-300 per cent	100-150 per cent	60-70 per cent
Quality	Very poor	Poor	Reasonable
Intention of Retailer	To cheat	To mislead	To freeload
Consumers	Unaware	Unaware	Want cheaper products
Identify	None	Only literate	Majority
Offer	None	Discounts	Schemes

Source: "Study on Fakes" by MART, 2003[6].

The facts given in Table 10.1 shows that spurious manufacturers market their products in all the three categories: duplicate, spell alike and look alike products. It also shows that retailers play an important role in misleading consumers in the rural market and take an advantage of their ignorance.

Factors Behind Sale of Spurious Products in Rural Market

On the basis of various studies, it is clear that there are various factors responsible for the sale of spurious products in the rural markets. The few factors which are most important in sale of fake and spurious products are:

- *Lack of Distribution Channel:* Most of the FMCG companies are lacking in penetration of the rural market due to lack of proper distribution channel system. Here, the local manufacturer of spurious product has an advantage over branded and original manufacturers. It is easy for most of the spurious manufacturers to cover the rural areas which have not even been explored by the original branded companies.

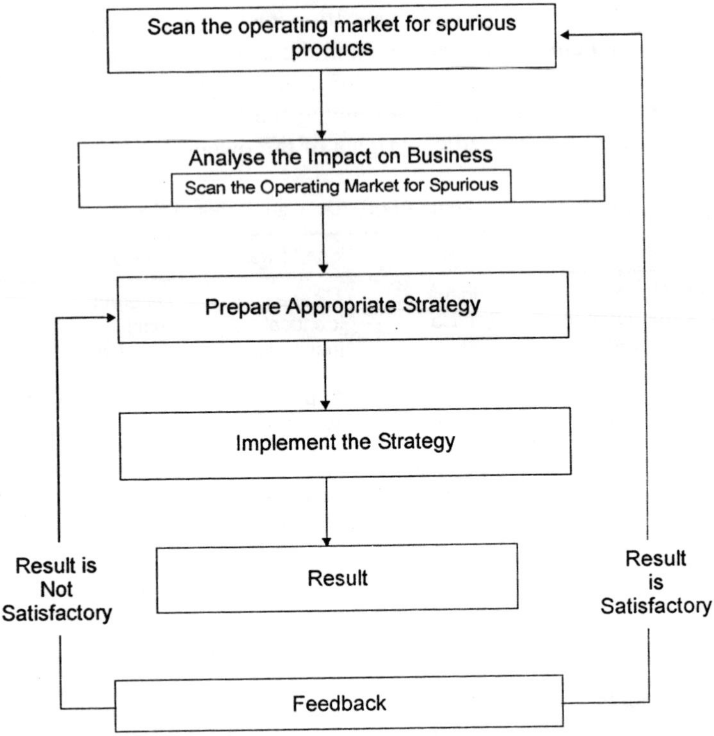

Figure 10.1: Strategic Framework: Countering Spurious Products.

- *Retailer's Influence*: In rural markets, retail store owner plays an important role in influencing the rural consumers to purchase the product. Rural marketing is a relationship based marketing and local retailers are having good interaction with the rural people. Moreover, the margin provided by spurious product manufacturers is much higher than the margin provided by the original branded manufacturers. This motivates the retailers to promote sale of fake products to their customers.
- *Lack of Awareness*: Rural consumers are less aware and less educated to differentiate between fake and spurious products from the original branded products. This is one of the main reasons for the sale of spurious products in the rural market.
- *Poor Economic Conditions*: A huge potential lies in the rural market but it is equally true that rural consumers are still living with the limited income and resources. They generally prefer

cheaper products over quality products. This is one of the reasons for the sale of spurious products in the rural market.

- *Scan the Operating Market for Spurious Products*: Crusade against the fake and spurious products starts with the scanning of the market where company is operating its business. If fake or spurious products are found during the inspection of the area of business operation they start collecting the data of retailers who are selling spurious products and also about the awareness level of the consumers who are purchasing these products.
- *Analyse the Impact on Business*: After collection of the data it is analysed to assess its impact on the business in terms of loss in sales and loss of goodwill. Both the sales and goodwill factors are equally important for any company because these two factors are the deciding factors behind the existence of any company.
- *Prepare Appropriate Strategy:* After analysing the impact of spurious and fake products on the business and goodwill of branded and original manufacturers the company prepares appropriate countering strategy to fight against the fake and spurious manufacturers by using available resources (Legal, human and money) and by increasing education and awareness level of consumers through various promotional campaigns.
- *Proactive Strategies* includes lobbying with the government departments at both Centre and State level in formulation and implementation of policy to protect the original brands under various laws like Trade Marks Act, 1999 and Trade Marks (Amendments) Rules, 2002, The Patents Act, 1970 and The Patent (Amendments) Rules, 2006, Copyright Act, 1957 and Copyright Rules, 1958 and International Copyright Order, 1999. It also includes the changes in the marketing mix (4 Ps of marketing) and labelling to protect against the counterfeiting.
- *Reactive Strategies* are the actions taken by the companies after being affected with the spurious and fake products. These strategies includes warning to the spurious product manufacturers, legal action against them and reactive changes in marketing mix like increase in the retailer's margin, extensive promotional campaign in the rural areas to educate rural consumers and increase in the extensive channels to make products available in the affected areas.
- *Implement the Strategy:* Implement the appropriate strategy or combination of strategies as per the situation, to lessen the impact on the business and capacity of the company.

- *Result:* After implementation of the appropriate strategy or combination of strategies it is time to monitor the result of action taken. If result is satisfactory then strategy is successful and simple monitoring from time-to-time is required but if results are not satisfactory then again search for appropriate strategy to fight against the fake and spurious product manufacturers is needed.
- *Feedback:* Feedback in the form of action if results are satisfactory. Once again the environment needs to be scanned to avoid future threats from manufacturers of spurious product. But, if results are not satisfactory then again appropriate strategy are to be prepared to counter the manufacturers of fake and spurious product.

Promotional Strategies

There are a number of strategies that can be adopted by the companies. Some low cost promotional strategies which can be adopted by the FMCG companies to create awareness among the rural consumers are: Wall painting, *Nukkad-Natak* (Street plays), addressing the issues in front of people during *Panchayat Sabha*, through vans and other vehicles. Awareness programmes through NGOs under CSR activity and joint venture with local/government schools to aware rural consumers about the issue and harmful effects of spurious products. Communication on packaging should be done in local language so that consumers can understand and differentiate between the original brands from the spurious one.

Conclusion

Rural markets in India are badly affected by the sales of spurious products. The rural consumers are unable to differentiate between the branded FMCG products from the spurious products available at retail shops. Although in last decade literacy level of rural consumers has seen a rise from 59 per cent (Approx.) to 69 per cent (Approx.), but still availability of spurious products indicates that there are other factors behind its sale. It is clear that rural market is flooded with spurious and fake products. Branded and original manufacturers are affected with the sale of spurious products as the retailers get higher margin from the manufacturers of spurious product, lack of awareness level among rural consumers to identify the fake products, poor distribution channel coverage of original and branded product manufacturers and also poor economic condition of the rural people to purchase quality products of high cost. To avoid all the hurdles every effected company has to take preventive actions by scanning the market and business environment to counter manufacturers of fake and spurious product. Apart from associating with Brand Protection Committee (BPC) every company specially FMCG companies have to co-operate in terms of fighting against fake manufacturers especially in the rural market.

NOTES

1. Gunjan Rana Sharma, 2004, "Counterfeit Defeat Brands", *Social Science Research Network.*
2. Kanan, K.V., 2005, "Strategies for Chocolate Companies to Kill Fake Products in Indian Rural Market", www.indianmba.com.Kashyap, Pradip, Ghosh Anirban and Vikram Bhalla, 2001, *Study on Fakes*, MART Research Centre, 2001.
3. Sridhar, G., 2007, "Countering Counterfeits", *International Marketing Conference on Marketing and Society,* IIMK, April, 2007.
4. Simi, T.B., 2009, "Combating Counterfeit Goods Compromising Development?", *CUTS Centre for International Trade, Economics and Environment,* 13/2009, September 2009.
5. Joshi, P., Sabharwal, P.C. and Manish Vishnoei, 2012, "Strategies to Counter Spurious Products with reference to FMCG in Rural Market", *Rural Marketing Millennium*, edited by Piali Haldar, Paramount Publishing House.
6. Kashyap, Pradip; Ghosh, Anirban and Vikram Bhalla (2001). *Study on Fakes*, MART Research Cantre.

WEBSITES

Brand Protection Committee—Facts and Figures, available at www.ficci.com/sector/5/Add_docs/factsnfigures.pdf (Retrieved on 16-09-2012).

www.censesofindia.gov.in

Express News Service, "High Number of Fake Products in WB", February 2008, available at www.expressindia.com/latest-news/High-number-of-fake-products-in-WB/274231/ (Retrieved on 13/09/2012)

Malavika Sharma, "Unilever Losing to Fakes Selling to Illiterate Indians: Retail", April 2012, available at www.bloomberg.com/news/2012-04-19/unilever-losing-to-fakes-selling-to-illiterate-indians retail.html?goback=%2Egde_1802091_member_109388240 (Retrieved on 01/10/2012)

Seema Seth, "Real World of Fakes!" August 2011, available at www.indianretailer.com/article/whats-hot/trends/The-real-world-of-fakes-532/ (Retrieved on 10-09-2012)

11

Prevalence and Awareness of Food Adulteration and Misbranding in a Rural Area of Kancheepuram District, Tamil Nadu

RADHIKA GANESAN

Introduction

Since medieval times there has been presence of food fraud in both developed and developing nations along with efforts which have been undertaken to stamp out occurrence of this fraud (Sudharshan *et al.*, 2008; Rao *et al.*, 2009). In addition, there is growing concern among food control authorities to promote the welfare of people and the main motivation behind promoting a clear control with respect to food manufacture as well as marketing to ensure that the needs of the consumer and the honest trader is protected (Rao *et al.*, 2007). The central point of all marketing activities is the consumer who is identified to be the largest economic group. With the increase in globalisation, there is an overflow in the number of new products available. There has been a notable shift in world food trade over the past three decades (Dhyani & Saklani, 1994). The importance given to classical food products including coffee, tea, sugar and cocoa has been reduced with increasing consumer demand for processed food as a result of diet upgrade (Kalpagam *et al.*, 2006).

Changes in consumer food habits around the world are associated with rising income, growing health consciousness and urbanization (Rae & Josling, 2003). Other aspects contributing to change in consumer habits involves international migration, communication revolutions and international tourism (Athukorala & Jayasuriya, 2005). There is increasing difficulty for consumers to select food items as a result of misleading advertisements, improper emphasis by traditional and modern media as well as rampant increase in food fraud (Bhat and Rao, 1997).

In developing countries like India, frauds in various consumer sectors are now commonly practiced and food is purposely contaminated with additives to increase bulk, attractiveness, disguise spoilage and increase profit. All food products targeted for adulteration are high commercial value products and/or produced in high tonnage around the world and have direct impact on national progress and production (GDP). These types of malpractices with respect to food make consumers the ultimate victim as they undergo suffering due to lack of food safety. Moreover, these malpractices are more prevalent among rural consumers as they are generally ignorant and also unorganised. Rural market in general comprised duplicity of branded goods (misbranding) and sub-standard goods and there are no quality checks on production and sale of such products.

The problems of food fraud in India take two main forms. First, it involves a direct method where merchants perform straightforward adulteration. This involves reducing the quality of food by adding some additives which involves insidious commercial debasement of food (Umali-Deininger & Sur, 2007) either due to intentional or unintentional in nature. Intentional adulteration is often wilful where the adulterator intends to increase his overall margin of profit. Sometimes, adulteration occurs unintentionally due to contamination as a result of ignorance, negligence or lack of proper facilities (Sri Lakshmi, 2003 : 313). The second category of food fraud involves passing off food under misleading brand names, descriptions as well as claims. This may also include concealment of nutritional content and labelling and occur mainly due to growth in the power of the marketing (Vidya & Rao, 2010 : 240). In order to keep their market share, or even stay in business, traders large and small have had to "swim with the tide"; hence the problems grow.

In order to prevent adulteration, the Ministry of Health and Family Welfare, has initiated a programme called as the Prevention of Food Adulteration Act (PFA) which is designed to be a basic Food Security Act where authorities take various samples and test them at regular intervals (Chadha, 2004; Bhat & Rao, 1997). Further, to protect the consumer from these frauds, Government of India has initiated legal measures particularly an initiation of the Consumer Protection Act, enacted on 24th December, 1986, where special emphasis is given to consumer education to ensure that people become aware about their rights and responsibilities especially among rural consumers. Despite these efforts, the levels of fraud still prevail in rural areas.

The awareness, knowledge as well judgement of food is found to be directly related to habits, attitude as well as perception of what "good food" entails which are often linked to social, cultural as well as economic influences (Wilcock *et al.*, 2004). This is found to explain why today a large number of studies which focus on food safety (Martin *et al.*, 2003; Mensah & Julien, 2011; Liu *et al.*, 2013), food adulteration, mislabelling and misbranding (Jacquet & Pauly, 2008; Karoui, 2012) is carried out more in developed countries. The consumer attitude towards food safety and food fraud is not found to be of great impact in a number of developing countries as previously the level of consumer impact was less (Wilcock *et al.*, 2004). However, this situation is rapidly changing with a number of researchers concentrating on improving consumer awareness of food products in India (Rao *et al.*, 2007; Rao *et al.*, 2009; Khapre *et al.*, 2011). Despite the fact, there is a paucity of reliable data with regards to adulteration, nutrition labelling awareness and misbranding in rural Tamil Nadu, as this data is more important to frame an appropriate policy and regulations. The aim of this study is to identify the prevalence of food adulteration, awareness towards food and nutrition labelling and misbranding in rural consumers in southern India.

Methodology

Study participants comprising 75 households were recruited using random sampling method from in and around Chunampet Village Clusters, Cheyyur Taluk, Kancheepuram district, Tamil Nadu (southern India). Individuals aged = 20 years were selected and structured questionnaire was administered. The study was conducted over a week period (August 17-23) using a trained nutritionist and research assistant across 8 different villages. A study was conducted in Tamil and hence questionnaire was translated to local regional language to ensure reliable information.

Food Adulteration, Misbranding and Food Labelling Awareness

In order to select a most commonly consumed foods, we used a 24-hour recall to understand their consumption quantity and quality of the foods consumed. The 24-hour recall covers all the information including brand, quality, place where consumed, quantity and household portion tool. A questionnaire was administered to 75 participants who both were purchasing and cooking food items. Further, ten most common shops nearby houses/villages areas were visited and bought ten (n=10) commonly consumed foods and packed products (n=15) as identified in 24-hour recall for adulteration and misbranding respectively. These shops were identified based on the choice of consumers participated in this study. To identify the level of adulteration among different food items we adopted protocol listed from Food Safety and Drug Administration (India) [Appendix 1]. However, an attempt was made to select only simple household procedures to ensure translation of research among rural consumers. An awareness of these products was captured under Nutrition labelling questionnaire.

Food and Nutrition Labelling Awareness

The questionnaire for this study was presented in four different parts including socio-demographic information, awareness of food adulteration, misbranding of products and food claims, nutrition and food label related issues. The preparation of this scale involved making use of items or statements which contain factual information with respect to consumer responsibilities and food adulteration. The protocol for the study was approved by the Institutional Ethics Committee of the Association of Health, Food, Nutrition and Dietetics (AFND) and informed consent was obtained from all study participants.

Statistical Methods

All analyses were conducted using the statistical software package SPSS, (12.0 version; SPSS Inc., Chicago IL). *Fischer's exact analysis* was used to assess the relationship between variables. All tests of significance were two-tailed and P values < 0.05 were considered statistically significant.

Results

About 15 consumed foods were identified from household grocery list and purchased in ten shops from eight villages. The foods were tested for adulterant as specified in the Food Safety and Drug Administration (FSDA) (Appendix 1). Table 11.1 shows the prevalence of Food Adulterant in these villages. The prevalence of food adulteration (in terms of purity)

Table 11.1: Prevalence of Food Adulterant (n=15)

Foods Items (n=15)	*Adulterant %*
Cereals	
Rice	10
Wheat	40
Semolina	80
Pulses	40
Coriander	60
Chilli Powder	20
Turmeric Powder	40
Asafoetida	60
Tea Powder	90
Coffee Powder	70
Honey	90
Milk	70
Salt	80
Iodised Salt	90
Sugar	60

ranged from 90 per cent for tea powder and iodized salt and lowest purity was obtained for rice with an approximately prevalence of 10 per cent. The most alarming was the amount of contamination in salt. The survey revealed that 70 per cent of the survey participants were found to be consuming adulterated milk. Moreover, food products such as pulses were found to have impurities that have carcinogenic properties. Wheat and rice another staple food of Indian residents also was found to have a large amount of impurities. Almost all the foods are obtained in unpacked form while only tea powder, chilli powder, honeys are obtained in packed form. The test results revealed an alarming amount of contamination in the daily diet of the survey participants.

Awareness of Consumers

The study included 75 participants and majority of the respondents were women (92%), one-third respondents were in the age group of 30-40 years (80%) and found to be illiterate (40%) or completed up to class 5 (29.3%) level of education. Most of the respondents were found to be home-makers (28%) with some of them being daily wagers (26.7%) or shop owners (24%). The home-makers made the decision with respect to food products being bought (38.7%) while small percentage (12%) of the families' decision was made by the husband or by a joint family system (20%). The purchase frequency of the respondents purchased their products on a daily (40%) to weekly (25%) basis with respect to products

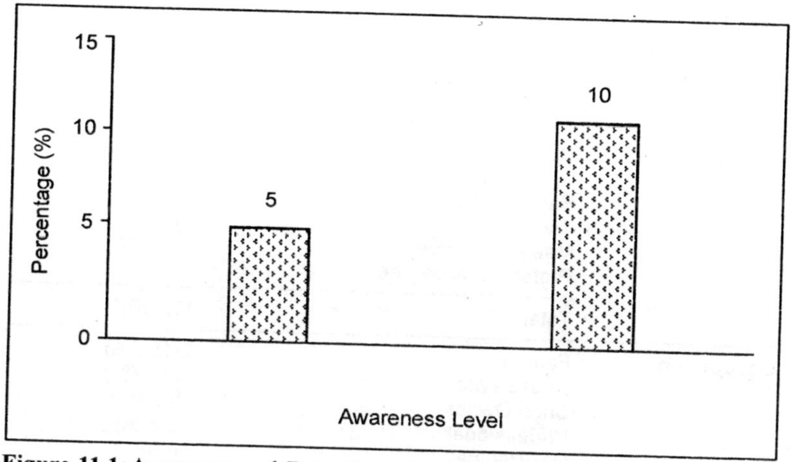

Figure 11.1: Awareness and Detection of Adulteration and Legal Procedures (n=75).

like spices while staples like wheat and rice were purchased on a monthly basis (70%). Most (90%) of the participants were found to purchase from local *kirana* stores and for major food products they depend on their own farming (data not shown).

Awareness of Food Adulterants

Participants were questioned on their knowledge of adulterants in food and found that 70 per cent of the participants were not aware of the concept while 64 per cent have not come across the presence of an adulterant in their food. The awareness of complaint procedures related to adulterated food was very low (5%) as observed in Figure 11.1. Awareness level was higher for literates than illiterates and was more among men rather than women. The knowledge of food adulteration was found to be highest among families that had the least number of sick people. A significant difference in perception of awareness of food adulteration and education ($\rho = 0.004$), occupation ($\rho = 0.045$), gender ($\rho = 0.027$), family income ($\rho = 0.030$) and number of sick members in the family ($\rho = 0.003$). Thus knowledge rights and responsibility related to food adulteration was found to be poor among this population.

Awareness of Food Claims and Food Safety

Product, nutrition and food label awareness level was only 2 per cent of the households. A few respondents gave importance to the nutritional

Table 11.2: Relationship between Awareness of Food Adulteration and Demographics.

	Variables	*Awareness of Food Adulteration n (%)*
Education	Up to class 12	8 (72.7%)
	Up to class 5	2 (18.2%)
	Bachelor's degree	1 (9.1%)
	Illiterate	0 (0%)
	Master's degree	0 (0%)
	Professional degree	0 (0%)
	Total	11(100%)
Occupation	Farmer	2(18.2%)
	House Wife	8(72.7%)
	Shop Owner	1(9.1%)
	Professional	0 (0%)
	Daily Wage	0 (0%)
	Total	11(100%)
Gender	Male	3(27.3%)
	Female	8(72.7%)
	Total	11(100%)
Family income	Less than 2000	3 (27.3%)
	2000-5000	7 (63.6%)
	5000-10000	1 (9.1%)
	More than 10000	0 (0%)
	Total	11(100%)
Sick family members[1]	0	8 (72.7%)
	1	2 (18.2%)
	2	1 (9.1%)
	3	0 (0%)
	Total	11(100%)

Note: 1. last six months; percentage values are in comparison with an unawareness group.

content of packaged foods (16%). Misleading statements in terms of (e.g. no added Mono sodium glutamate) were observed among 25 per cent of the branded products surveyed. Since in the present study only 2 per cent were aware, a further comparison was not made with socio-demographic variables. The respondents identified that they did not read any information presented on packaged products and often were found to be misled by advertisements.

Awareness of Misbranding

The percentage of misbranding prevailing in the rural area was obtained from the shops. Most misbranding items are fried snacks (e.g. Kir Kir for KurKure), chocolates (e.g. Kir Kat for Kit Kat and Daily Milk for Dairy Milk) and biscuits (Milk Shakthi Bikis for Milk Bikis). Figure 11.2 shows that majority of the shops (75%) showed presence of counterfeit products and that the number of counterfeit products was highest among snacks. Awareness of concept of misbranding was only among 5 per cent of respondents. The respondents indicated that they only looked for product colour and packaging style when they purchased processed goods and rarely looked at the labelling. Only few respondents (10%) gave importance to verifying if the product was original (e.g. by identifying the correct brand logo/symbols) as observed in Figure 11.3. A significant difference in perception of awareness of food claims and safety and education ($\rho = 0.034$), occupation ($\rho = 0.016$), gender ($\rho = 0.021$), family income ($\rho = 0.036$) and number of sick members in the family ($\rho = 0.024$) as observed from Table 11.3.

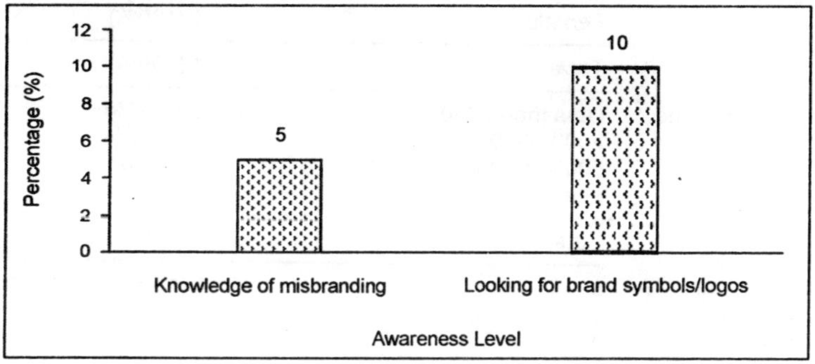

Figure 11.2: Awareness of Misbranding.

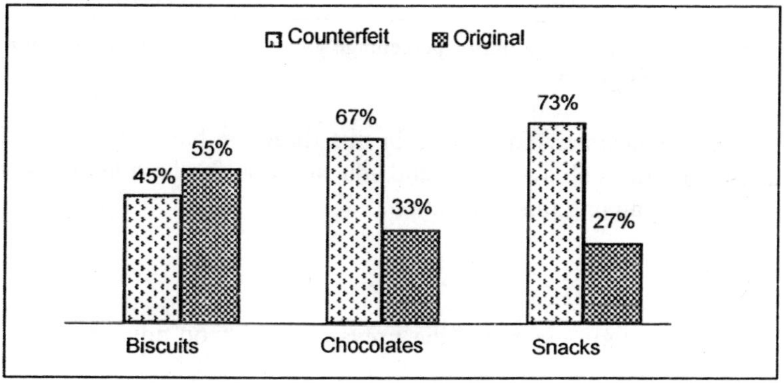

Figure 11.3: Misbranding Trends in Kirana Shops.

Table 11.3: Relationship between Awareness of Food Adulteration and Demographics.

	Criteria	Awareness of Misbranding N (%)
Education	Illiterate	4 (100%)
	Up to class 5	0 (0%)
	Up to class 12	0 (0%)
	Bachelors degree	0 (0%)
	Masters degree	0 (0%)
	Professional degree	0 (0%)
	Total	**4 (100%)**
Occupation	Farmer	0 (0%)
	Housewife	4 (100%)
	Shop Owner	0 (0%)
	Professional	0 (0%)
	Daily Wage	0 (0%)
	Total	**4 (100%)**
Gender	Male	0(0%)
	Female	4 (100%)
	Total	**4 (100%)**
Family income	Less than 2000	2 (50.0%)
	2000-5000	2 (50.0%)
	5000-10000	0 (0%)
	More than 10000	0 (0%)
	Total	**4 (100%)**
Sick family members*	0	4 (13.8%)
	1	0 (0%)
	2	0 (0%)
	3	0 (0%)
	Total	**4 (100%)**

* $P < 0.05$; *B:* last six months; percentage values are in comparison with an unawareness group.

Thus, consumer movements in this direction have to be actively encouraged through awareness and education on food adulteration and misbranding among this population.

Discussion

The present study examined the prevalence of food adulteration and misbranding in Tamil Nadu and surprisingly the study found high percentage of food adulterants and misbranded products in the rural area. There is a poor awareness among consumers with reference to prevalence of food adulterant, food safety and laws related to food. Generally, it can be observed that adulteration rate increases when there is a food shortage. As the prices of food products keep increasing there is a demand for cheaper products and this is when adulteration increases as dishonest dealers tend to supply the consumers with adulterated food products at cheaper prices which the public unknowingly consume (Sundaram, 1985).

A study by Roday (2002) showed that food adulteration was higher in smaller cities like Jalgaon, Nanded and Jalna when compared to bigger cities such as Nagpur, Pune, Amaravati, Solapur etc. while another study has revealed a significant increase in the amount of food adulteration in Nepali villages (Subedi, 2001) in particular over 66 per cent of the food samples that were being tested showed positive for food adulteration. In this study, the number of products which showed signs of adulteration was quite high indicating that over the last three decades the situation has remained marginally the same.

There were a number of studies that showed that home-makers were typically the ones who tend to purchase food for the entire family (Nimkar 1976; Pande, 2000). The studies also revealed that home-makers tend to take almost all the decisions related to purchase of food except in their financial aspects. In the present study apart from the woman others including her husband and the joint family system also take decisions hence efforts to promote knowledge should be directed towards all sections of the population. In addition, the present study correlated the awareness level and number of sick people and results showed people who are unaware about adulterants and food safety issues are more affected by infections like diarrhoea, food poisons, cold etc.

Fake products are more prevalent in this village but in general consumers are not aware and buy these products by looking at their colours and package but not reading the labels. In the present study only five per cent of the consumers reported that they look at the labels. Thus, it can be established that in order to meet the challenges that customers face today, there should be increased knowledge and awareness with respect to issues of food safety, misbranding and health claims. It can be promoted that the best defence any consumer has against these issues is knowledge of his/her rights as a consumer and of the remedies which exist to resolve these problems when they occur. Fake products cause damage to leading companies' sales and brand image. Fake products also create problems to consumers' health. Hence, the MNCs and other leading companies that are worse affected by fake brands have to promote awareness among the rural population with respect to buying these products. "Knowledge and awareness about adulterated foods, laws and its rights related to adulterated food is crucial in a society where technology heightens opportunities for perpetrators of fraud deception and misrepresentation" (Garman & Jonest, 1992).

Food claims are found to transfer information from manufacturers to consumers with respect to nutritional and positive benefits, which can be obtained with respect to consumption of different components/ constituents in food products (Brookes, 2010). However, if food claims fail to achieve a specific objective due to misinformation of the contents of the product then it would result in a negative impact on market efficiency (Hawkes, 2004; Mason & Scammon, 2011). Consumer misunderstanding and lack of proper information availability is found to invalidate the tremendous effort in terms of financial and human resources that the food industry and other developed countries are making to communicate food nutrition content responsibly.

The present study had several limitations. Firstly, being a cross-sectional study, it does not allow us to make a cause and effect inference particularly the prevalence of food adulterant and its impact on health of consumers. Secondly, the sample size is low to assess the accurate prevalence of villages and moreover sample is restricted only to few villages of particular district. Hence, this may not be representative of entire Tamil Nadu. Further, only structured questionnaire has been adopted, it would have been useful if more of qualitative information has been collected to assess their perception and attitude towards food safety. However, this study also has several strengths. It was first study to assess the prevalence of misbranding, counterfeit products and awareness of food labelling among south Indian rural consumers. Further, we had assessed relationship between per capita incomes, education of respondents, food borne illnesses with magnitude of adulteration in each household. Furthermore, the research also showed that not much studies have focused on the awareness of the consumers when it comes to food adulteration while there are studies that provide detailed analysis on the amount of contamination that happens in most of the food samples; however, studies dealing with the awareness of respondents in rural areas in relation to food adulteration are severely lacking. This is one of the main reasons as to why the investigator felt it was necessary to educate respondents on the existing adulteration practices of retailers and manufacturers and to instil knowledge on detecting food contamination among women.

In conclusion, the study reported low awareness of food safety and food labelling and high prevalence of food adulterant among south Indian rural consumers. Health education in food safety to avoid food adulteration and mislabelling issues is both possible and cost-effective, but it should be culture specific and should respond to technological, economic and social situations that prevail in a particular society or cultural groups. Identification of educational needs and lacunae in knowledge and perceptions is the first step towards developing educational material.

Acknowledgements: We thank the GuiRes Healthcare Private Limited, Chennai for the field studies. Ms. Kalai Chitra and Ms. Akriti Mendiratta for their assistance in conducting field study and preparation of Manuscript.

Appendix 1

Food Adulteration Protocol

Food items	*Household Protocol*	*Result*	*Adulterant*
Wheat Flour	Sprinkle on water surface/Shake sample with dil HCl	Bran will float on the surface/effervesecence indicates chalk	Present (Excess bran/chalk powder)
Rice	Rice is immersed underwater/handpicking	Rice will float whereas impurities will sink	Present (Stones/Grit)
Semolina	Spread a small quantity (2 tsp) of sample on a chapter, and draw magnet over it	Iron flakes if present will cling to the magnet.	Iron/Flakes
Sugar	Mix sugar with water	Sugar will dissolve leaving any impurities to settle down	Present (Chalk powder/dirt)
Pulses	Shake 5 gms: of the pulses with 5 ml of water. Add a few drops of hydrochloric acid.	The appearance of pink colour in the solution.	Present (Metanil yellow/Lead Chromate)
Coriander Powder	A teaspoon of Coriander powder is mixed in a glass of water (100 ml)	Impurities and substandard materials float on the surface	Present (Dung)
Chilli Powder	Take a tea spoon full of chillies powder in a glass of water	Coloured water exhibit presence of artificial colour. Any grittiness that may be felt on rubbing the sediment at the bottom of glass confirms the presence of brick powder/sand, soapy and smooth touch of the white residue at the bottom indicates the presence of soap stone.	Present (Brick/salt/talc powder)
Salt	Mix water and Salt in a glass	Salt dissolves while impurities settle down	White powdered
Iodized Salt	Cut a piece of potato, add salt and wait minute and add two drops of lemon juice	If Iodized salt blue colour will develop, there will not blue colour	Common Salt
Turmeric Powder	2 gms of Turmeric powder is mixed in a test tube with water and few drops of HCl	Appearance of bubbles in Turmeric powder	Present (Chalk/Brick Powder) or metanil yellow
Asafoetida	Shake little portion of the same with water and allow to settle	Soap stone or other earthy material will settle down at the bottom	Present (Resins)

(Contd.)

Food items	*Household Protocol*	*Result*	*Adulterant*
Tea Powder	Tea powder is laid on the table and a magnet is moved over it.	Iron based impurities will stick to the magnet	Present (Iron flakes/fillings)
Pepper Corns	Sample is spread over a table and observed keenly using one's own sight.	Papaya seeds can be identified	Absent
Coffee Powder	Coffee powder is sprinkled on a clear glass water	Coffee powder will float while impurities will sink while leaving a trace behind them	Present (Chicory Powder)
Honey	Add a few drops of honey into a glass of water	Some of the honey dissolves in the water while pure honey forms thin thread like structures and settles down	Present (Molasses sugar)
Milk	The presence of water can be by putting a drop of milk on a polished slanting surface	The drop of pure milk or flows slowly leaving a white trail behind it, whereas milk adulterated water will flow immediately without leaving a mark	Water

REFERENCES

Athukorala, P. and Jayasuriya, S., 2005, "Processed Foods Exports from Developing Countries and Food Safety related market access issues: aims and scope of the Research Project", *Background Chapter Prepared for the Workshop on International Food Safety Regulation and Processed Food Exports from Developing Countries: A Comparative Study of India and Thailand*, Research Information Systems, New Delhi.

Bhat, R.V. and Rao, R.N., 1997, 'Food Regulation', *Food Safety*, Bangalore: The Bangalore Printing and Publishing Co. Ltd., pp. 118-39.

Brookes, G., 2010, "Economic Impact Assessment of the European Union (EU)'s Nutrition and Health Claims Regulation on the EU Food Supplement Sector and Market." *European Health Claim Alliance*, GBC Ltd., UK.

Chadha, 2004, *The Prevention of Food Adulteration Act and Rules.*

Dhyani, A. and Saklani, A., 1994, "To Assess Awareness of Consumers towards Consumer Protection Laws", *J. Marketing,* 23(7-8), pp. 9-12.

Garman and Jonest, 1992, "Older American's Knowledge of Consumer Rights and Legal Protection", *J. Consumer Study and Home Eco*, 16, pp. 283-291.

Hawkes, C., 2004, *Nutrition Labels and Health Claims: The Global Regulatory Environment* World Health Organisation, Geneva.

Jacquet, J.L. and Pauly, D., 2008 "Trade Secrets: Renaming and Mislabelling of Seafood Original Research Article", *Marine Policy,* 32(3), pp. 309-318.

Kalpagam, P., Sudershan, R.V., Subba Rao, G.M., Vishnu Vardhana Rao, M., Rao, P., *et al.* (2006) *"KABP Study on Food and Drug Safety in India: A Report, Food and Drug Toxicology Research Centre"*, Hyderabad: National Institute of Nutrition.

Kamala, S., 1974, "Food Authenticity", *Baroda Journal of Nutrition,* 49(1).

Karoui, R., 2012, "Food Authenticity and Fraud", *Chemical Analysis of Food: Techniques and Applications,* pp. 499-517.

Khapre, M.P., Mudey, A., Chaudhary, S., Wagh, V. and Dawale, A., 2011, "Buying Practices and Prevalence of Adulteration in Selected Food items in a Rural Area of Wardha District: A Cross-sectional Study", Online *J. Health Allied Scs,* 10(3), p. 4.

Liu, S., Xie, Z., Zhang, W., Cao, X. and Pei, X., 2013, "Risk Assessment in Chinese Food Safety Review Article", *Food Control,* 30(1), pp. 162-167.

Martin, T., Dean, E., Hardy, B., Johnson, T. and Jolly, F., *et al.*, 2003, "A New Era for Food Safety Regulation in Australia Original Research Article", *Food Control,* 14(6), pp. 429-438.

Mason, M.J. and Scammon, D.L., 2011, "Unintended Consequences of Health Supplement Information Regulations: The Importance of Recognizing Consumer Motivations", *Journal of Consumer Affairs,* 45 (2), pp. 201-223.

Mensah, L.D. and Julien, D. 2011, "Implementation of Food Safety Management Systems in the UK Original Research Article", *Food Control,* 22(8), pp. 1216-1225.

Motarjemi, Y. and Moaref, A., 2000, *Food Borne Disease: A Focus for Health Education*, Geneva: World Health Organization.

Naik, Y., 2010, "25% of Milk in State Adulterated", *The Times of India*, Available at: http://timesofindia.indiatimes.com//city/mumbai/25-ofmilk-in-state-adulterated/articleshow/2127308.cms (Accessed on: 2 December, 2010)

Nimkar, A., 1976, "Food Buying Practices of Unemployed and Employed Home-maker", *The Indian Journal of Home Science,* 10(1), Coimbatore: Home Science Association of India.

Pande, U., 2000, *A Study of Ascertaining Buying Practices of Consumable Goods among Low Income Group*, Vallabh Vidyanagar: P.G. Department of Home Science, S.P. University.

Rae, A. and Josling, T., 2003, "Processed food trade and developing countries: protection and trade liberalization", *Food Policy,* 28, pp. 147–166.

Rao, S.C., 2010, "Food Adulteration Goes Unchecked", *The Times of India,* Available at: http://timesofindia.indiatimes.com//city/hyderabad/Foodadulteration-goes-unchecked/articleshow/13507365.cms

Roday, S., 2002, *Food Hygiene and Sanitation,* New Delhi: Tata McGraw-Hill Publishing Company Ltd., pp. 248-249.

Srilakshmi, B., 2003, "New Age International", *Food Science*, p. 313.

Subba Rao, M. G., Sudershan, R.V., Rao, P., Rao Mendu, V.V. and Polasa, K., 2009, "Focus Group Studies on Food Safety Knowledge, Perceptions, and Practices of School-going Adolescent Girls in South India Original Research Article", *Journal of Nutrition Education and Behaviour*, 41(5), pp. 340-346.

Subba Rao, G.M., Sudershan, R.V., Rao, P., Rao, V.V. and Polasa, K. 2007, "Food Safety Knowledge, Attitudes and Practices of Mothers—Findings from focus group studies in South India", *Appetite*, 49(2), pp. 441-449.

Subedi, 2001, Available at: http://www.nepalnews.com.np/contents/englishdaily/ktmpost/2001/may/05/index XI.htm.

Sudershan, R.V., Subba Rao, G.M., Pratima Rao, M., Rao, V.V. and Polasa, K., 2008, "Food safety related perceptions and practices of mothers—A case study in Hyderabad, India Original Research Article", *Food Control*, 19(5), pp. 506-513.

Sundaram, S., 1985, *Consumer Protection in India*, Delhi: B.R. Publishing Corporation, pp. 66-77.

Umali-Deininger, D. and Sur, M., 2007, "Food safety in a globalizing world: Opportunities and Challenges for India", *Agricultural Economics*, 37, pp. 135-147.

Vidya and Rao, D.B., 2010, *A Text Book of Nutrition*, Discovery Publishing House.

Wilcocky, A., Pun, M., Khanonax, J. and Aung, M. 2004. "Consumer Attitudes, Knowledge and Behaviour: A Review of Food Safety Issues." *Trends in Food Science and Technology*, 15, pp. 56-66.

12

Fake Branding in Pharmaceuticals

A Study of Select Rural Villages in Telangana Region

SURESH CHANDRA Ch

Introduction

Consumer is the most influencing personality for determining the success or failure of products and services whose purchasing is often influenced strongly by internal and external factors and often provide room for the companies to effectively influence and motivate them to purchase. The branding is one of the valuable components of marketing of the products and services which involve reinforcing a good reputation, encourage loyalty, assure quality, convey a perception of greater worth, allowing a product or service to be priced higher and grant the buyer a sense of affirmation and entry into an imaginary community of shared values. Rural consumers in India account for more than 70 per cent of total population who get easily influenced by the marketers because of low literacy level, occupation, geographic location and lack of better exposure to media.

Fake brands are part of a pervasive material and it is regarded as an inherently second rate and potentially shady activity in practice. The transactional properties of fake brands are based on material properties, log and label included, and interpersonal relationships between manufacturers, buyers, and consumers. Fake branding is the process whereby the companies encompass the success of existing successful brand names to their products and services in order to grow and sustain in the market. Fake branding involves introducing the product which is not genuine with an aim to achieve sales by going with the reputation of the existing brands. The unregistered fake brands are spoiling the market share of the registered original brands in the market and especially the urban and rural differentiation is giving the life to many fake branded products in the Indian market. The fake products in the market are available and can be divided into distinct categories, *viz.*, (a) Look-alikes, (b) Spell-alikes, and (c) Duplicates. Brand piracy is another existing problem which is putting huge challenges to the existing brands.

Objectives of the Study

The main objective of the study is to investigate the impact of the fake brands in pharmaceuticals on the consumers of select rural villages. The objective is segmented to the following heads:

1. To study the overview of Indian pharma industry with special reference to fake brands in pharmaceuticals.
2. To analyse the impact of fake pharmaceuticals on the rural consumers of select villages.
3. To examine the perceptions of rural consumers on fake pharmaceutical products in select rural villages.

And finally, the study will provide the findings and suggestions on the basis of field observations.

Methodology of the Study

The study is based on both primary and secondary data sources. The primary data is collected from the field observations of select rural villages of North Telangana region of Andhra Pradesh State (i.e. Regonda in Warangal District, Pagideru village in Khammam District and Ellanthakunta in Karimnagar District). The secondary data is collected from the select research chapters, books, journals, newspaper reviews and internet sources. For the purpose of collecting the primary data from the sample respondents, convenience sampling is applied in order to determine the target rural consumers.

Indian Pharmaceutical Industry: Fake Pharmaceutical Products

The Indian pharmaceutical industry traces its roots to the 1903 with the formation of Bengal Chemical and Pharmaceutical Works in Calcutta by Prof. C. Roy. Alembic Chemicals has created founder stone as the first

Indian Pharma manufacturing company primarily engaged in production of tinctures and alcohol at Baroda in the year 1907. The early part of 20th century remained unsuccessful for Indian Pharma Industry and post-Independence has given the life to the industry which has resulted in exports to foreign countries. The earlier Patents Act, 1911 (regarded as Indian Patents and Designs Act, 1911) under the rule of Britishers has recognised the product and process patents. Due to the monopoly status enjoyed by the MNCs, the drug prices remained high during this period. But later, the Government's introduction of new Patent Act in 1972 enabled Indian firms to use the "reverse engineering process" to manufacture drugs without paying royalty to the original patent holder. The Act, along with the Drug Price Control Order, provided little incentive to the MNCs to introduce new pharmaceutical products in India. During this period, the production of bulk drugs, generic and branded goods has also increased. Low cost and high-volume production has helped the Indian pharmaceutical industry in opening up the export channels to many developed and developing countries. Economic liberalisation in 90s enabled the industry to become what it is today. The year 1995 recorded another milestone for the Indian pharmaceutical industry. One of the agreements under the World Trade Organisation (WTO) required complying with the provisions of the Trade Related Intellectual Property Rights (TRIPS). The TRIPS agreement reintroduced product patent in India. Further, during this period, tariff and non-tariff measures have come down.

The Pharmaceutical industry in India at present is the world's third-largest in terms of volume and stands and 14th in terms of value. Sale of all types of medicines in the country is expected to reach around US$ 19.22 billion by 2012. Pharmaceutical Council of India (PCI) is actively engaged in providing pharma education and research for the young Indian pharmacy learners. Further, the Indian Drug Manufacturers Association (IDMA) and Indian Pharmaceutical Association (IPA) are strengthening the industry with innovative and effective strategies.

The pharma industry contains the production of Branded and Generic drugs which are considered as its two eyes. The generic drugs (which are named based on the composition) exports from India crossed over 200 countries but the usage of Branded drugs (a specific name used for identity and marketing by big pharma companies) is more than the generic drugs and the sale of generic pharma products is less than 40 per cent in India. This has given rise for the fake pharma producers to tap the market through its counterfeits. According to the Report of *Times of India*, the fake brands are accounting to the counterfeiters cost of Rs. 2500 crore a year in Indian consumer products industry. The report also concluded that Government is losing the revenue of Rs. 900 crore every year, mainly by way of unpaid taxes and duties. According to the World Health Organization (WHO) Report, 20 per cent of the medicines sold in India are fake ones. And according to the report of Director General of Health Services and Ministry of Family Welfare and Health, India, there are more than 10,000 drug manufacturers and more than six lakh outlets that sell fake drugs. The statistics are clearly showing the rising of fake pharmaceutical products in rural and urban markets. In view of these objectives, the present chapter will provide an observational based study on the impact of fake pharmaceutical products on rural consumers.

Impact of Fake Pharmaceutical Products on Rural Consumers—Field Based Observations and Survey Results

From the field survey on select rural villages of three districts of Telangana region, the following fake branded pharmaceutical products were found. Most of the fake branded pharmaceutical products found in the three select villages of Telangana region are from medicinal background. The above mentioned pharmaceutical branded products have huge reputation in the market but due to non-availability in remote areas of rural regions, the fake brands found dominating (Table 12.1).

The survey results revealed that 71 per cent of the rural consumers are not able to recognise the fake brands. Further, majority of the select rural consumers are having the background of VII standard and S.S.C. which is also another influencing factor for inability to identify the fake branded pharmaceutical products (*see* Table 12.2).

The Chi-square test is applied to analyse the association between educational qualification of the rural consumers and their awareness regarding recognition of fake pharmaceutical branded products. The test results are given in Table 12.3.

Reasons for the Growth of Fake Brands

Very few countries have specific regulatory mechanism to counter-attack the counterfeits in FMCG and pharmaceutical drugs. Especially in India, lack of efficiency in regulatory environment has led to an opportunity for fake brands to exploit the lack of protection for many products. Ineffective drugs in rural villages are causing inconvenience to the patient in many

Table 12.1: List of Original and Its Corresponding Fake Branded Pharmaceutical Products found in Field Survey

Sl. No.	*Name of the Original Brand*	*Name of the Fake Brand*
1.	Zandu Balm (Original brand belongs to Zandu Pharmaceutical Company)	Zanda Balm (Fake manufacturer with unknown address and identity)
2.	Fair and Lovely Fairness Cream (Original brand belongs to Hindustan Unilever Limited Company)	Faire and Lovely, Fair and Lonely (Unrecognised fake brand with unnoticeable address)
3.	Vicks (Original brand belongs to P and G Company)	Vikks (fake brand with the same quantity and package found in the rural villages)
4.	Colgate Tooth Paste (Original brand belongs to Colgate and Palmolive Company Limited)	Colkate Tooth Paste (fake brand with similar identity)
5.	Chloroquine Phosphate Tablets (IPCA Manufacturers)	Chloroquine Phosphate Tablets (IFCA manufacturers)
6.	Desogestreal and Ethinyl Estradiol Tablets (Novelon)	Desogestreal and Ethinyl Estradiol Tablets (Femilon)
7.	Dichlofenol (Agron Pharma)	Agron Remedies Pvt. Ltd.
8.	Cetirizine (Cipla and other major pharma companies)	Agron Remedies Pvt. Ltd.
9.	Berozeldon	Unapproved and unlicensed drug sold in PHCs in Telangana region in Agron Remedies Pvt. Ltd.
10.	Joint-S	Completely manufactured and sold by Visiting Orthopedician (Declared as unapproved formula based and unlicensed drug sold in Warangal District by Drug Inspectors)
11.	Zincovit (Apex labs)	Zinkovit (fake and unregistered tablets available from Hindusthan Nutraceuticals, Hyderabad)

Source: Field Survey.

cases. The field survey results have clearly shown that the rural consumers are facing many problems. Right from side-effects, the fake pharmaceutical products has exposed the life of the consumers to various harmful impacts like getting itches, skin diseases, extreme sweat and thirst, change of skin colour, Osteoporosis, Anuria, Dysphagia etc. Apart from that the widespread use of substandard antibiotic drugs could lead to a potentially explosive increase in the prevalence of drug-resistant bacteria. The toxic nature of pharmaceuticals is causing immediate and harmful effects in those exposed to them. Field survey results about the reasons for

Table 12.2: Rural Consumers' Ability to Recognise Fake Pharmaceutical Products

Sl. No.	*Educational Qualification of the Consumers*	*Rural Consumers Response on Fake Pharmaceutical Products*		
		Able to Recognise the Fake Brands	*Not Able to Recognise the Fake Brands*	*Total*
1.	Illiterate	2 (11.7%)	15 (88.2%)	**17**
2.	Up to Class VII	8 (18.1%)	36 (81.9%)	**44**
3.	S.S.C.	8 (25%)	24 (75%)	**32**
4.	Under-graduates	12 (60%)	8 (40%)	**20**
5.	Post-Graduates	4 (57%)	3 (43%)	**7**
	Total	**34 (28.4%)**	**86 (71.6%)**	**120**

Source: Field Survey.

Table 12.3: Chi-Square Test Results

H_0: There is no significant association between educational qualification of the rural consumers and their awareness on recognition of fake pharmaceutical branded products.
H_1: There is a significant association between educational qualification of the rural consumers and their awareness on recognition of fake pharmaceutical branded products.
Chi-square table value at 4 degrees of freedom and 5 per cent level of significance = 9.49.
Chi-square calculated value from the given data = 17.4446.
Result: **Accept H_1, i.e., there is a significant association between educational qualification of the rural consumers and their awareness on recognition of fake pharmaceutical branded products.**

preferring fake branded pharmaceutical products in rural villages is given in Table 12.4.

In Table 12.4, statistics have clearly revealed that lack of knowledge showed major factor for preferring the fake branded products. Further, non-availability of original brands also emerged as major concern for the rural consumers for preferring the fake branded pharmaceuticals.

Two-way ANOVA was applied in order to analyse the significant difference in the opinion of the rural consumers and the significant difference in the opinion of rural consumers with reference to preferring of fake branded pharmaceutical products of three select villages (*See* Table 12.5).

Table 12.4: Opinion on Preferring the Fake Branded Pharmaceutical Products

Area of Rural Consumers	*Rural Consumers' Opinion on Preferring the Fake Branded Pharmaceutical Products*				*Total*
	Lack of knowledge	*Non-availability of original brands*	*Recommendations from RMPs and PHCs*	*Affordable price*	
Regonda (Warangal District)	13 (32.5%)	8 (20%)	10 (25%)	9 (22.5%)	40
Ellanthakunta (Karimnagar District)	10 (25%)	19 (47.5%)	6 (15%)	5 (12.5%)	40
Pagideru (Khammam District)	18 (45%)	12 (30%)	8 (20%)	2 (5%)	40
Total	**41 (34.1%)**	**39 (32.5%)**	**24 (20%)**	**16 (13.3%)**	**120**

Source: Field Survey.

Table 12.5: ANOVA Test Results

ANOVA of Two-Way Classification						
Source of Variation	***SS***	***Df***	***MS***	***F***	***P-Value***	***F Crit***
Rows	10.66667	1	10.66667	**1.04918**	0.413412	**18.51282**
Columns	152.3333	2	76.16667	**7.491803**	0.117761	**19**
Error	20.33333	2	10.16667			
Total	183.3333	5				

Decision: H_1 (Alternative Hypothesis is accepted both for the Rows & Columns).

The test results have clearly shown that Alternative Hypothesis is accepted for both cases. Hence, there is a significant difference in the opinion of the rural consumers with reference to preferring of fake branded pharmaceutical products.

The survey results with reference to rural consumer's awareness levels on different factors about pharmaceutical drugs are given in Table 12.6.

Survey statistics given in Table 12.6 clearly shows that majority of the rural consumers are completely unaware in recognizing original and fake pharma brand, spelling of the pharma drug, quality grades, components and manufacturers. With reference to the awareness about

Table 12.6: Rural Consumer's Awareness on Different Factors about Pharma Products.

Factors Considered	*Fully Aware*		*Aware to Some Extent*		*Completely Unaware*		*Total*	
	f	%	f	%	f	%	f	%
Ability to Identify Original and Fake Pharma Brand	8	9.6%	43	51.6%	69	82.8%	**120**	**100%**
Knowledge about Spelling of the Pharma Drug	3	3.6%	36	43.2%	81	97.2%	**120**	**100%**
Quality Grades	11	13.2%	42	50.4%	67	80.4%	**120**	**100%**
Components/Ingredients	8	9.6%	36	43.2%	76	91.2%	**120**	**100%**
Knowledge about Manufacturing Date (MFD) and Expiry Dates (EXP.)	32	38.4%	57	68.4%	31	37.2%	**120**	**100%**
Awareness on Caution	21	25.2%	63	75.6%	36	43.2%	**120**	**100%**
Awareness about dosage	23	27.6%	69	82.8%	28	33.6%	**120**	**100%**
Awareness about the manufacturers	11	13.2%	45	54.0%	64	76.8%	**120**	**100%**
Awareness about Consumer Protection Act, 1986 and the consumer rights against unethical practices	19	22.8%	56	67.2%	45	54.0%	**120**	**100%**

Source: Field Survey.

dosage and caution more than 70 per cent opined that they are somewhat aware about them. Fully aware consumers were found in very less percentage. Only 38 per cent of them opined that they are aware about Manufacturing and Expiry dates of the drugs.

Perception of Rural Consumers towards Fake Pharmaceutical Products

The data clearly shows that there is variation among the rural consumers in terms of their income level. The survey results have clearly shown that majority of the rural consumers, i.e., 50 per cent of them are from the income range of Rs. 2500-5000. On question of action taken by them against fake pharmaceutical products, majority of them have opined that "that they did not take any action". This statistics clearly indicates the ignorance and dependency on the existing available pharmaceutical brands which are fake in nature and are dominating the decisions of rural consumers of three select villages (See Table 12.7).

Table 12.7: Observations on Rural Consumers' Perception towards Action against Fake Pharmaceutical Products

Income range of Rural consumers (per month in rupees) (₹)	*Rural Consumers Perception towards Action Against Fake Pharmaceutical Products in Rural Villages*				
	Returned the products	*Asked for compensation*	*Reported to Police and sued case*	*Did not take any action*	*Total*
Less than ₹ 2500	7 (32%)	4 (26.6%)	2 (26.6%)	12 (18.2%)	**25**
₹ 2500-5000	5 (20%)	1 (6.6%)	2 (26.6%)	52 (78.9%)	**60**
₹ 5001–7500	5 (20%)	4 (26.6%)	1 (13.3%)	10 (15.1%)	**20**
₹ 7500 and above	6 (24%)	2 (13.3%)	1 (13.3%)	06 (9.1%)	**15**
Total	**23**	**11**	**06**	**80**	**120**

Source: Field Survey.

The Chi-square test is applied to analyze the association between Income range of the rural consumers and their perception towards action against fake pharmaceutical products in rural villages. The test results are given in Table 12.8.

Table 12.8: Chi-Square Test Results

H_0: There is no significant association between Income range of the rural consumers and their perception towards action against fake pharmaceutical products in rural villages.
H_1: There is a significant association between Income range of the rural consumers and their perception towards action against fake pharmaceutical products in rural villages.
Chi-square table value at 9 degrees of freedom and 5 per cent level of significance = 16.9.
Chi-square caliculated value from the given data at 4 degrees of freedom and 5% level of significance = 24.4500.
Result: **Accept H_1, i.e., there is a significant association between educational qualification of the rural consumers and their awareness on recognition of fake pharmaceutical branded products.**

Rural Consumers' Perception on Measures to Overcome Fake Branded Pharmaceutical Products

From the rural consumers of 3 selected villages of Telangana region, it was found that 37.5 per cent of them perceive that increasing regulation over fake brands is the best measure. Further 25.83 per cent and 20 per cent of the rural consumers have opined that period i.e. inspection by medical inspectors and increasing rural awareness with the co-ordination of policy-makers and village committees are the best measures to overcome from the influence of fake branding in pharmaceuticals in rural villages (*See* Table 12.9).

Table 12.9: Rural Consumers Perception on Measures to Overcome from Fake Branded Pharmaceutical Products

Area	*Perceptions of Rural Consumers on Best Measure to Overcome from the Influence of Fake Branding in Pharmaceutical Products in Rural Villages*				*Total*
	Awareness Campaigns by the Pharma Companies and Doctors	*Increasing Rural Awareness by Policy-makers and Village Committees*	*Increasing Regulation over Fake Brands*	*Periodic Inspection by Medical Inspectors*	
Regonda (Warangal District)	5 (12.5%)	10 (25%)	10 (25%)	15 (37.5%)	**40**
Ellanthakunta (Karimnagar District)	7 (17.5%)	8 (20%)	19 (47.5%)	6 (15%)	**40**
Pagideru (Khammam District)	8 (20%)	6 (15%)	16 (40%)	10 (25%)	**40**
Total	**20 (16.6%)**	**24 (20%)**	**45 (37.5%)**	**31 (25.83%)**	**120 (100%)**

Source: Field Survey.

Two-way Analysis of Variance is made in order to analyse whether there is a significant difference in the perception of rural consumers of select districts and perception of the rural consumers with reference to the measures to overcome from the problem of lapsation. The test results are given in Table 12.10.

From the test results, it was found that there is a significant difference in the perceptions of rural consumers of select districts. And also, there is a significant difference in the perception of rural consumers with reference

Table 12.10: Two-way ANOVA Results

ANOVA of Two-way Classification						
Source of Variation	*SS*	*df*	*MS*	*Ftab*	*p-value*	*F crit*
Rows	0.166667	1	0.166667	0.023256	0.892789	**18.51282**
Columns	134.3333	2	67.16667	9.372093	0.096413	**19**
Error	14.33333	2	7.166667			
Total	**148.8333**	**5**				

to the measures to overcome from the problem of fake branded pharmaceutical products.

Findings and Suggestions

The pharmaceutical companies and industry relies to a great extent on the brand awareness to generate revenue which in-turn cannot usually sell directly to its end consumers. In order to protect the consumers against fake branded pharma products especially from rural villages, anti-counterfeiting strategy needs to be coordinated across the whole medical profession. As more than 70 per cent of the people in India lives in villages hence, there is a responsibility on all sections of society including importers, distributors, repackagers, physicians, pharmacists, and finally patients (consumers) themselves. Rural consumers' education and income levels are one of the important factors affecting their awareness and preference of pharma products. Hence, the Government as well as pharma brand owners must get into the act of providing information and awareness campaigns to literate rural consumers about pharmaceutical products.

Though, the policy-makers' role is very crucial in safeguarding the rural consumers but there is a definite need for consumerism for identifying their problems especially deceiving from fake pharmaceutical products. Further, selling the pharmaceutical products in the respective local language and providing authenticated strips is a healthy measure to counter-attack counterfeits. The Government needs to encourage and regulate the pharma companies for non-clonable ID nanotag for all pharma drugs manufactured. A committee set-up by the Indian Ministry of Health has approved a proposal to put 2D barcodes, and scratch-off labels on medicines. QR codes (quick response) can also be tested and it helps anyone with a camera enabled phone and web access to scan the code and take it instantly to the pharma company website to authenticate the drug. Further, the Healthcare Centres must ensure qualitative pharma products and it must also guarantee for prescripted medicines in all rural places. The role of medical representatives, NGOs and educated consumers is also very vital to effectively eliminating fake branded pharmaceutical products in rural areas and to safeguard rural consumers.

REFERENCES

Davison, Marks, 2011, *Pharmaceutical Anti-Counterfeiting—Combating the Real Danger from Fake Drugs*, Canada: Wiley & Sons, Inc., pp. 24-27.

Dr. Sarangapani, A., 2009, *Rural Consumer Behaviour in India—A Study of FMCGs*, New Delhi: Laxmi Publications, pp. 54-59.

http://articles.timesofindia.indiatimes.com/2012-07-29/special-report/32923254_1_generic-drugs-quality-and-efficacy-pioneer-drug

http://indiatoday.intoday.in/story/government-cracks-down-on-fake-drugs-menace-in-india/1/201183.html

http://www.bbc.co.uk/news/business-15208595

http://www.sunday-guardian.com/business/delhi-is-the-national-capital-for-fake-products

Kothar, C.R., 2006, *Research Methodology—Methods and Techniques*, New Delhi: New Age International Publishers, 2nd edition, pp. 233-236.

McCartney, Sarah, 2006, *The Fake Factor—Why We Love Brands but Buy Fakes*, Cyan Commumication 3-7.

Rajesh Kumar, B. and Satish, S.M., 2007, *Growth Strategies of Indian Pharma Companies*, Hyderabad: ICFAI University Press.

The World Medicines Situation, World Health Organization Report, 2004.

SECTION III

Changing Taste and Preferences of Rural Consumers

13

Changing Lifestyle and Consumption Patterns of Indian Rural Households

An Analytical Study

ZEESHAN AMIR AND ALI GHUFRAN

Due to globalisation and liberalisation, economic development in the urban areas is much faster as a result of which rural people are migrating cities in search of livelihood. Despite this fact, the major portion of Indian population still resides in rural India, and everybody is eyeing the next wave of growth to rural household. The Indian rural population which was 72.19 per cent in the year 2001 reduced to 68.84 per cent as per 2011 Indian Census Report. Out of this, 18.62 per cent lives in the State of Uttar Pradesh itself and their main occupation is agriculture and related occupations. The standard of living of a household (a group of persons who normally live together and take their meals from a common kitchen unless the exigencies of work preventing any of them from doing so) can be understood from their consumption pattern, and the qualities of consumption budget which clearly indicate the level of welfare of the household. Food consumption pattern of household depends on many factors like level of education, assets, occupation and demographic characteristics and it is an important barometer of individual welfare and well-being in any region.

Lifestyle is a term to describe the way a person, household and society live. It reflects the attitude, interests, activities, values and allocation of income. It also means the expression of self-image which is extended through the use of goods and services. The change in consumption pattern is observed due to changes in consumer taste, preference and income at micro level and structural shift in the overall environment at macro level. It ultimately affects the buying behaviour of consumers.

Objectives of the Study: The objectives of the present study are as follows—

1. To study the socio-economic factors and their influence on lifestyle and consumption pattern.
2. To study the food consumption behaviour of rural households.
3. To study the fashion adoption trend among rural households.
4. To examine the media habits and entertainment modes of rural households.
5. To explore the use of technology in the consumption of life-style goods among rural households.

Hypothesis: The two hypotheses are being framed and tested by the researchers in the background of the following contentions:

1. The researchers observe that the fashion consciousness is gradually reflected by the use of branded items in post neo-liberal era which in turn is an outcome of ever-increasing affluence of the rural consumers.

   H_{01}: The preference of branded outfit is independent of the family income.
2. Use of technology has exposed a common man to the broader spectrum of social needs and comfort of day-to-day life. Interactive media like internet has occupied an important place in the 'information seeking' based lifestyle of an individual irrespective of the livelihood he/she live with.

   H_{02}: Internet usage is independent of the occupation.

Research Methodology

The present study is a descriptive study. A structured questionnaire based on nominal scale has been used as the research instrument to collect the primary data. A total of 225 questionnaires were distributed among the respondents of Lucknow city of Uttar Pradesh having rural background. Convenience random sampling is being applied in this study. Respondents were selected from the data base of the universities of Lucknow. 200 workable questionnaires were sorted out for the analysis. The responses were tabulated and cross-tabulated to infer the results with respect to the stated objectives and hypothesis. The association of socio-economic variables was tested using chi-square test.

Profile of the Respondent Households

The profile of the sample household for subject study can be seen in Table 13.1 depicting demographic variables as well as percentage distribution of the respondents.

Table 13.1: Rural Households Profile

Demographic Variables	*Category*	*%age Distribution*
Absolute Number of Respondents	Male and Female	200 (100%)
Gender Ratio	Male	656 (53.25%)
	Female	576 (46.75%)
Age of Family Members	Below 25 Years	554 (44.97%)
	Between 26-40 Years	340 (27.59%)
	Between 41-50 Years	202 (16.40%)
	Above 50 Years	136 (11.04%)
Occupation of the Head of Family	Self-employed	20 (10.00%)
	Business	76 (38.00%)
	Service	36 (18.00%)
	Farming	68 (34.00%)
Total Family Monthly Income	Less than Rs. 5,000	24 (12.00%)
	Between Rs. 5,001-Rs. 10,000	28 (14.00%)
	Between Rs. 10,001-Rs. 15,000	32 (16.00%)
	Above Rs. 15,000	116 (58.00%)
Qualification of the Family Members	Illiterate	146 (11.85%)
	Primary Education	246 (19.97%)
	High School	276 (22.40%)
	Intermediate	260 (21.10%)
	Graduate and Above	304 (24.68%)
Marital Status of Family Members	Married	556 (45.13%)
	Unmarried	676 (54.87%)
Knowledge of English Language	Male	60 (40.54%)
	Female	88 (59.46%)

Data Analysis

The analysis of the workable questionnaire reveals the following trends:

1. Food Habits and Consumption Pattern

The food habit and consumption pattern have been analysed taking into account the factors like motivational factors affecting purchase, decision-maker, expenditure on food items other than the staple food, preference for homemade *vs.* readymade food items, consumption of junk fast food. A great shift has been observed in the post-liberalisation era towards the consumption of fruits, confectionaries and of course, the fast food items due to cross-cultural value adoption among the Indian households. Increasing trend of consuming more food prepared outside of the home, from restaurants and grocery stores has also been observed in the rural areas.

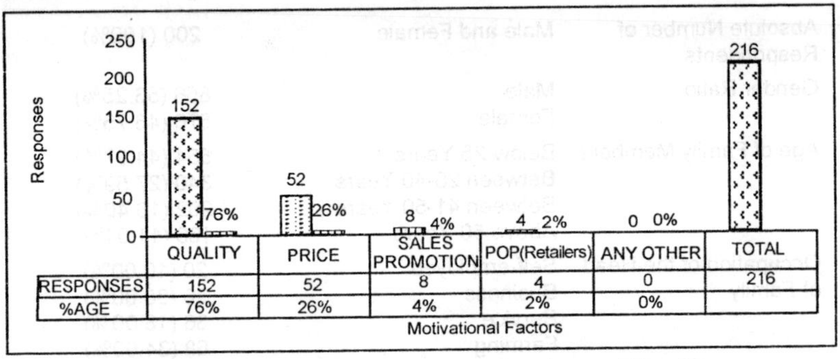

Fig. 13(i): Motivational Factors Affecting the Purchase of Food Items.

Figure 13(i) revealed that majority of respondents (76%) agree that the quality is a major factor to buy a particular food item followed by price (26%), while sales promotion and point of purchase have a little influence to motivate the buyer to purchase a particular food item.

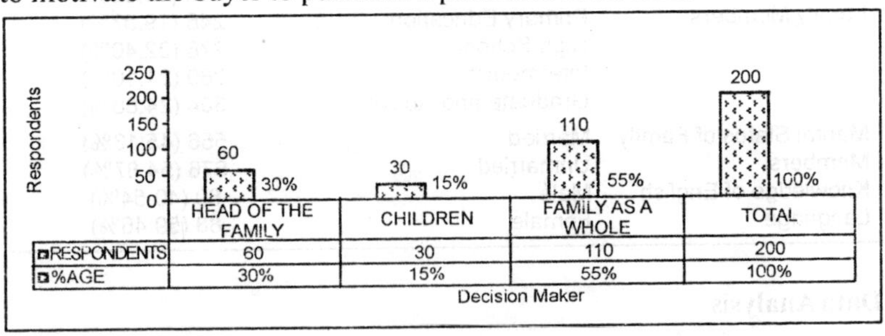

Fig. 13(ii): Role of Family Members in Purchase of Specific Food Items.

Figure 13(ii) revealed that a great deal of household consumption decision-making is not in the hands of one person but family as a whole (55%) which may lead to good outcomes, it can also be a source of even handedness within the family. On the other hand, head of the family (mainly male) and children have an influence on decision as 30 per cent and 15 per cent respectively.

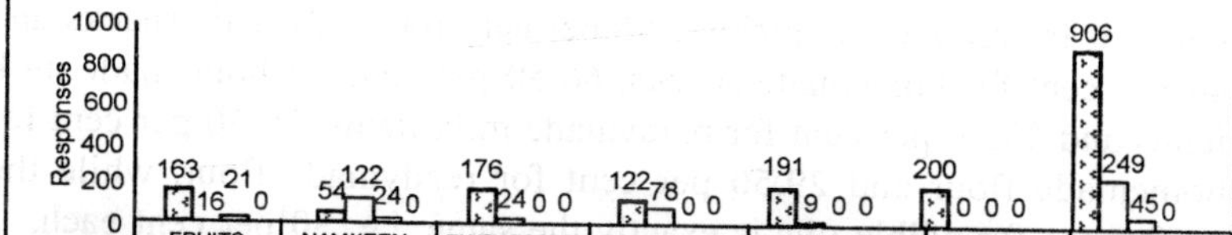

	FRUITS	NAMKEEN	FANCY FOODS	COLD DRINKS	CONFECTIONARY	OTHERS	TOTAL
5 to 20%	163	54	176	122	191	200	906
20 to 35%	16	122	24	78	9	0	249
35 to 50%	21	24	0	0	0	0	45
50 to 65%	0	0	0	0	0	0	0

Household Items

Fig. 13(iii): Households Expenses on Items other than Staple Foods.

It is exhibited in Figure 13(iii) that maximum 95.50 per cent of household spend 5 per cent-20 per cent of the expenditure to buy confectioneries followed by fancy food items like fast food or junk food (88%). *Namkeen* has got the share of 20 per cent–35 per cent of the expenditure done on accessory food items by 61 per cent of rural households. The consumption of fruit has also been seen increasing as is evident from the figure shows that 81.50 per cent households spending between 5 per cent–20 per cent. Overall we can say that within 5 per cent–35 per cent of total expenditure the rank order of consumed items is confectionery, fancy food, cold drink and fruits. Biscuits/*Namkeen* is very commonly consumed with tea, cold drink etc. Hence, the expenditure on this comes at 1st rank having expenditure bracket of 20 per cent–35 per cent. The consumption of biscuits/*namkeen* with cold drink seen to be most favoured combination.

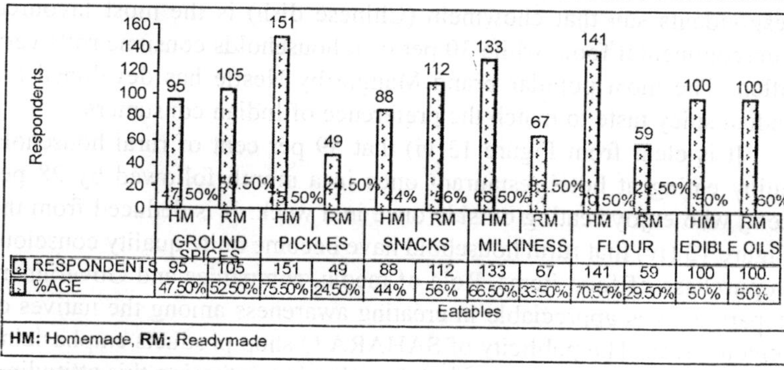

	GROUND SPICES HM	GROUND SPICES RM	PICKLES HM	PICKLES RM	SNACKS HM	SNACKS RM	MILKINESS HM	MILKINESS RM	FLOUR HM	FLOUR RM	EDIBLE OILS HM	EDIBLE OILS RM
RESPONDENTS	95	105	151	49	88	112	133	67	141	59	100	100.
%AGE	47.50%	52.50%	75.50%	24.50%	44%	56%	66.50%	33.50%	70.50%	29.50%	50%	50%

Eatables

HM: Homemade, **RM:** Readymade

Fig. 13(iv): Preference for Homemade or Readymade Products.

It is evident from Figure 13(iv) that 52.50 per cent respondents prefer readymade ground spices to homemade spices which is 47.50 per cent. Similarly, the preference is 75.50 per cent for homemade and 24.50 per cent for readymade pickles, 56 per cent for readymade snacks and 44 per cent for homemade snacks, 66.50 per cent for homemade milk items and 33.50 per cent for readymade milk items, 70.50 per cent for homemade flour and 29.50 per cent for readymade flour, while the preference for edible oils is exactly the same, i.e. 50 per cent each.

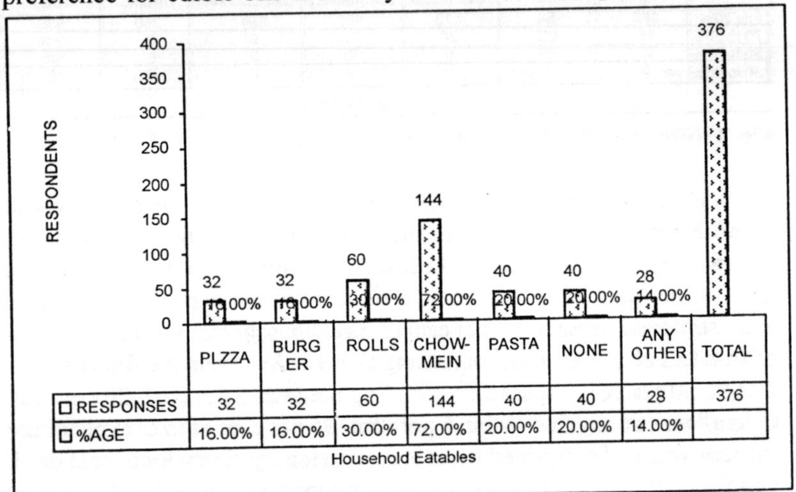

Fig. 13 (v): Household Consumption of Fast Food Items.

It is inferred from Figure 13(v) that the maximum 72 per cent respondents say that chowmein (Chinese dish) is the most favoured intercontinental food, while 30 per cent households consume rolls very often. The most popular brand Maggie by Nestle has developed the Indian spicy taste to match the preference of Indian consumers.

It is clear from Figure 13(vi) that 39 per cent of rural household enjoy eating at hotel/restaurant once in a month followed by 28 per cent, who enjoys eating outside once in a week. It is deduced from the Figure 13 (iv) that rural household have become quite quality conscious in purchase of food items. Role of media, companies and Government departments is appreciable in creating awareness among the natives of remote areas. The publicity of SAHARA Q shop products emphasizing quality and harmful effects of adulteration is reinforcing this attitudinal change by associating the products with health value.

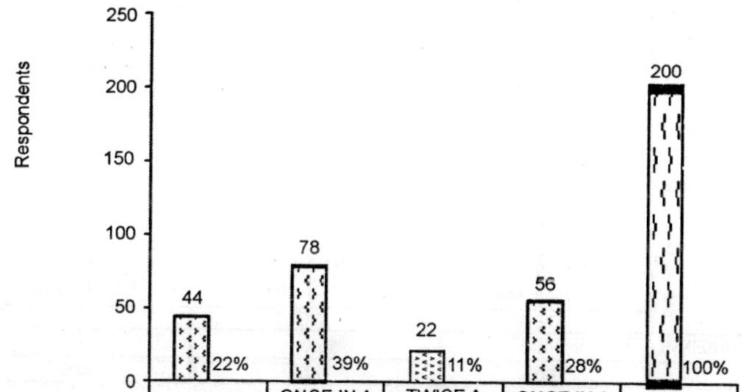

	NEVER	ONCE IN A MONTH	TWICE A MONTH	ONCE IN A WEEK	TOTAL
RESPONDENTS	44	78	22	56	200
%AGE	22%	39%	11%	28%	100%

Eating Options at Hotel/Restaurant

Fig. 13(vi): Eating at Hotel/Restaurant.

Expenditure on food accessories indicates the affluent behaviour of rural household. Use of readymade powdered spices and snacks adds to the ease and comfort in making food which was not accepted in the rural households in the past. This again shows the changed attitude towards the women who may save time to articulate her through other productive activities. Family decision in making the purchase of food items in this study further consolidates the role of women in rural household. Rural household still prefer home-made pickles, milk items, flour and edible oil as generally they have the facilities and resources to ensure the purity in these items. Trend of eating outside is catching up with rural households as responded by nearly 67 per cent respondents. Chowmein (Noodles) are the most popular intercontinental food in Indian community. It is found that rural households are also becoming health value conscious and non-traditional in picking and consuming the food items.

2. Fashion Adoption Trend

Now the marketing potential for fashion items in the rural part of the country is also growing especially in the villages of north India due to surplus income and exposure to the changing world through TV and other interactive media.

Figure 13 (vii) revealed that 60 per cent of the rural household prefer

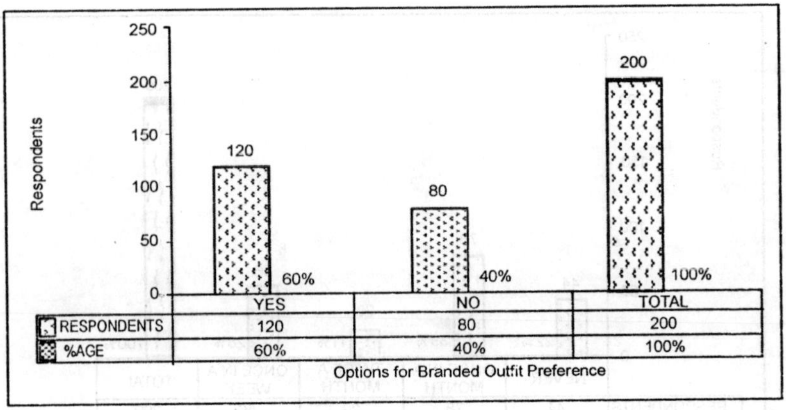

Fig. 13(vii): Preference for Branded Outfit.

branded outfits while 40 per cent do not bother about the branded one and stick to their traditional outfit stitched by the nearby tailoring shop.

Table 13.2: The Preference of branded outfit is independent of the Family Income

Sl. No.	*Options/Income Group*	*Yes*	*No*	*Total*	*Chi-Square Value*
1.	Less than Rs. 5000	2 (14.40)	22 (9.60)	**24**	51.67* Significant
2.	Between Rs. 5001 to Rs. 10000	12 (16.80)	16 (11.20)	**28**	
3.	Between Rs. 10001 to Rs. 15000	14 (19.20)	18 (12.80)	**32**	
4.	Above Rs. 15000	92 (69.60)	24 (46.40)	**116**	
	Total	**120**	**80**	**200**	

*Degree of freedom 3, Level of Significance 5%.

H_{01} has been tested for Table 13.2 by using Chi-square test at 5 per cent significance level. The calculated value (51.67) has been found significant at 5 per cent significance level. The results reject the Null hypothesis in favour of Alternate hypothesis saying that the preference of branded outfit depends upon family income.

It is revealed from Figure 13(viii) that 42 per cent of rural household prefer to change their outfit as per the fashion while 58 per cent voted against that by saying that they do not want to change their outfit with the changing fashion.

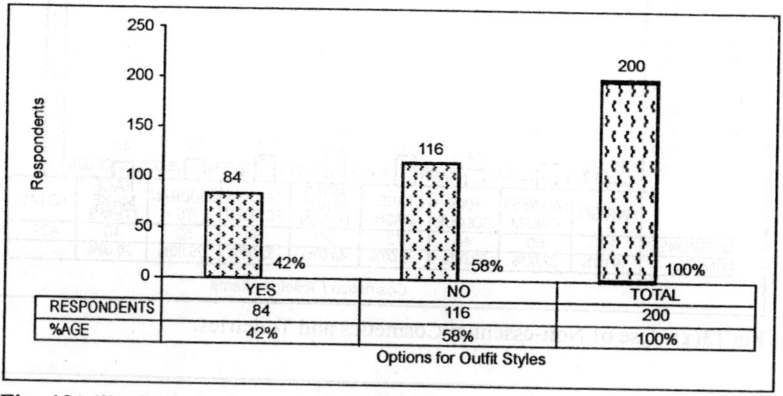

Fig: 13(viii): Fashion oriented Outfit Styles.

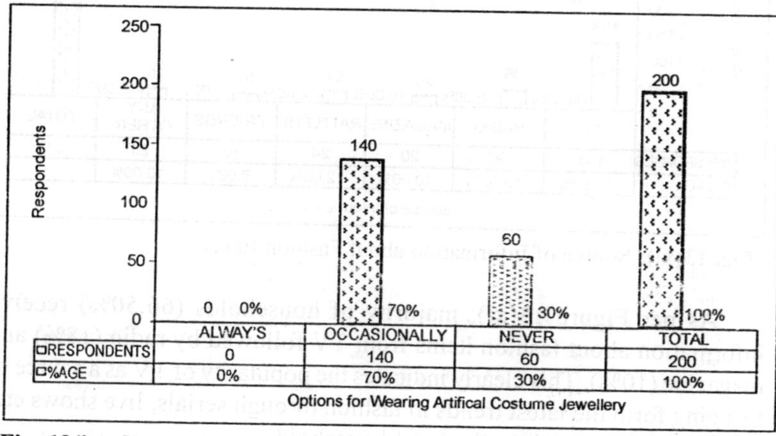

Fig: 13(ix): Use of Artificial Costume Jewellery among girls.

Figure 13(ix) extends that 70 per cent female folks of rural households, wear artificial jewellery occasionally while the remaining 30 per cent never wear it.

Figure 13(x) exhibits that 40 per cent households use after shave lotion followed by face wash (36%), fairness cream and talcum powder (32%), deodorant 26 per cent, Hair colour 22 per cent and face make up items 20 per cent. Hair gel is having the lowest preference by just 10 per cent.

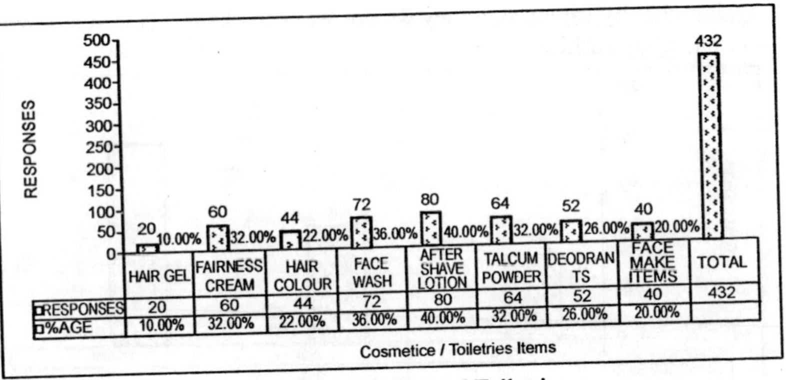

	HAIR GEL	FAIRNESS CREAM	HAIR COLOUR	FACE WASH	AFTER SHAVE LOTION	TALCUM POWDER	DEODRANTS	FACE MAKE ITEMS	TOTAL
RESPONSES	20	60	44	72	80	64	52	40	432
%AGE	10.00%	32.00%	22.00%	36.00%	40.00%	32.00%	26.00%	20.00%	

Fig 13(x): Use of Non-essential Cosmetics and Toiletries.

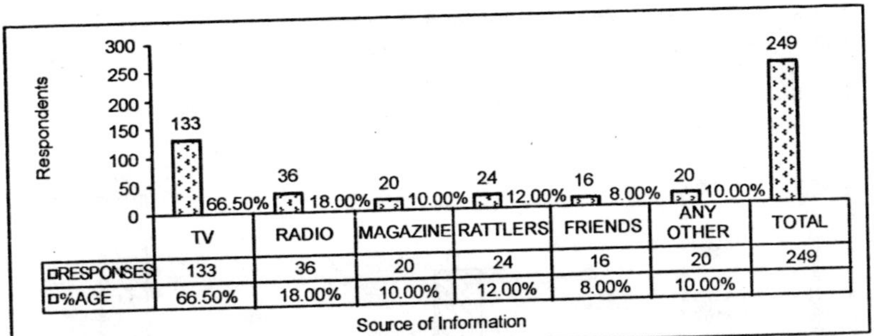

	TV	RADIO	MAGAZINE	RATTLERS	FRIENDS	ANY OTHER	TOTAL
RESPONSES	133	36	20	24	16	20	249
%AGE	66.50%	18.00%	10.00%	12.00%	8.00%	10.00%	

Fig. 13(xi): Source of Information about Fashion Items.

As per Figure 13(xi), majority of households (66.50%) receive information about fashion items from TV followed by radio (18%) and magazine (10%). This clearly indicates the popularity of TV as a source of bringing forth the latest trends in fashion through serials, live shows etc. and penetrating reach to the rural households.

It is revealed from Figure 13(xii) that more than 50 per cent of the rural households still think that their normal outfits are trendy and acceptable in the group that belongs to. In the categories of Jeans and T-shirts high percentage of households use stylish and latest design to portray the fashionable look.

It is inferred from Figures 13(vii)–13(xii) that substantially high percentage of households prefer branded outfit. However, they do not change their outfits as fast as the fashion changes. Hence, brand conciousness among rural household suggests the marketer to strategise their promotional campaign based on image building which could be

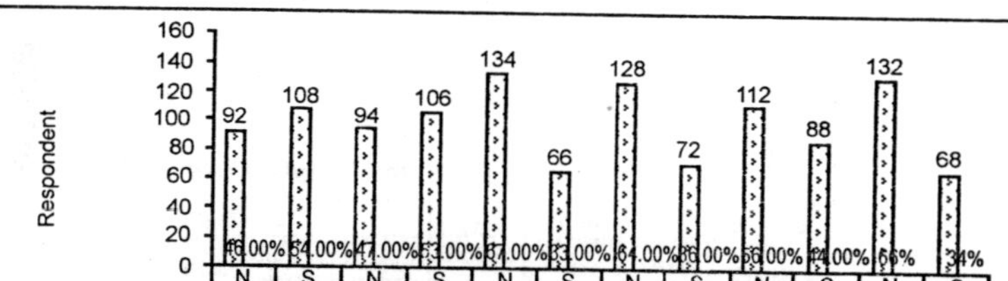

	JEANS N	JEANS S	TEES N	TEES S	SHOES N	SHOES S	SHALWAR N	SHALWAR S	JUMPER N	JUMPER S	TROUSER N	TROUSER S
RESPONDENTS	92	108	94	106	134	66	128	72	112	88	132	68
%AGE	46.00	54.00	47.00	53.00	67.00	33.00	64.00	36.00	56.00	44.00	66%	34%

N: Normal, **S:** Stylish

Fig. 13(xii): Products used for Fashionable Look

differentiated from the competing brands. The choice of branded items depends upon the income as revealed from the analysis. Rural consumers do not wait for the special occasion to buy new clothes rather whenever they get the outfit of their choice in the market, they buy it. This behaviour again refers to the increasing disposable income in the hands of rural consumers. The favoured cosmetics and toiletries are after-shave lotion, fairness cream and talcum powder which happened to be traditionally used by urban population but now has become the lifestyle of rural consumers also. TV is the most popular source for getting informed about the upcoming fasion trends being disseminated through serials, live shows, advertisements, celebrity endorsement etc. Except Jeans and T-Shirts, rest of the lifestyle outfit products are used in traditional way among the rural consumers. That may be because of the late adoption of radically different style of shoes, shalwar-jumper etc. Artificial jewellery is also occasionally worn by the rural women that indicates the non-acceptance and negative perception towards bold look of women in day-to-day life.

3. Media Habits and Entertainment Modes

Due to the increase in literacy rate and penetration of conventional media, the perception and attitude of rural consumer is moving towards proper consumerism. The reach of TV and satellite has made noticeable impact on the lifestyle of rural household as they get exposed to cluster of latest information. In post-liberal era, the culture of shopping at Mall has been taken as entertainment accompanied with eating at restaurant/ hotels.

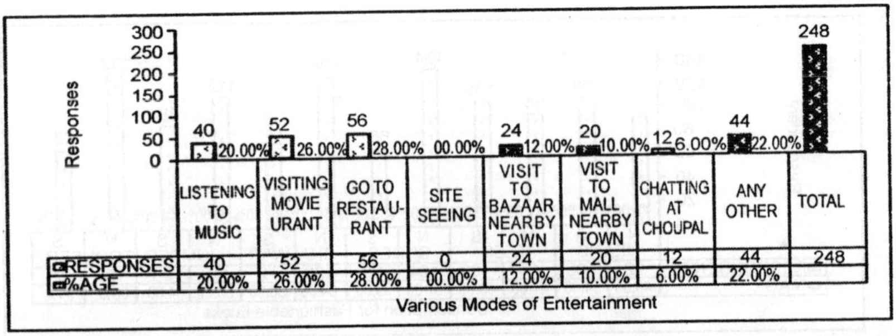

Fig. 13(xiii): Preferential Modes of Family Entertainment.

It is inferred from Figure 13(xiii) that in order to entertain themselves in leisure time 28 per cent rural people prefer to go to nearby restaurant followed by 20 per cent visit nearby movie hall, 22 per cent prefer to listen music of their choice, while 10 per cent to 12 per cent used to visit either bazaar or mall situated in nearby town, and finally, 6 per cent mainly the old ones prefer to chat with their friend at *choupal*. The remaining 22 per cent are not certain about utilising their leisure time, they may go for any of the above options or find suitable to remain in their house and play with their children.

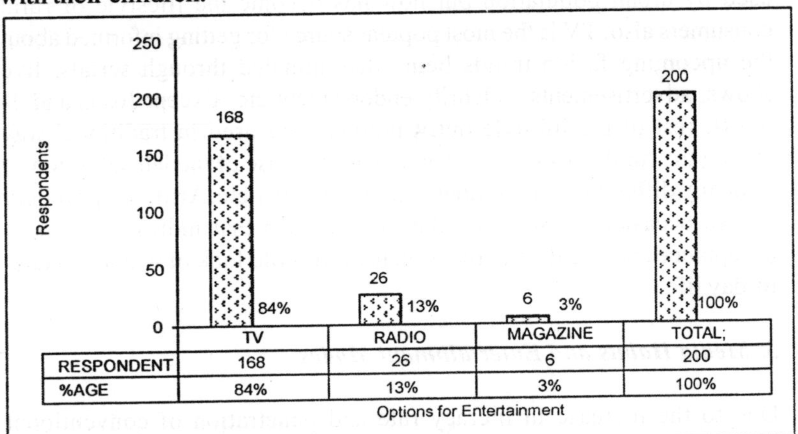

Fig. 13(xiv): Popular Media for Entertainment.

It is clear from Figure 13(xiv) that a big majority of 84 per cent prefer TV as a media for entertainment followed by radio and magazine, which are just 13 per cent and 3 per cent respectively. Whether the person is young or old, male or female, prefer TV to other media for entertainment.

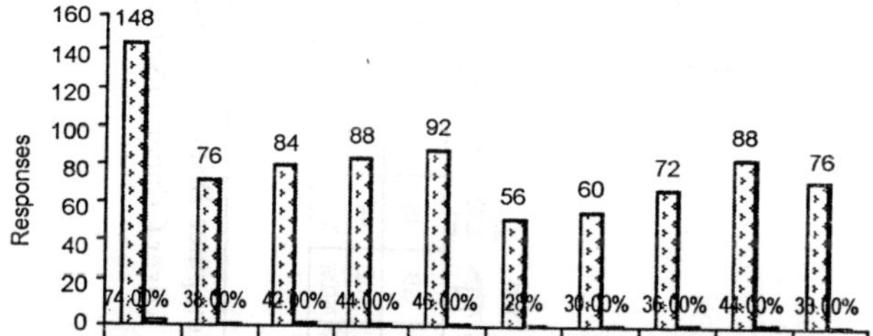

	TV				RADIO			MAGAZINE		
	Serial	Movie	Music	Sports	Music	Derma	Sports	Filmy	General	Stories
RESPONSES	148	76	84	88	92	56	60	72	88	76
%AGE	74.00%	38.00%	42.00%	44.00%	46.00%	28%	30.00%	36.00%	44.00%	38.00%

Options for Preferred Programmer on Different Media

Fig. 13(xv): Favourite Programme on Different Media.

It is evident from Figure 13(xv) that TV serials are the preferred media having 74 per cent audience in its favour followed by 44 per cent for sports, 42 per cent for music and 38 per cent for movie. In the case of radio, the preferred programme is music (46%) followed by sports commentary (30%) and drama (28%). For the print media, i.e. magazine, 44 per cent prefer general information to read followed by 38 per cent stories and film news 36 per cent.

It is exhibited from the Figures 13(xiii)–13(xv) that recreational activities and out of home visit to restaurant and movie hall are towards higher trend. TV is found to be the most favoured media and the market analysis also shows the increasing percentage of rural households having TV sets in their houses. Serials and family dramas are being watched by nearly 74 per cent rural household followed by music on radio and general information in magazines. Reading habits are missing among consumers as only 3 per cent households have rated it as their favourite media.

4. Use of Technology in the Consumption of Lifestyle Goods

The Indian customers are increasingly adapting their preferences to the new technologies. The technology has entered the day-to-day life of rural households too in the form of gadgets used to make the life easy and comfortable. The rural population is ready to use the technologically interfaced services like mobile and internet, high utility products like automobiles to laptop.

As per *Times of India* report (September 2012) rural consumption outpaces urban India and the same is revealed from Figure 13(xvi) that most of the rural households are almost using the same gadgets which

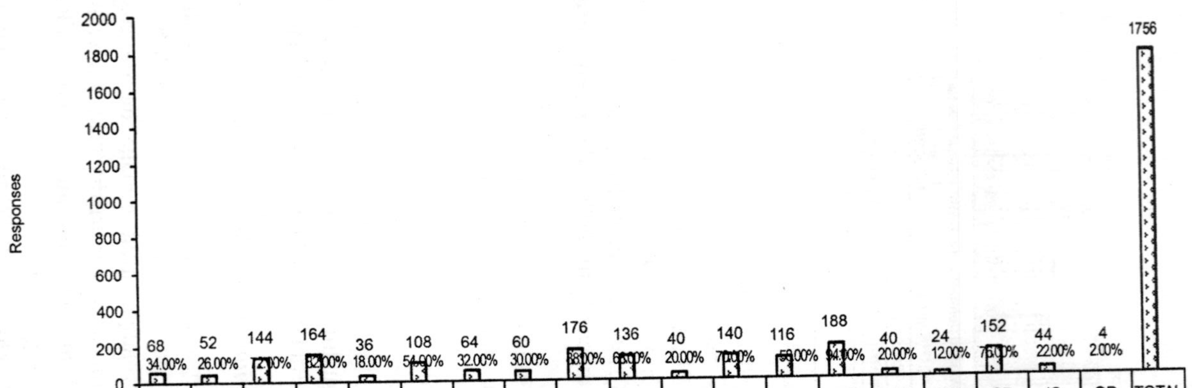

	RF	WM	AC	TW	FW	CM	DS	WP	MO	LT	GR	TV	RD	FN	MG	ON	GB	IS	OR	TOTAL
RESPONSES	68	52	144	164	36	108	64	60	176	136	40	140	116	188	40	24	152	44	4	1756
%AGE	34.00%	26.00%	72.00%	82.00%	18.00%	54.00%	32.00%	30.00%	88.00%	68.00%	20.00%	70.00%	58.00%	94.00%	20.00%	12.00%	76.00%	22.00%	2.00%	

Options for Household Gadgets

RF: Refrigerator, **WM:** Washing Machine, **AC:** Air Cooler, **TW:** Two Wheeler, **FW:** Four Wheeler, **CM:** Computer, **DS:** DVD System, **WP:** Water Purifier, **MO:** Mobile: **LT:** Laptop, **GR:** Geyser, **TV:** Television, **RD:** Radio, **FN:** Fan, **MG:** Mixer Grinder, **ON:** Oven, **GB:** Gas Burner, **IS:** Insulation Stove, **OR:** Others.

Fig. 13(xvi): Gadgets as Indicator of Standard of Life

their urban counterparts are using like; fan (94%), having mobile (88%), having two wheeler (82%), having gas burner (76%), having air coolers (72%), having laptops (68%), having radio (58%), having computers (54%), having refrigerators (34%), having DVD system (32%), having water purifier (30%), having washing machine (26%), having induction stove (22%), having geyser (20%), having geyser and mixer grinder (20%), having four wheeler (18%), having oven (12%), while 2 per cent are having other household gadgets. As per NSSO (2011-12) data, more than 50 per cent of country's TV's, fans, mobiles and 2 wheelers are in rural areas and the same one can easily find by having a glimpse shown in Figure 13(xvi).

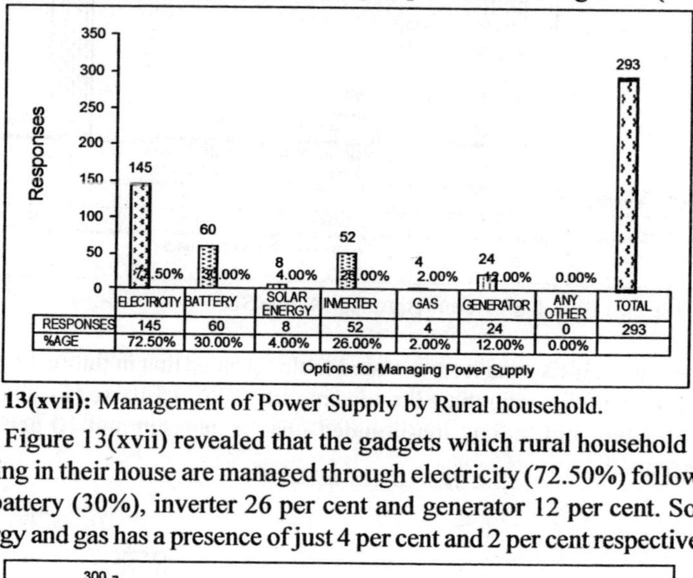

	ELECTRICITY	BATTERY	SOLAR ENERGY	INVERTER	GAS	GENERATOR	ANY OTHER	TOTAL
RESPONSES	145	60	8	52	4	24	0	293
%AGE	72.50%	30.00%	4.00%	26.00%	2.00%	12.00%	0.00%	

Fig. 13(xvii): Management of Power Supply by Rural household.

Figure 13(xvii) revealed that the gadgets which rural household are having in their house are managed through electricity (72.50%) followed by battery (30%), inverter 26 per cent and generator 12 per cent. Solar energy and gas has a presence of just 4 per cent and 2 per cent respectively.

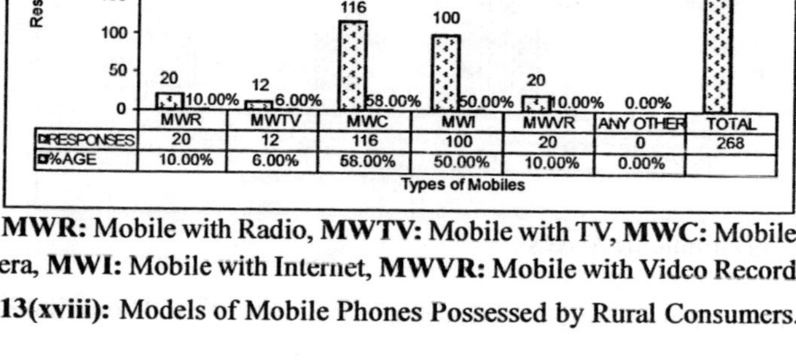

	MWR	MWTV	MWC	MWI	MWVR	ANY OTHER	TOTAL
RESPONSES	20	12	116	100	20	0	268
%AGE	10.00%	6.00%	58.00%	50.00%	10.00%	0.00%	

MWR: Mobile with Radio, **MWTV:** Mobile with TV, **MWC:** Mobile with Camera, **MWI:** Mobile with Internet, **MWVR:** Mobile with Video Recording.

Fig. 13(xviii): Models of Mobile Phones Possessed by Rural Consumers.

It is extended from Figure (xviii) that most of the rural households are presently using mobile with camera (58%) followed by mobile with internet (50%), mobile with video recording and radio 10 per cent, and mobile with TV only 6 per cent.

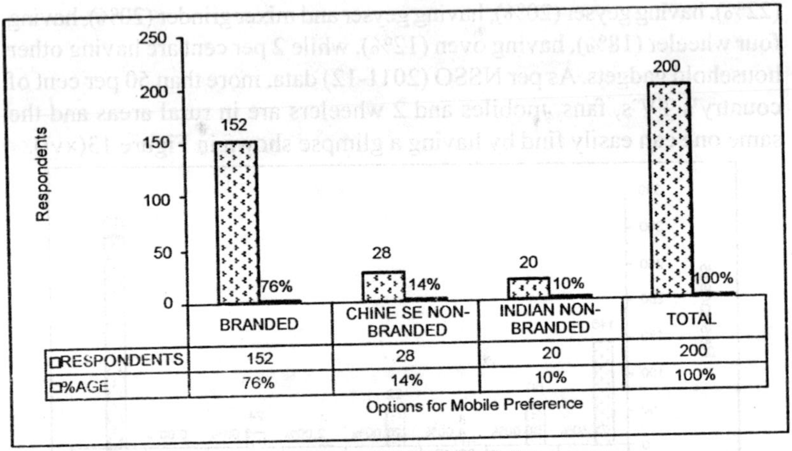

Fig. 13(xix): Branded vs. Non-Branded Mobile Set.

Figure 13(xix) and its associated table revealed that in future the rural household prefer to purchase branded mobiles (76%) followed by Chinese non-branded and Indian non-branded just 14 per cent and 10 per cent respectively.

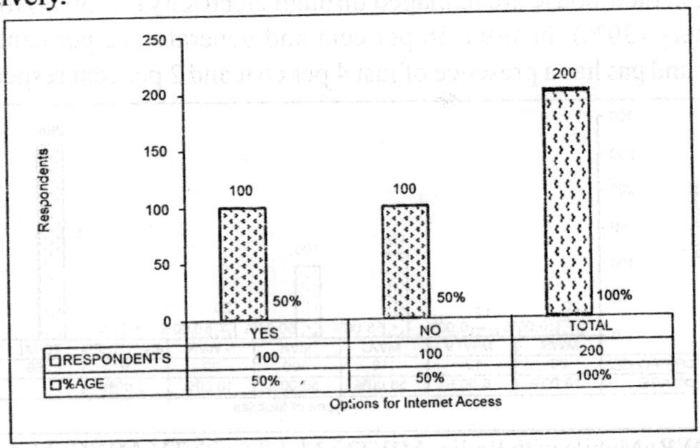

Fig. 13(xx): Internet Access.

It is clear from Figure 13 (xx) that 50 per cent of rural household have internet access at home while the same percentages of households are not accessing it. In this regard second hypothesis H_{02} has been tested by using Chi-square test at 5 per cent significance level, and rejected with the conclusion that internet usage is dependent on the occupation.

Table 13.3: Internet usage is Independent of the Occupation

Sl. No.	*Options/Occupation*	*Yes*	*No*	*Total*	*Chi-Square Value*
1.	Self-Employed	8 (10.00)	12 (10.00)	20	
2.	Business	48 (38.00)	28 (38.00)	76	
3.	Service	20 (18.00)	16 (18.00)	36	12.16* Significant
4.	Farming	24 (34.00)	44 (34.00)	88	
	Total	**100**	**100**	**200**	

* Degree of freedom 3, Level of Significance 5%.

H_{02} has been tested for Table 13.3 by using Chi-square test at 5 per cent significance level. The calculated value (12.16) has been found significant at 5 per cent significance level. The results reject the Null hypothesis in favour of Alternate hypothesis saying that the internet usage is dependent on occupation.

It is evident from the analysis of the Figure 13 (xvi–xx) that the Oven, Mixer grinder and washing machine are not commonly used by the rural households. Substantially, high usage of Fan (94%), mobile (88%), two wheelers (82%), TV (70%) and laptop (68%) show that living standard is more shifted to the utility based consumption. We can deduce that gradually the items taken as luxury items in past, are now perceived as necessity to live a comfortable and productive life. In this region of Uttar Pradesh still the power supply is managed through electricity rather than battery or inverters. Since, battery and inverter require electricity for recharging, hence, we can say that irregular and insufficient supply of electricity are the reasons for not using inverters. Camera is the most demanded feature in mobile handset. Internet services are also preferred by the rural households. It all refers to the lifestyle products that can match the self-image of the consumers, no matter if they stay in the rural areas. It is the mind-set which is taking turn towards comfortable and stylish lifestyle conditioned with utility and economy based behaviour.

Conclusion and Policy Implications

The pyramid structure of Indian customer market has been flattened with huge middle class at the centre and economically deprived class at the bottom. A great shift has been observed from lower end to next upper level of rural and urban market. The affluent behaviour of rural household can be judged as outcome of MNREGA and intervention of technology in agriculture sector and increasing rate of literacy level. The study reveals that lifestyle of rural households is changing but with gradual pace to have conformity with the social, economic and cultural values. Better infrastructure and extensive awareness through media can turn them to huge market of future.

REFERENCES

Dholakia, R.R., 1999, "Going shopping: Key determinants of shopping behaviours and motivations", *International Journal of Retail Distribution Management.*

Dubey, Jayashree and Patel, Rajni P., 2004, "Ads that Work with Youth", *Indian Management*, Vol. 43, No. 10.

Kashyap, P. and Raut, S., 2008, *The Rural Marketing Book,* New Delhi: Biztantra.

Kaur, H. and Kaur, R., 2002, "Fashion Awareness Among Rural and Urban Adolescents", *Journal of Social Research*, Vol. 43, No. 1.

Nagaraja, B., 2004, "Consumer Behaviour in Rural Areas: A Micro-level Study on Buying Behaviour of Rural Consumers in Kavali Mandal", *Indian Journal of Marketing*, Vol. 34, No. 11.

Panda, Tapan, 2006, "The Myth of Indian Rural Market: Challenges and Illusions," *Marketing Mastermind.*

Rajan, R.V., 2007-08. *The New Face of Rural Marketing: Marketing white book,* New Delhi: Business World.

Ramana Rao, P.V., 1997, "Rural market problems and prospective", *Indian Journal of Marketing*, Vol. 27.

Selvaraj, A., "Rural Consumers' Behaviour Regarding Non-Durable Goods: A Study in Erode District of Tamil Nadu", *Indian Journal of Marketing,* Vol. 37, No. 12, 2007.

Shukla, R.K., 1997, *New Perspectives in Rural Marketing*, New Delhi: National Publishing House.

14

Changing Tastes and Preferences of Rural Consumers

Emerging Paradigm in Indian Market

P. N. SINGH

Introduction

Rural marketing has become the latest mantra of most corporates including MNCs who are in race to capture the large Indian market. The rural market consists 70 per cent of the population. This is the reason why marketers are focusing on the emerging and easily approachable rural markets. Logically, they have convincing arguments in justifying their actions. Although, there is a huge scope for enhancing sale in the rural markets for a variety of products, yet the marketers have not spent much time in understanding the numerous hurdles in rural marketing.

Due to the changing face of the Indian economy, the needs, tastes and expectations of the rural people are changing. The rural market has a huge demand base and offers great opportunities to marketers. With empowerment of the rural people and rise in education, employment, higher purchasing power, better media exposure, better connectivity with outside world rural market provides a massive unexplored pool of consumers. To be successful in the rural market, companies will have to be innovative and sensitive towards devising appropriate marketing strategies. Traditional urban marketing strategies will have to be localised as per the demands of the rural market. In view of the large investments made by the Government in rural infrastructure thereby pushing income and demand level, the marketing prospects are bright in rural India.

According to McKinsey report by 2020 rural India will be a market worth US $ 500-600 billion. Rural consumption levels are also anticipated to equal current urban levels by 2017. The economy is vibrant, incomes are rising and the habits, preferences and attitudes of rural India are changing rapidly.

The chapter analyses the emerging paradigm of the Indian rural markets and how the marketers have been able to have an impact in the rural segment through effective marketing strategies by overcoming the roadblocks in rural selling. The chapter examines some of these issues by looking at the village structure, the rural consumer, his current product usage and suggests indicative marketing strategies to be employed in rural marketing.

Population (in crores) based on Census 2011

	2001	*2011*	*Difference*
India	102.9	121	18.1
Rural	74.3	83.3	9
Urban	28.6	37.7	9.1

Rural India accounts for 69 per cent of India's population, 56 per cent of national income, 64 per cent of total expenditure and a third of total savings. Rural India has about 6,38,365 villages spread over 32 lakh sq. km. Rural demand in FMCG, automobile and retail is growing at a faster pace than anticipated due to rise in its consumption patterns which is creating demand. Based on the types of products currently seen and the rising aspirations of the rural consumers, product proliferation may take many directions. Consumers need to be made aware about more sophisticated and better products as they too aspire for more than just the basic functions of the products. Indian rural sector is much diversified both in terms of culture, values and geography; therefore, to achieve success, brands will have to devise strategies using various rural folk media to reach them in their own language and in large numbers. Appropriate mix of conventional and non-conventional media like, television, radio, audio-visual, vans, cinema commercials, wall paintings, intensive door-to-door campaigns, live demonstrations, distribution of samples can be used as an effective media to increase sales.

In rural areas, HUL promoted its products through demonstration Vehicles, rural fairs and festivals. Local entertainment forms like "*Nautanki*" (A form of entertainment, comprising a mix of dance, dramas, skits etc. by a group of people.) in Uttar Pradesh Asian Paints launched its Utsav range during the pre-Dipawali season in which the salesmen took the opinion leaders in villages and painted the village post-office, library or the house of the *pradhaan* to demonstrate that paint does not peel off. This is because wall Paintings are quite effective in catching attention of rural consumers.

To reach the rural audience customization and regionalisation of the promotional message is required. Regionalisation of advertising campaigns by many leading multinational companies indicates a healthy trend for the advertising business as well. Companies like, ITC, Wipro etc. are harnessing full potential of technology by using IT tools for rural marketing. Organisations can make use of product demonstration to communicate about product benefits to villagers. Demonstration may be 'Method-demonstration' like, on launch of Dalda (vanaspati Ghee brand). The company demonstrated by fried *pakodas* on the street corners to convince people that it can be used for frying. The other approach was 'Result-demonstration' in which to prove its safety LPG was introduced for cooking. Integrated campaigns which are low in cost, scale and are interactive in nature, aid in enhancing brand penetration. Therefore, frequency of usage is required to be developed for the rural market.

Although, the rural market does offer a vast untapped potential, it should also be recognised that it is not that easy to operate in rural market because of several problems. Most MNCs are, therefore, accepting the challenges of the rural markets with the help of the 4As, i.e. *availability, affordability, acceptability* and *awareness.* Over the years, India's largest MNC, Hindustan Lever, a subsidiary of Unilever, has built a strong distribution system, to reach the interiors of the rural market for selling products like Sunsilk and Clinic shampoos in small, inexpensive packets, as product cost is major considerations which determine purchase decision in rural segment. It has also launched a variant of its largest selling soap brand, Lifebuoy at Rs. 2 for 50 gm. The move is mainly targeted at the rural market. Rural India accounts for nearly half of HUL's revenue.

Objectives of the Study

1. To understand the basics of rural market.
2. To explore the potential of rural market.
3. Difference in rural customer taste and preferences from the urban customer.
4. Factors that determine the buying decision-making of the rural customers.

5. To analyse the various parameters of potential of rural market.

Salient Features of Rural India

Some common characteristics that do exist amongst most of the rural markets in India are as follows:

1. *Population:* 83.3 per cent of the villages have a population of less than 2000 (Census of India, 2011).
2. *Levels of Education:* Although the percentage of literates has increased from 36 in 1981 to 67 in 2011, there is still approximately 60 per cent of the rural population lies below the middle education bracket (Kashyap & Raut, 2010).
3. *Occupation Pattern:* Almost 74 per cent of the rural population depends on cultivation or wages for their living (NCAER, 2010).
4. *Changing Characteristics*: In terms of occupation, consumption and buying behaviour change prominently from urban to rural in locations with population more than 10,000.

The study is confined to two villages of Mirzapur district in Uttar Pradesh i.e. Hallia and Jamalpur. In both these villages, people are mainly engaged in agriculture or own shops or are in Government service. The profile of the respondents is given in Table 14.1 (a, b, c, d).

Table 14.1 (a): Respondents' Gender

Response	*No. of Respondents*	*% of Respondents*
Male	69	64.48
Female	38	35.52

Gender-wise analysis shows that 64.48 per cent respondents are male and rest of them are females. It means rural markets are being dominated by male.

Table 14.1(b): Respondent's Age

Response	*No. of Respondents*	*% of Respondents*
Less than 20 years	9	8.41
21-30 years	20	18.69
31-40 years	33	30.84
41-50 years	28	26.16
50 years and above	17	15.88

Table 14.1(c): Occupational Profile of Respondents

Agriculture		60
Shopkeepers		10
Service:	Engineers	2
	Bankers	4
	Army Personnel	6
	Teachers	10
Other Services		15
	Total	**107**

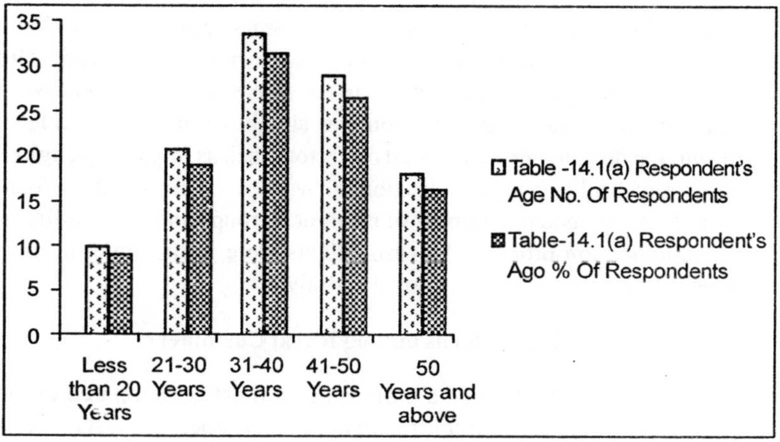

Table 14.1(d): Educational Profile of Respondents

	Male	*Female*
Illiterate	5	14
Under Matric	21	7
Matric	18	8
Higher Secondary	9	5
Graduate	10	2
Post-Graduate	6	2

It is found that monthly income of the respondents range between Rs. 2000-Rs. 8000, which is 60 per cent of the sample population, indicating respondent's affordability of making purchases (Table 14.2).

Research Methodology

The data for the present study have been collected by interviewing the respondents using a structured and unstructured questionnaire. Keeping

Table 14.2: Respondents Monthly Income

	No. of Respondents	*% of Respondents*
Less than Rs.2000	10	11.21
Rs.2001- Rs.5000	39	36.44
Rs.5001- Rs.8000	25	23.36
Rs.8001- Rs.10000	15	14.01
Rs.10001- Rs.15000	11	10.28
More than Rs.15000	7	6.54

in view the time and availability of the respondents, group interviews and interviews at the individual level have also been conducted. The observation method has also been used wherever conditions were favourable for the same. Information was sought from the respondents on the buying decision process based on factors such as impact of religion, customs and traditions, participation of women in buying decisions, impact of advertisements, impact of reference groups and the validity of the communication process. All respondents were forthcoming in their response to the various aspects of the study.

Trends and Prevailing Patterns among Rural Customers

Rural consumers, tend to lead a more relaxed lifestyle compared to the urban counterparts and exhibit little urgency. Consumers in rural markets of the two villages tend to have greater trust in products and services endorsed by the Government and its agencies. They tend to be more brand loyal, as habits once formed are difficult to change and they tend to feel a pride in getting a good deal rather than paying premium prices for products and services.

A number of leading rural marketing organisations in Uttar Pradesh are implementing a series of initiatives designed to help the corporates looking for new markets. Rural communities tend to be closer than urban societies and reference groups have a greater importance. Relatives and people from the same caste are important reference groups. Joint families still exist in villages although the trend is towards the nuclear families. In village "Hallia", the consumption is driven to a large extent by the occupation and income of the consumers. Low income levels and inadequacy of credit facilities also affect the consumption patterns. Another important factor that affects demand in rural areas is the instability of the income of the farmers, which is linked to the seasonality of agricultural production as well as to the unpredictability of the harvest. Similarly, the landless labourers and daily wage earners get their remuneration on a day-to-day basis and therefore, they purchase smaller quantities of products at a time, mostly on a daily basis.

It is found that in comparison to the urban counterparts, the rural consumers have different interpretations of colours, symbols, and social activities. The cultural values and norms have a strong influence in determining buying and consumption behaviour in the rural areas. There are restrictions on the type of food and the type of intoxicants that can be consumed in the villages. Similarly, women occupy a more traditional place in rural areas and therefore, western apparel may not be accepted in the rural markets. However, the rural youths are open to any new ideas, and are largely influenced by the urban consumption patterns. As the exposure to mass media and information technology is increasing, rural consumers are more informed about products and services and their dependence on traditional reference groups is decreasing.

Rural Marketing is an evolving concept, and as a part of any economy it has untapped potential, and this has now been realised by marketers. Improvement in infrastructure and reach, promise a bright future for those intending to go rural. Any macro-level strategy for these markets should focus on availability, accessibility and affordability. Constant scanning and sieving of ideas and plans is essential and attention needs to be focused on market research that tries to reduce the uncertainty in dealing with these markets. More specifically, in relation to rural areas, demand is seen to a highly price elastic. And there is need to break the price barrier.

There is no doubt that divide exists between urban India and Rural Bharat. However, with the silent revolution taking place a seamless integration of rural and urban markets is underway. Once this happens, the gulf that divides the two markets will become narrower. For this, change needs to be engaged and managed. The overall marketing mix framework for rural markets must, therefore, focus on plugging the segments with the right product, using value for money pricing, selecting the most appropriate channel of distribution, building long-term relationships with the customers and finally, using the power of emotional brands.

Findings

Factors that Determine the Buying Decision

The respondents of both the villages make their decision in consultation with the elders and the ladies of the house. Views of the women in the family are given due respect and consideration. The house lady, i.e. the '*Grihani*' is emerging as a strong pillar in the family life. The youngsters too have considerable respect for the women in their families, perhaps this is a part of their culture.

However, the youngsters make their own independent decisions for purchasing items for their personal use like clothes etc. Sixty per cent of the respondents in the age group of above 35 years made their buying decisions especially for the consumer durable items keeping in with the religious beliefs. No purchase of consumer durables was being made in the inauspicious month according to the Hindu mythology. Items of daily use like Ghee, Oil, etc. were not bought on Tuesdays. As a matter of belief, haircut was avoided on Monday and Tuesday. Similarly, clothes too were not being washed on Tuesday and Thursday. However, fifteen per cent of the respondents, in the age group of 15 to 35 years, did not subscribe to these beliefs. These are the ones who are educated.

Level of Awareness

The villagers are well aware of the availability of the products and visit the city for making purchases for marriages and social functions. This helped them to have better choice though they are not sure about the quality of service. They go for such purchase decisions as it enhances their social status and prestige.

Conclusion

1. Regional languages play a vital role in rural marketing in both the villages.
2. The decision to purchase goods is taken by the male head of the household followed by the spouse.
3. Advertisements through electronic media are preferred over other methods of communication by majority of the villagers. About ninety per cent of the respondents in different age groups opined that they were interested in advertisements on the television.
4. Rural customers are increasingly becoming brand conscious as well as price and discounts conscious.
5. Marketers can benefit to a large extent if they value the rural consumers as their customers.
6. Participation of women of the family in buying decisions is increasing in the villages.
7. Even if goods are available locally, consumers prefer to go to the city Mirzapur, as it gives them a better deal and choice as well.

8. The youngsters prefer to make independent buying decisions for the products, for their own use but certainly like to consult the family members, if it is a family utility product.
9. The consumers of village 'Jamalpur' usually do not experiment with a new product unless something triggers them.
10. Though people of 'Hallia' are not much aware about the MNCs, they welcome the companies that enter villages with a social commitment.
11. The rural customer upholds his traditions and customs in high esteem.
12. Rural consumer prefers to purchase from the city for occasions such as marriages and social functions

REFERENCES

Allen, R. Kathleen, 2005, *Bringing New Technology to Market*, 1st Reprint edition, Prentice Hall Publication, pp. 1-21.

Dogra, B. and K. Ghuman, 2008, *Rural Marketing: Concept and Practices*. New Delhi: Tata McGraw-Hill.

Gopalaswamy, T.P., 1997 *Rural Marketing: Environment, Problem, and Strategies*. New Delhi: Wheeler Publishing.

Iyer, Vidya, 2010, Rural Marketing", *SIES Journal of Management*, Vol. 6, Issue 2; pp. 4, 110.

Kashyap, P. and S. Raut, 2006, *The Rural Marketing Book*, New Delhi: Biztantra.

Kotler, P., K. Keller, A. Koshy and M. Jha, 2007, *Marketing Management: A South Asian Perspective*. New Delhi: Pearson Prentice Hall.

Paninchukunnath, Ajith, 2010, *3P Framework: Rural Marketing in India*, January-March, pp. 54-67.

Singh, Nirvikar, 2004, *Information Technology and Rural Development in India*, University of California, Santa Cruz, USA, April.

Vaswani, L.K., R. Aithal, D. Pradhan and G. Sridhar, 2005, "Rural Marketing in Development Paradigm", *International Journal of Rural Management*, 1 (2): 245-62.

Velayudhan, S.K., 2002, *Rural Marketing: Targeting the Non-Urban Consumer*. New Delhi: Response Books.

15

Marketing Strategy in the Context of Changing Tastes and Demand of Modern Rural Consumers of India

SANGHAMITRA CHOUDHURY AND SHAILENDRA KUMAR

Introduction

Rural India is growing and this is evident from the increase and change in the consumption pattern of the rural people. Considering that rural India comprises 41 per cent of India's middle class and accounts for 58 per cent total disposable income accounting for consumption and with approximately 7 out of 10 consumers residing in rural India, the rural buyers are spurring growth and driving demands. The companies of late have started recognizing the potential of rural market. They have started focusing on the changing tastes and demand of the new modern rural consumers. The modern rural Indian consumers have also started making demands for those premium products which were earlier exquisitely meant to cater to the demand of the niche urban market. Hence, a proper Marketing strategy is the need of the hour. The basic objective of this research work is to study the potential and growth of the Indian rural market and to suggest changes in the age old marketing practices followed by the Indian companies.

Potential of the Indian Rural Market

Rural Market has great potential and it is still largely untapped. The consumer culture is fast spreading in the rural India where 69 per cent of the total population resides. This increase in consumerism is driving not only big Indian corporate houses but also multinational organisations towards rural India. The potential of the Indian Rural Market can be understood under following heads:

Size of the Rural Market and Penetration

The size of the Indian rural market is twice the size of the entire market of USA and Rural India is a home to 12.2 per cent of world consumers. The number of rural supermarkets (*haats*) in India is 42,000 which exceeds the total number of retail chain stores in the US (35,000). As per Census 2001, there are total 6,40,867 villages in India and of those 1,59,667 villages are most populous and hold nearly 65 per cent of the total rural population. Thus, a large portion of rural population can be reached merely by focusing on 25 per cent most populous villages of India (i.e.1,59,667 villages).

Increasing Income and Purchasing Power

Increased industrialisation in the rural areas and establishment of SEZs (Special Economic Zones) along with the introduction of several Government schemes like MNREGA (Mahatma Gandhi National Rural Employment Guarantee Act), NRLM (National Rural Livelihood Mission) etc. along with the agricultural development programmes of the Government have helped in increasing the income of the rural people. This in turn has resulted in increase in disposable income and purchasing power of the rural people. Rural income constitutes approximately 56 per cent of the total income and is growing at a much higher pace of 5.6 per cent per annum whereas the urban income is growing at a pace of 5.4 per cent per annum. According to ASSOCHAM, the consumer durable market in rural India is likely to witness an annual growth of 40 per cent in 2011-12 due to higher disposable income of the rural India that has brought in lifestyle changes. A survey by the National Council of Applied Economic Research reveals that there are 33 million households in rural India with a monthly income of Rs. 1,000 or more. Interestingly, there are only 25 million urban households in this bracket. Table 15.1 clearly indicates the rising rural prosperity.

There has been a significant change in the sectoral share of rural workforce. In 1983, Agriculture employed 81.49 per cent of the total rural mass which reduced to 70.08 per cent in the year 2004-05. The less dependency upon agriculture for livelihood is reducing the risk associated with agriculture and also increasing the income of the rural people. Table 15.2 clearly shows the shift towards Non-Agriculture sector for employment.

Table 15.1: Rising Rural Prosperity

Income Group	*1994-95*	*2000-2001*	*2006-07*
Above ₹-1,00,000	1.6%	3.8%	5.6%
₹-77,001-1,00,000	2.7%	4.7%	5.8%
₹-50,001-77,000	8.3%	13.0%	22.4%
₹-25001-50,000	26%	41.1%	44.6%
₹-25000 and below	61.4%	37.4%	20.2%

Source: http://www.rimisp.org

Table 15.2: Sectoral Share of Rural Workforce

Rural Employment	*1983*	*1987-88*	*1993-94*	*1999-2000*	*2004-05*
Agriculture	81.49	77.46	78.39	76.16	70.08
Non-Agriculture	18.51	22.54	21.61	23.84	29.92

Source: National Sample Survey Organisation (NSSO).

Improving Infrastructure

Earlier it was believed that since rural markets are very widely dispersed and not well connected hence reaching them is quite costly. But the notion has now changed. Remoteness is no longer a problem. The improvement in the road and rail network along with the increase in the tele density has facilitated a systemised product distribution system to village. Improvements in the infrastructures have promoted the companies to expand their business and network in rural India.

Increasing Awareness and Literacy among the Rural Consumers

The literacy gap between rural and urban India is reducing very significantly. The increase in literacy rate among the rural masses has resulted in their greater awareness about consumer issues. As a result, they have now started demanding even those products which were earlier supposed to be exquisitely meant for niche urban market.

Table 15.3 shows the bridging literacy gap between rural and urban India.

Table 15.3: Literacy gap between Rural and Urban India.

Year	*Age Group*	*Literacy Rate Urban Areas*	*Literacy Rate Rural Areas*	*Difference in rural/urban areas (%age points)*
1961	5 and over	54.43	22.46	31.97
1971	5 and over	60.22	27.89	32.33
1981*	5 and over	64.85	34.04	30.81
1981*	7 and over	67.20	36.00	31.20
1991**	7 and over	73.08	44.69	28.39
2001***	7 and over	79.92	58.74	21.18
2011	7 and over	84.98	68.91	16.07

* Excludes Assam.

** Excludes Jammu & Kashmir.

*** Census of India, 2001.

Increasing Consumerism and Changing Lifestyle

The age old habits and lifestyle of the rural people of India has changed significantly. Therefore, the consumption pattern of the Indian rural consumer is fast changing. They are now using toothbrush and paste instead of *neem* or charcoal powder. Uses of consumer durable goods along with other daily commodities have increased very rapidly. The advent of media and globalisation has significantly changed the lifestyle of Indian rural mass.

Table 15.4: Percentage Share in Total Monthly Per Capita Consumer Expenditure (MPCE) by Group of Items in Rural and Urban Areas of India

Item Group	*Share in Total Consumer Expenditure in*									
	Rural					*Urban*				
	1987-88	*1993-94*	*1999-2000**	*2004-05*	*2009-10*	*1987-88*	*1993-94*	*1999-2000**	*2004-05*	*2009-10*
Food Total	64.0	63.2	59.4	55.0	53.6	56.4	54.7	48.1	42.5	40.7
Non-Food Total	36.0	36.8	40.6	45.0	46.4	43.6	45.3	51.9	57.5	59.3
Total Expenditure	**100.0**	**100.0**	**100.0**	**100.0**	**100.0**	**100.0**	**100.0**	**100.0**	**100.0**	**100.0**

Source: National Sample Survey Organisations (ON189).

Table 15.4 clearly shows that the Indian rural consumers have reduced their expenditure on food articles and increased expenditure on non-food articles. The expenditure on food articles in Rural India was 64 per cent of the total expenditure in the year 1987-88 whereas in the year 2009-10, the expenditure on the food articles declined to 53.6 per cent of the total expenditure in the year 2009-10. On the other hand, the expenditure on non-food items increased from 36 per cent in 1987-88 to 46.4 per cent in the year 2009-10. This clearly shows that the Indian rural economy is no more a subsistence economy and the disposable income of the rural consumers have increased significantly in recent years which has made them spend more on non-food items and thus spur the demand.

If we talk about the changing lifestyle of the rural people we can see that the rural people have increased their expenditure on beverages. The expenditure on beverages was 3.9 per cent of the total monthly per capita consumer expenditure in the year 1987-88 and it rose to 5.6 per cent of the total monthly per capita consumer expenditure in the year 2009-10 whereas during the same period the total per capita monthly consumer expenditure in urban India almost remained constant. However, what concerns is that the consumers are decreasing their expenditure on food and cloths whereas the expenditure on beverages and tobacco is increasing. This is a clear indicator of the changing lifestyle of the Indian rural people. Table 15.5 shows average monthly per capita expenditure by group of items (based on MMRP) in Rural and Urban Areas of India.

Table 15.5: Average Monthly Per Capita Expenditure (MPCE) by Group of Items (Based on MMRP) in Rural and Urban Areas of India (July 2009—June 2010)

*Item Group**	*Expenditure per Person per 30 days (Rs.)*		*Percentage to Total*	
	Rural	*Urban*	*Rural*	*Urban*
Food Total	600.36	880.83	56.98	44.39
Non-Food Total	453.29	1103.63	43.02	55.61
All items ($MPCE_{MMRP}$)	**1053.65**	**1984.46**	**100.00**	**100.00**

Abbr: MMRP: Modified Mixed Reference Periods.

*: Estimates based on data collected with reference period 7 days for some item groups, 365 days for some item groups and 30 days for the rest.

Source: National Sample Survey Organisation (ON189).

Marketing Strategy to be Followed

The rural market dynamics is largely different from that of the urban market dynamics. Marketers should try to understand the psychology of rural consumers before designing the product for them. The goods designed for the urban market and then pushed into the rural market may not attract the rural consumers.

Modifying Marketing Mix

Success of business depends upon the Marketing-mix proposed by E. Jerome McCarthy. These four elements have guided marketers for long in formulating their marketing strategy and successfully tapping the market. However, the dynamics of the rural market is quite different from the urban market, therefore, the marketing mix strategies followed for the urban market should be modified before applying it to the rural market.

1. Product Mix

Product is the key to firm's success. The product must be suitable enough to cater to the need and requirement of the rural customers. It is not necessary that if the product is successful in urban areas, it will be equally successful in the rural areas. Product features (size, shape, colour, weight etc.), qualities, brand name, packaging, labelling, services, and other relevant aspect must meet the needs, wants and capacity of the rural buyers. Necessary changes must be made in the product to make it successful in the rural market. Gone are the days when products were sold solely on their brand name. Today, people want value for their money. The company should focus more on quality and consumer satisfaction index. Most of the rural consumers prefer those products which offer more features at reasonable price. Durability of the product along with the after sale value of the product is equally important for the rural people. Due to various factors there is an increase in their income, therefore, rural people have started showing preference towards premium products.

Specifically-Designed Products do help in many cases:

- Ghari detergent cake.
- Eveready's Jeevan Sathi Torch.
- Titan-Sonata watches.
- Chik shampoo.
- TVS heavy duty moped, TVS Star series etc.
- Atlas and Hero cycles etc.

2. Price Mix

Rural market is very price sensitive. Value for money is the key to success in the rural areas. The income and socio-cultural realities should be properly considered while developing the product strategy for the rural market. Some key things which should be kept in mind while formulating pricing policies for the rural markets are:

(a) Rural consumers are very price sensitive, and price plays a major role in their buying decisions. Pricing policies should be formulated with utmost care and caution.
(b) Since, the rural market is price sensitive hence pricing, discounts, sale, rebates, credit and installment facilities etc. are very important while setting and altering prices.
(c) Products which are low in price do help in many cases in marketing the product but there is no generalization in this regard. Even high priced premium products are now in demand in the rural areas due to increase in rural prosperity.
(d) Some companies follow the strategy of reducing the price of their product by reducing product size and by decreasing quality. This approach may work some time for some products but not all the times with all the products. For example, selling the shampoo in sachets increased the popularity of shampoo. The main strategy should be of selling value brands and not cheap brands.
(e) *Example:* Chik Shampoo, Hero Honda, and Lifebuoy.

3. Place Mix

Cost of reaching the outlets in rural market is higher in comparison to reaching the outlets in urban market because of the geographical spread of rural India.

(a) Distributing goods and commodities in the rural market is a herculean task due to poor infrastructure and vast geographical spread of the rural market.
(b) Choosing suitable mode of transportation, locating warehouses at strategic points, sufficient insurance, maintaining adequate inventory, maintaining sufficient number of retail outlets at different regions and deploying specially trained sales force are some of the critical decisions in rural distribution.

(c) A distinct feature of the rural market is the presence of *Haats* and rural *melas*.

Traditional *Haats* and *Melas* in India

There are 47,000 *haats* in India and a large number of *melas* are organised every year. These *Haats* and *Melas* are the economic, social and cultural nerve centres of rural India. The first comprehensive study of these traditional *Haats* and *Melas* was undertaken by MART in 1995 at the initiative of Government of India. The report has helped put *haats* and *melas* firmly on corporate marketing map.

Haats

Haats are periodic markets in rural India where people assemble at least once in a week to buy or sell products. It is estimated that each *Haat* caters to the need of a minimum 10 to maximum 50 villages and from these villages on an average 4000 persons visit the *haats* to meet their daily needs.

The people in rural India receive their wages on weekly basis hence the *haats* are also organised mostly on weekly basis and the sellers at *haats* are typically mobile. Since, the payment days in rural areas differ from village to village hence, sellers at *haat* sell in one *haat* on one day and move to the other *haat* on the next days. *Haats* are scheduled on the day when the employees get their "*Hafta*" (wages). People visit *haats* because these *haats* offer more variety and choice of bargain. These *haats* are also like a social hub where people expect to meet the villagers from other areas after week long hard work.

Advantages of Companies Marketing through *Haats*

- *Haats* are being organised in rural India for thousands of years, and still continue to cater to the requirement of large section of rural people. *Haats* not only cater to the need of the retail customers but they also serve the interest of large number of retailers and sub-wholesalers who buy from the *haats* for their village stores.
- There are approximately 47,000 *haats* conducted in rural India. These rural super markets are much larger than all the world's K-marts and Wal-marts put together.

- *Haats* are the nerve centre of Rural India. *Haats* are seen as a place for social, cultural and economic interchange.
- The most attractive thing for the marketers is that the sales in the rural *haats* take place on cash basis. This is unlikely in the village shops where large number of transactions take place on credit basis. Apart from the 90 per cent cash sale, 5 to 7 per cent is conducted on barter system and the rest 3 to 5 per cent is on credit.
- The system of distribution through *haats* is very efficient and has not lost popularity for thousands of years. This speaks volumes of the rigidity and strength of this rural marketing system.

Melas

In India large number of *melas* are organised every year. These *melas* have commercial, religious and cultural significance. However, due to certain limitations it is not possible for the companies to focus on every *mela*. The companies should try to target those *melas* only which are very popular and can generate interest and awareness about the company's product in the rural market. *Melas* attract people in thousands. India's largest *mela* is the *Maha Kumbh Mela* which attracts close to 70 million people. *Vali Yatra Mela* which is held since the time of the 'Ramayan' has over 3,000 stalls. Sonepur *Mela* of Uttar Pradesh, Pushkar *Mela* in Rajasthan are some of the big *melas* organised in India. The average sale per day at a *mela* is more than Rs. 30 lakhs. This speaks of the heavy volumes in which trade takes place in these *melas*.

Advantages to Companies in Using *Melas*

- The foot fall in *melas* is very high. High participation of women and children increase the significance of *melas* for the companies. This is the place where women and children can be easily targeted because in the villages the women are often restricted from going out alone for shopping.
- The people in *melas* are in festive mood and hence the companies could try rural folk or puppet show to promote their product.
- Visitors in *melas* hold cash to buy the products and majority of the transactions are cash based transactions. *Melas* are also

hot spots for launching new products and creating awareness about the new product.

- The major difference between *mela* and *haat* is that *mela* is generally used to promote and sell durable goods which are high in price and new to the market whereas in *haats* mostly agro related products are sold with lesser stalls selling durable goods.

4. Promotion Mix

Promotional strategies are of paramount importance and play a vital role in the success of any product. Therefore, the mode of promotion should be selected properly such that it suits the expectation of the rural people. There are various modes of promotion in rural areas. For exmpale:

(a) Mass Media reaches approximately 57 per cent of the rural population and is a powerful mode of promotion. Advertisement through television can attract large number of rural people as the number of television sets in rural India is increasing. The advertisement through television and radio is one of the easy modes to reach the target audience.

(b) Van/vehicle campaigns, edutainment films generating word of mouth publicity through opinion leaders, colourful wall paintings etc. techniques have proved to be effective.

(c) To attract rural mass puppet-shows, dance, dramas, and mythological songs specially developed for product-promotion purpose, are now being used in rural markets.

(d) Mural paintings, hoardings, pamphlets, music CDs etc. are another effective medium of rural advertising and promotion. It is a cost effective and appealing medium of promotion.

(e) Publicity through word of mouth is very popular among rural areas. Opinion leaders play a key role in popularising products and influencing rural markets. Educated rural youths play a influential role in the rural society.

(f) Due to increase in number of mobile phones and the penetration of internet in rural India, mobile advertisement and e-advertising is also gaining popularity.

Promotional Strategy

Firms must be very careful in choosing the medium for communication. Only 16 per cent of the rural population has access to a vernacular newspaper, therefore, the audio-visuals must be planned to convey the right message to the rural folks. The rich traditional media forms like folk dances, puppet shows etc., with which the rural consumers are familiar and comfortable, can be used for high impact product campaigns.

Top Media in Rural Markets

- *Print Media: Dainik Jagran* is the largest selling newspaper and *Saras Salil* is the largest selling magazine in the rural India.
- *Mass Media:* TV and Radio are popular mode of entertainment in rural India and the number of TV sets is fast increasing in rural India. Some popular channels in rural India are:
  (a) Doordarshan which has deepest reach in the rural India.
  (b) Private channels like Zee, Star and movie channels are fast gaining popularity in rural India.
  (c) Infotainment channels like Discovery Hindi, Animal Planet, National Geographic etc. are also very popular because they have started offering their services in many Indian languages.

Due to poor signal in the rural areas people are now switching from cable to satellite TV. This is because of the hassle-free dish connection of the satellite TV. Some popular DTH companies like Tata Sky, Airtel, Videocon, Sun TV etc. are fast spreading their arms in rural India. As a result of these, the viewership in the rural areas has increased substantially.

Some Cases of Rural Marketing

Some of the companies and advertising agencies have started using innovative traditional methods of advertising in the rural areas. Puppet shows are being organised in Punjab and folk media like *Ragini* is used in Haryana to promote Virat cement. Folk media *Pala* and *Daskathia* in Odisha for promoting safe electricity consumption and tooth pastes of Colgate Palmolive, Baul songs in West Bengal for advertising insecticides are some of the other notable examples of innovative advertising techniques to lure the rural masses.

Rural *melas* and weekly *haats* have become a very popular medium of advertising by media agencies. Companies use some popular forms of entertainment like puppet shows, *nautanki*, *ragini*, *bhangra*, *qawalli*, *biraha*, and traditional dance shows to attract the rural masses and promote their products. The media agencies conceive stories in which the characters are shown using the product of the company in order to make an impact on the mind of the rural people. Some big companies like HLL, P and G, Titan, Colgate Palmolive, Tractor manufacturing companies etc. have already started using innovative advertising techniques for promoting their brands.

Beyond 4Ps of Marketing

The whole dynamics of rural market is so different that one needs to think beyond 4Ps. Recently, some marketers have reduced their dependency upon 4Ps and are advocating 4As of marketing instead of traditional 4Ps. The 4As of Marketing are:

(a) *Affordability:* The companies should strive to make affordable products for the rural markets. Making affordable product does not mean making cheaper product but instead it means that the product should be made keeping in view the buying capacity of the target customer.

(b) *Acceptability:* Making the product according to the need and want of the customer. The customers should feel comfortable with the product and they should not hesitate in buying that product.

(c) *Availability:* Making the product available to the customer at the right time and at the right place.

(d) *Awareness:* Making the customer aware of the products through awareness programmes, running commercials on TV, Radio and using innovative methods like mural paintings, folk songs, folk dance, dramas, role plays, pamphlets etc. Live demonstration of the product can make the customer more aware about the product.

Conclusion

The taste and demand of the Indian rural consumer is changing very rapidly and hence the age-old marketing strategies adopted by the corporate companies may not work well. A paradigm shift in the marketing strategy of the companies planning to operate in the rural areas is the need of the hour. Excessive reliance on the 4P model will be of no use for the companies which plan to operate successfully in the rural areas. The companies should make certain changes in the 4P model and reduce their overall dependency upon this model in order to successfully market their product in the emerging rural India.

REFERENCES

Balakrishnan, Ravi, 2004, "Rustic Never Sleeps", *The Economic Times*, 4 February.

Bamzai, Sandeep, 1999, "Marketers Now Target Bharat", *Business India*, 6–17 September.

David, Robin, 2000, "T.V. Transforming Rural India: Study", *The Times of India*, 13 February.

Ecksus, R.S., 1955, "Factors Proportions in Underdeveloped Countries", *American Economic Review,* Vol. 45, September, pp. 539-65.

Ganguly, Dibeyendu, 2001, "Rasna Flows Straight into Rural Heart to Boost SDC", *The Economic Times*, 16 April.

http://censusindia.gov.in/2011census

http://en.wikipedia.org/wiki/Literacy_in_India

http://www.nlm.nic.in/tables/scenario.htm

Iyer, Sriram K., 2000, "Henkel to Charm Rural India *via* Economy Packs", *The Economic Times*, 27 September.

Jensen Robert and Oster Emily, 1977, "The Power of TV: Cable Television and Women's Status in India", *Journal of Economics,* Vol. 35, October, pp. 130-134.

Joseph, Lancelot, 2005, "Finding a Niche", *Business India*, 18–31 July.

Kashyap, Pradeep, 1998, "Selling to the Sons of the Soil", *Strategic Marketing*, August–October 1(4).

Kumar, Shailendra, 2012, "Marketing Paradigm in the Emerging Indian Rural Market", *ICON BHU.*

Moore, William E., 1955, "The Social Framework of Economic Development in Transition, Values and Socio-Economic Development", edited by Braibanti, R., and J. Spengler, Durham: Duke University, pp. 539-65.

National Council of Applied Economic Research, National Survey of Household Income and Expenditure (NSHIE)/Market Information Survey of Households (MISH), NSHIE, New Delhi, 2011.

Peter, P.K., 2010, *The Great Indian Consumer,* New Delhi: Concept Publishing Company (P) Ltd.

Statistics India, Census of India, 2011. Retrieved from http://censusindia.gov.in/2011 census

Statistics literacy, Literacy in India 2011. Retrieved from http://en.wikipedia.org/wiki/Literacy_in_India

Velayudhan, Sanal Kumar and Suri, B., 1996, "Rural Market Response—A Tentative Study", *Management and Labour Studies*, Vol. 21, No. 1.

16

Consumer Behaviour and Rural Marketing

A Case Study of Ghaziabad District of Western Uttar Pradesh

MEENU AGRAWAL AND NITISH AGGARWALA

Introduction

The ultimate objective of all production is consumption for the satisfaction of varied needs of man. A free market economy provides freedom to the consumers to buy and consume goods of their choice, buying preferences of the consumers send signals to the producers to produce various commodities in required quantities. Producers, therefore, produces only those commodities which are desired by the consumers. Consumer behaviour relates to likes and dislikes and expectations and motivations of the consumers. Every consumer differs from the other because his/her preferences for commodities are generally different. Consumer behaviour, as a matter of fact, is influenced by individual desires, product quality, situational characteristics and needs, habits, attitudes and experiences which determine his/her lifestyle.

In recent years behaviour of the consumer has changed. A few decades ago consumer was a silent person who uncomplainingly purchased the goods from any place. But this is not so today. Now the consumer is the choice empowered. Consumer behaviour is also changed owing to enhanced awareness, information technology and more importantly governmental intervention through legislations. Thus, the manufacturers are more cautious in dealing with consumers of their respective products. The rural consumers in India account for about 73 per cent of the total consumers. In India, a large number of rural consumers' lifestyle has changed/turned dramatically and the process of change is on. The buying behaviour of the rural consumers is influenced by several factors such as socio-economic conditions, cultural environment, literacy level, occupation, geographical location, efforts on the part of sellers, exposure to media etc.

In India, the consumers are generally ignorant and they are also not organized. Under these circumstances, the sellers or manufacturers, exploit the consumers. These factors also give rise to hoarding, black-marketing, economic corruption and cheating of the consumers. Though the consumers in India have been provided with various safety measures against their exploitation but they avoid such measures against the undue behaviour of the traders. The communication networks have, now multiplied. With the advent of technological revolution, production, marketing, advertising and consumption functions have assumed new dimensions and distribution channels have become quite efficient and quick. Media has approached the consumers so that they may base their consumption functions on rational criteria. The emergence of corporate sector has made the marketing activity as a professional activity and it is, now impersonal as the consumers and producers are situated at a distance.

In modern times, marketing is all about branding, brand positioning and creating a rise in the already exciting segments. The major task of marketers is to position the brand in the minds of the different segments of consumers by developing a message. Consumers in India are being trodden in the fight among brand perceptions. Marketers have needed to caution themselves against evaporation of important brands in the sea of brands. Some times ago, the rural areas were impregnable because of the lack of basic infrastructural facilities but now they are no more untouched from brands attach. Though the purchasing power in rural areas is poor, yet the people there have more curiosity to know, buy and consume new brands. These developments in India have helped in the upliftment of the Indian economy. The purchasing power of the people in India, within 15 years of economic liberalisation, has increased that was never before. It is assumed that in India, demand of various goods and commodities will be high, in days to come, in comparison to the rest of the world. This phenomenon has been realised by the Government and paths are being paved to meet future challenges and reap the benefits that will surely change the fate of the country for ever.

As per Census of India, 2001, 73 per cent of India's population is rural. Over the last three decades there has been a marginal reduction in the rural population. However, they continue to be a tradition bound community with religion, culture and traditions strongly influencing their consumption habits. Nearly 60 per cent of rural income is from agriculture. The rural prosperity and discretionary income with rural consumers reveal that in recent years, rural consumers have been increasingly drawn into the saving habits. It has been estimated that as much as 70 per cent of rural household save a part of their income.

The rural consumers are not only scattered but also diverse and heterogeneous. They are diverse in terms of religion, social, cultural and linguistic factors. It can be said that heterogeneity is No. 1 hallmark of the rural markets. In India, half a dozen religions, 33 languages, 1650 dialects and diverse sub-cultures characterize the rural consumer. However, extent of exposure of rural consumers to urban lifestyles also influences their buying habits. Thus, it has to be recognized that all rural consumers do not share a common buying behaviour. There are rural consumers who can afford high priced brands and are also willing to buy. There is, therefore, a great scope and need for segmenting the rural market on the basis of buying behaviour.

The rural market in India, constituting 742 million people is the largest potential market in the world. Thus, there are tremendous opportunities for rural marketing. However, there are some issues such as low level of literacy, poor reach of mass media, poor infrastructure, poor understanding of rural customers etc. that are hindering large-scale advent in the rural markets. It is very pertinent to point out here that to become a better consumer and a more informed citizen, it is best to analyse the purpose behind advertisements, packages, designs, prices and other marketing activities. This is the only way by which, consumers can make efforts to protect their interests and take care of their welfare. It has been felt that consumerism in developing countries differs from that of the advanced countries since the indigenous characteristics of the markets and importing of goods from developed nations shape it. In a developing economy like India ever-increasing population and limited supply of goods have led to the weak bargaining power of the consumers.

Objectives of the Study

1. To investigate the main characteristics of Consumer Behaviour and Consumer Protection measures taken in Ghaziabad district.
2. To study factors responsible for success/failure for buying and selling of goods and services by the consumers and producers.

3. To examine the marketing strategy and delivery system according to the needs of the consumers in the district.
4. To study the role of Consumer Organisations in Consumer Communication.
5. To examine rural consumers' current knowledge, attitudes and practices regarding quality of goods, brands and places etc.
6. To draw conclusions of the study and suggest remedial measures for bringing improvement in consumer behaviour in rural areas of the district and to make the rural masses aware of their rights.

Study Area

This study is based on certain objectives which include investigation of main characteristics of consumers' behaviour and consumers, protection in Ghaziabad district, examination of marketing strategy and delivery systems in the study area, role of consumers' organizations, evaluation of current knowledge, attitudes and practices regarding quality of goods, brands, places etc. of rural consumers and to suggest measures to improve the behaviour of the rural consumers and to make consumers aware of their rights.

For understanding the marketing behaviour of rural consumer a study was undertaken in select villages of Ghaziabad district. From 16 villages 320 households were selected. The survey of the sampled area reflected a number of characteristics of the consumers' behaviour and it was found that consumers in the area are not well aware about the ways to properly safeguard their interest as buyers. Awareness enlarges the knowledge of the consumers about the various products they need. Due to unawareness the consumers are generally cheated by the traders in the market.

Table 16.1: Factors Influencing the Consumers' Behaviour in the District (Respondents—320 Households)

Sl. No.	*Factors Influencing Consumers' Behaviour*	*No. of Answering Respondents (Households)*	*Percentage of Respondents*
1.	Personal Factors	170	53.1
2.	Psychological Factors	25	7.8
3.	Cultural Factors	30	9.4
4.	Social Factors	50	15.6
5.	Information Factors	45	14.1
	Total	**320**	**100.0**

Source: Personal Survey of the Area.

Table 16.2: Personal Factors Influencing the Consumes' Behaviour in the District (Respondents—170 Households)

Sl. No.	*Personal Factors influencing Consumers' Behaviour*	*No. of Answering Respondents*	*Percentage*
1.	Age	25	14.7
2.	Level of Education	35	20.6
3.	Occupation	30	17.6
4.	Economic Position	50	29.4
5.	Living Style	20	11.8
6.	Personality Traits	10	5.9
	Total	**170**	**100**

Source: Personal Survey of the Study Area.

Table 16.1 indicates that the consumers' behaviour in the district is mostly influenced by personal factors as 53.1 per cent of the respondents admitted the influence of this factor on their buying behaviour. However, social factors influence on their behaviour is equally important. Psychological factors exercise the least influence on their behaviour but cultural factors influence more consumers than the psychological factors.

Personal factors influence the behaviour of the consumers in several ways. Table 16.2 shows the influence of each component of the personal factors on consumers' behaviour in the study area.

Table 16.3 shows that in the district out of 170 respondents, whose behaviour is influenced by the personal factors, 29.4 per cent admitted that their economic position influenced their behaviour. They said that the poor economic position had put several restrictions in buying products for consumption. It was not possible for them to go beyond their economic means and thus, they never insisted on purchasing a particular brand. However, education level influenced the behaviour of 20.06 per cent of the respondents and that of 17.6 per cent was influenced by their occupations. Age also had influence on the behaviour of the consumers. It was observed that the influence of lifestyle and personality traits of the respondents (consumers) had no significant influence on their buying behaviour. Personal discussion with the respondents revealed that information factor was gaining importance in guiding the consumers in buying the products. The present age is the age of information technology; hence it effect on consumers' behaviour is universal.

The consumers in the rural areas lack knowledge about the prices, merits of different products, adulteration and misrepresentation by the sellers etc. It was found that the attitude of the consumers in the study

Table 16.3: Reply of Respondents regarding Rural Marketing Strategy

Sl. No.	*Query*	*Yes/No*	*No. of Respondents*	*Percentage*
1.	Whether the business organisations distributed samples of their products and/or other gifts in their areas.	Yes	208	65%
		No	112	35%
2.	Whether any literature about their products was distributed by business houses to convince the consumers?	No	320	100%
3.	Whether such business concerns were successful in changing their attitude towards their products by rectifying the doubts and assuring about their quality and reasonable price.	Yes	64	20%
		No	256	80%
4.	Whether advertisement campaigns of these concerns were attractive/ charming.	Yes	224	70%
		No	96	30%
5.	Are you satisfied with the marketing strategies of the business concerns/traders.	Yes	160	50%
		No	160	50%
	No. of Respondents		**320**	

Source: Personal Survey of the Study Area.

area towards, the products was not logical and lacked conviction and therefore the decisions taken were not based on sound footings. In most of the cases, the consumers had no knowledge of the brands of the products. They were also not in a position to distinguish a product from another. Lack of information was mainly responsible for their state of affair in the sampled area.

Further, the response of the respondents with regards to communication and its impact on their behaviour was also studied. Almost all of them admitted that the best source of information to the consumers is mass media, as it has created awareness and changed their buying behaviour. They, however, said that the mass communication media has broken their deep-rooted behaviour to a very little extent. The respondents recognized only the following sources of communication, (a) cinema, (b) T.V., (c) Radio and Newspaper, (d) Publicity Vans, (e) Demonstrations, (f) Decorated bullock-carts carrying advertisement panels, and (g) puppet shows. Other means of communication were not known to them. 80 per cent of the respondents stated that their family members had taken interest in product publicity programmes and these had affected their buying behaviour. Thus, they found the product advertisements/publicity programmes to be useful. In rural areas of the district, the standard of living of the households has not changed much due to their low level of earnings and rising prices. However, some of the respondents were aware of the new products that they purchased from the neighbouring urban maıkets.

It is beyond doubt that these days advertisement is a very powerful means of mass communication. The traders or producers have not spared even the remote areas of the district to create demand for their products through advertisement in various ways. Thus, the impact of mass communication media on the consumers—rural/urban has been very affective. The way of life is changing but the consumers in rural areas are not aware of their exploitation by the traders in a very refined manner.

Rural Marketing Strategy

"Rural Market is the key to survival in India." It is a fact that the rural market in India is the largest potential market. The opportunities in rural marketing have tremendously increased due to the rising aspirations of rural people for a better quality of life. As a result, consumption pattern has changed with a change in their lifestyle and attitudes. However, all is not well in the rural market. There are a number of issues that are hindering large-scale advent of marketers in the rural markets are as follows:

1. Lack of Adequate Understanding of Rural Consumer,
2. Inadequate Data on Rural Market,
3. Poor Infrastructure,
4. Low Level of Literacy,
5. Poor Reach of Mass Media in Rural Areas, and
6. Producer Marketing Strategy.

The most important question that arises at this stage is as to how the business organisations make their rural marketing strategies to attract the potential consumers towards their products or services. It is a fact that a single strategy cannot serve the purpose in this regard. The marketing departments of the big business houses conduct intensive survey and research before formulating the marketing strategies. The marketing strategy for consumers who have indifferent attitudes about the product or service should include such efforts, which may change their attitudes towards the positive side and tell the different merits and uses of the products. The company or business organisation should adopt a separate marketing strategy for those consumers who have negative attitudes towards their products. In such a case, the marketing strategy should be able to convince and explain to the consumer as to how their products or services are better than others.

The consumers who have rational attitude may be satisfied by good quality of product at reasonable prices. For such consumers, the marketing strategy should be very rational. However, the consumers who have irrational attitude may be attracted by charming packing, free gifts, attractive advertisements etc. For such consumers, the marketing strategy should be very specific. It is very important to point out here that only those organisations or producing firms touch the zenith of success, which are successful in reading the behavioural complexities of potential consumers and act accordingly at the appropriate time in the market, which they have selected.

During survey of the study area, several questions were asked from the respondents and their replies were recorded. The respondents were asked whether they were aware of the strategies adopted by the traders to attract the rural folks towards their products. It was encouraging to note that most of the consumers had knowledge about it but they were ignorant about any survey being conducted by the business concerns in their area. The respondents reply on other queries is summarised in Table 16.3. The findings indicate that 65 per cent of the respondents admitted that business concerns distributed samples of their products and other gifts in their area. However, 100 per cent of them agreed that the business houses did not distribute any literature to convince them about their products. Moreover, 80 per cent of the respondents attitude could not be changed by the business houses although 70 per cent of them admitted that the advertisement campaigning of the business houses in their area was attractive and impressive. However, 50 per cent of the respondents were not satisfied with the marketing strategies of the business concerns/traders.

Problems in Rural Marketing

In rural markets sellers as well as buyers face several problems, which are very complex and serious in nature. The sellers and buyers in these markets come from the rural community, which is not only ignorant but unaware also. The sellers themselves have no knowledge about the merits or demerits of the products, which they sell to the consumers. They cannot convince or satisfy the buyers by telling the various uses of the products which the consumers purchase. The buyers in these markets do not have a choice as only select products are available in the market. Generally, in these markets the products, manufactured by the local producers, are sold. As brand specific products are costly, neither the sellers nor the buyers prefer to buy or sell such products.

In these markets, the buying behaviour of the consumers is very rigid and therefore, not easy to change their attitude. The campaign by the mass media has not been very successful in such markets. Illiterate, ignorant and unaware sellers and buyers in these markets normally have no idea about the new and improved products. Poverty and other compulsions of the consumers do not allow them to think about new and expensive products, which are frequently sold in the urban markets. The buying behaviour of the poor consumers in the area is not rational and therefore, they hesitate in buying new and modern products. Therefore, these consumers suffer from inferiority complex owing to social and economic repression.

In the study area the big farmers are well to do. Their standard of living is quite high as also their incomes. Thus, they buy standard quality goods to fulfil their needs. But mostly they purchase the goods from the urban markets and do not depend upon the rural markets. They have T.V., refrigerators, coolers, telephones etc. of standard brands. They wear branded clothes.

As a matter of fact, the rural markets are meant for poor rural consumers whose consumption needs are very limited. In rural markets, the consumers are exploited by the traders in several ways such as:

(a) The goods sold by the businessmen in these markets are generally underweighed or undermeasured.
(b) Sub-standard quality goods are sold at higher prices.
(c) Expiry date medicines and defective or duplicate home appliances are sold to the consumers.
(d) Adulteration in foodstuffs is a common practice.
(e) Artificial scarcity of several products is created in these markets for the purpose of charging high prices from the consumers.
(f) The consumers are given false or incomplete information only to exploit them.
(g) The behaviour of the traders/sellers in the rural markets towards the consumers is very rude. There is no remedy for the poor consumers against such behaviour.
(h) To cheat the consumers, the products are not properly packed and labelled.

Result of Survey of the Study Area

Though the Government has enacted a number of legislations over the years to protect the interests of the consumers, yet the consumers feel that the efforts of the Government are not enough to check widespread malpractices of the traders and sellers in the country. It is a fact that the Government action will be successful only if the consumers are aware of their rights and use the redressal machinery effectively. A study conducted in Ghaziabad district of Uttar Pradesh about the protection of consumer rights has brought to notice several results, which have been analysed in Table 16.4.

The complaints were lodged regarding defective goods. The results were in the favour of complainants.

(a) Table16.4 reveals that 78 per cent consumers (respondents) were unaware about the meaning of Consumer Protection.
(b) Only 31 per cent consumers could tell that the consumer protection was essential.
(c) 94 per cent respondents admitted that there was no Consumer Organisation in their area.
(d) 100 per cent consumer had no idea about the Essential Commodities Act, 1955, Drugs and Cosmetic Act, 1940, and Sales of Goods Act, 1930. Moreover, 75 per cent had no knowledge about the Prevention of Food Adulteration Act, 1954, the Standard of Weights and Measures Act, 1985, and the Consumer Protection Act, 1986.
(e) 94 per cent consumers were unaware about the consumer courts established at different levels.
(f) No respondent could explain the main function of consumer courts satisfactorily.
(g) 87 per cent consumers were unaware about the role played by the Government to improve the consumers' awareness.
(h) 98 per cent consumers lodged no complaint before the grievance redressal court at the district level. However, the result in 2 per cent cases, who lodged complaint before the District Forum, was in their favour.
(i) 100 per cent consumers were unable to explain anything more about the consumers' protection and about the safety/security of consumers.

Table 16.4: Results of Survey of the Study Area Regarding Awareness of the Consumers about the Protection of their Right

Sl. No.	*Question*	*Reply Yes/No*	*No. of Respon-dents – (320)*	*%*
1.	Whether you know:	Yes	70	22%
	What is meant by Consumer Protection?	No	250	78%
2.	Whether Consumer Protection is Essential?	Yes	100	31%
		No	160	50%
		Ignorant	60	19%
3.	Whether there is any consumer organization in your area?	No	300	94%
		Ignorant	20	6%
4.	Whether you know about the following main Consumer Protection Acts/Laws instituted in India?			
	(a) The Essential Commodities Act, 1955	No	320	100%
	(b) The Drugs and Cosmetic Act, 1940	No	320	100%
	(c) The Sale of Goods Act, 1930	No	320	100%
	(d) The Prevention of Food Adulteration Act, 1954	Yes	80	25%
		No	240	75%
	(e) The Standards of Weights and Measures Act, 1985	Yes	80	25%
		No	240	75%
	(f) The Consumer Protection Act, 1986.	Yes	80	25%
		No	240	75%
5.	Whether you know about the consumer courts established in the country to protect the interests of consumers?	Yes	20	6%
		No	300	94%
6.	What is the main function of the Consumer Courts (District Forum, State Commission, Natoinal Commission, Supreme Court)	No respon-dents could explain	—	—
7.	Whether you know about the role played by the Government to improve consumer awareness?	Yes	40	13%
		No	280	87%
	Whether you lodged any complaint before the District Forum? (If yes nature of complaint and its result)	Yes	5	2%
		No	315	98%
8.	Whether you know anything more about the protection of consumer rights?	No	320	100%
9.	Any other information you would like to give about consumers safety/security	No	320	100%
		Total Respondents = 320		

Source: Personal Survey of the Area.

Major Findings

The survey reveals that the awareness of the consumers about the protection of their rights/interests is very poor and unsatisfactory. Due to poverty, illiteracy and ignorance in the rural area of the district, the people living there are very lethargic and insensitive to their own welfare as consumers. Consumer behaviour is mainly influenced by personal factors (53%), while social factors influence 15.6 per cent of the respondents and 14.1 per cent of them are influenced by information factors. On the other hand, 70.8 per cent of the respondents are guided by psychological factors and 9.4 per cent by the cultural factors. Thus, personal and social factors dominate in influencing the behaviour of the consumers. In terms of personal factors, economic position is the most important factor, which influences the behaviour of 29.4 per cent of the respondents. Level of education and occupation also influenced 20.6 per cent and 17.6 per cent of the respondents respectively.

The study has brought very interesting results. The results reveal that (a) 78 per cent of the respondents were unaware as to what was meant by consumer protection; (b) only 31 per cent of them could tell that the consumer protection was essential; (c) 94 per cent of them admitted that there were no consumer organisations in their area whereas 6 per cent were ignorant about them; (d) 100 per cent of the respondents had no knowledge about the Essential Commodities Act, 1955, Drugs and Cosmetics Act, 1940, and Sale of Goods Act, 1930 and 75 per cent of the respondents had no knowledge about the Consumer Protection Act, 1986, Standard of Weights and Measures Act, 1985, and Prevention of Food Adulteration Act, 1954; (e) 94 per cent of the consumers were unaware about consumer courts established at different levels; (f) Only 20 per cent of the respondents could explain the main function of the Consumer Courts; (g) 87 per cent of the respondents were unaware of the role played by the Government to enhance consumers' awareness; (h) 98 per cent of them had not lodged any complaint before the grievance redressal courts at the district level while of the 2 per cent, who lodged the complaint, it was decided in their favour; and (i) 100 per cent of the consumers could not explain anything about consumers' protection and safety/security measures.

Thus, the analysis reveals that the awareness among the consumers about the protection of their rights is very low. The consumers in the study area are, in fact unconcerned and insensitive about their own welfare.

Suggestions

The following suggestions are made to improve the awareness and behaviour of the consumers and to provide them with effective protection mechanism so that exploitation of rural consumers in the markets can be reduced:

1. It has been observed that lack of proper consumers' education is the major drawback in our society. If the consumers are well educated, vigilant and alert they are safe and their rights and powers remain intact.
2. The consumer movement should be made as a people's movement to develop awareness, vigilance, safety measures and alertness among the consumers effectively.
3. The Government should provide all possible help to consumer organisations.
4. Awareness meetings involving urban and rural consumers should be organized. These meetings can be arranged by the NGOs, Consumer Courts, Schools and Colleges, and Government departments.
5. Awareness programmes through communications and electronic media should be emphasised.
6. Print media like newspapers, magazines, posters should be used to create awareness.
7. The Government should declare at least one full year as "Consumer Awareness Year".
8. In rural areas awareness camps should be organised with the help of Gram Panchayats and posters and booklets should be distributed free of charge.
9. The decisions of the Consumer Disputes Redressal Agencies (CDRAs) should be given wide publicity.
10. Consumer behaviour must be separately judged for rural and urban sectors and separate guidelines be formed for their protection.
11. In rural areas where the illiterate, ignorant and poor people reside, the State Government and local administration should understand their problems as consumers and take effective measures to educate so that their exploitation at the hands of the traders/sellers is stopped.

"Consumer Empowerment" has a long way to go. This is the most appropriate time to act. We should prepare ourselves and usher a new era of "Consumerism". The State government, the concerned district authorities, NGOs, businessmen and consumers themselves should take steps in the right direction to achieve the goal.

REFERENCES

Advani and Rani, 1991, "The Consumer Protection Act, 1986: Scope and Remedies", *Consumer Confrontation,* July-August 1991.

Agarwal, V.K., 1989, Consumer Protection in India, New Delhi: Deep & Deep Publication.

Agrawal, Meenu, 2005, *Consumer Behaviour and Consumer Protection in India,* New Delhi: New Century Publications.

Ahluwalia, Sanjeev, 2002, "Can Consumers Reform Utilities", *Economic Times,* Newspaper, 3 June, 2002.

Amarchand, D., 1980, An Introduction to Marketing, New Delhi: Vikas Publishing House Pvt. Ltd.

Bludell, R., 1988, "Consumer Behaviour, Theory and Empirical Evidence—A Survey", *The Economic Journal,* 98, March, pp. 16-65.

Consumer Behaviour in Indian Context, 2005, S. Chand Publication, II edition.

Consumer Protection in India, 1985, Delhi: B.R. Publishing Corporation.

Gupta, Anil, 1986, *Consumption Behaviour in India: A Study of All-India* Consumption, New Delhi: Anmol Publications.

Hawkins, Del. I., *et al.*, 1986, *Consumer Behaviour—Implications for Marketing Strategy,* Taxes: Business Publications, Inc.

Himachalam, D., 1998, *Consumer Protection and the Law*, New Delhi: APH Publishing Corporation.

Holloway, Robert J., *et al.*, 1971, *Consumer Behaviour—Contemporary Research in Action*, Boston: Hughton Mifflin.

Kumar, Niraj, 1999, *Consumer Protection Act*, New Delhi: Himalaya Publishing House.

Laisram, Indira, 1999, "How Regal is Indian Consumer?", *Deccan Herald*, 7th January, 2000.

17

Awakening Rural Consumers Towards Sustainable Development

A Case Study

BASANTA KUMAR

Introduction

The Consumer movement has taken a new direction after the Asian Conference on "Millennium Development Goals (MDGs) and the Consumer Movement" organised jointly by Consumer International (CI) Asia Pacific and UNCTAD in Kuala Lumpur on 23 August, 2005. All the leaders of 21 Asia Pacific member countries of CI in the conference going beyond the legal definition of "consumer" have accepted a wider sense of the term to further the goal of "consumer movement". The common understanding is, "we shall not be constrained by the legal definition of consumer found in many Asian Consumer Protection Statutes. We shall serve the needs of all consumers, including those unable to consume and living below the poverty line as well as consumers who are victims of the inequality of bargaining power in the market place. We agree to adopt over-arching theme to our individual and collective efforts to achieve the MDGs and that these shall be *Pro-Poor, Pro-Rural* and *Pro-Women*. We realise that consumption must be equitable and ecologically sound and shall promote patterns of consumption and lifestyles that are sustainable and will not undermine the interests of the poor. We agree that the consumer movement needs to work with other civil society organisations to expose corrupt practices that deny consumers, access to basic goods and services, equality and justice in their lives. We recognise that corruption is a scourge that undermines development and denies consumers their right to basic goods and services and call on our governments to take effective measures to end corrupt practices in the public and private sector." This chapter is based on the wider connotation of consumer and the commitment of the leaders of the consumer movement to explore the scope of awakening the rural consumers for sustainable consumption in a highly corruption prone environment.

Research Issues

Corruption is anti-consumer and anti-development; it hurts mostly the rural and hard core poor. It delays, distorts and diverts economic growth. The higher the level of corruption, the lower is the level of their development. Corruption both causes and thrives upon weaknesses in key economic, political and social institutions and the poor people have very few options. In the development process, people or the consumers get involved in corrupt practices while making their choice—even in the daily routine administrative tasks cannot be performed without a bribe.

The rural development strategies of the Governments both at the States and Centre, focus on seven major flagship programmes such as Mahatma Gandhi National Rural Employment Guarantee Scheme (MGNREGS), National Rural Livelihood Mission (NRLM), Indira Awas Yojana (IAY), National Rural Drinking Water Programme (NRDWP), Total Sanitation Campaign (TSP), Integrated Watershed Development Programmes (IWDP), Pradhan Mantri Grameen Sadak Yojana (PMGSY) and Rajiv Gandhi Grameen Vidyutikaran Yojana (RGGVY). These programmes are essentially meant for creating gainful employment opportunities and to improve the quality of lives of rural masses. The positive side of these programmes is that rural India has been well connected by roads under PMGSY; poor people have found *pucca* shelter under IAY; power connectivity has been extended to BPL people even in remote villages under RGGVY; safe drinking water has been provided under NRDWP; women are being empowered through their self-help groups and their federated institutions for enabling them to increase household income through sustainable livelihood under NRLM; and sustainable earning provisions have been made through implementation ofMGNREGS.

Thus, the flagship development projects have changed the lifestyle of many rural people. The increased Government spending on rural jobs scheme, housing, health care and rural roads infrastructure has raised the aspirations of rural consumers to enjoy better quality of life by spending extra income in converting their *kuccha* dwellings into *pucca* houses, availing private tuitions for kids, and buying branded products. However, due to increased income inequality the developmental impacts of these programmes have shown adverse effects on people's quality of life leading to higher incidence of poverty and its impeding progress in health and education and contributing to crime and ultimately threatening the political stability of the country. With poor knowledge about their rights, duties and responsibilities as sensible consumers, rural consumers are still subjected to harassment and exploitation in the process of sustainable consumption and this is a major cause of concern. Some of them also get involved in corrupt practices. The awakening programmes implemented by the Government have not produced desired results. The Working Group of 12th Plan on "Consumer Awareness and Education" has found that consumer awareness level in the country is low and the main reasons are: (i) vastness of the country with more population below poverty line; (ii) economic inequality; and (iii) low level of literacy and ignorance. The situation in rural areas is dismal causing rural consumers subject to more exploitation by the trade, industry and service providers. Inclusive growth strategies of the Government among others warrant for creation of national awareness programme at district and taluka levels targeting vulnerable consumers such as women and children, youth, farmers and rural families and middle and working class. Hardly any independent research on consumer awareness at grassroots level is found. This research gap triggers the present study.

Objectives

The objectives of this chapter are: (i) to ascertain the magnitude of involvement of rural people in corrupt practices; and (ii) to suggest mechanisms for empowering the consumers with their rights, duties and responsibilities.

Methodology

This research work is based on a micro-level case study covering two villages in Athmallik block in the Angul District of Odisha. The first village was a remote village with more tribal population, road connectivity under PMGSY and power connection under RGGVY and the second village was a village in the mainstream with comparatively better infrastructure, education and awareness. The distance between these two villages was 4 kilometres. These two villages were selected for the reason that both were dependent on each other—first village was dependent on the second village for consumption of essential commodities and for pursuing higher education of kids and the second village depended on first village for forest products for regular household consumption. Besides, "consumer club" was established in the school of both the villages in 2007. Though these are now defunct, it was expected that the club activities might have impacted the villagers to gain some knowledge about consumer protection. A brief demographic profile of these villages was prepared to decide the suitable process of choosing the respondents to get as accurate feedback as possible.

Given the exploratory nature of this study, convenience sampling was adopted for this research. Since, corruption is a sensitive issue people were reluctant to reveal the facts. To make them comfortable with our approach, first of all interaction process was started with the villagers in the second week of September with a video show of film "Swades" and another on RTI Act, 2005. These were followed by general discussion on Government policies and strategies on rural development projects to make them aware and sensitise them about their role and responsibilities in the developments taking place around them. This helped in getting appropriate feedback in the next stage of the survey.

It was necessary to understand the extent to which consumers know about the development projects undertaken in these villages which could be an insight into the magnitude of their involvement in corrupt practices. As such, to achieve the desired objective Participatory Rural Appraisal (PRA) techniques, consisting of in-depth interview of individual respondents with semi-structured questionnaires, group discussions, community meetings with mapping techniques and observation methods, were employed. For these purposes, the respondents were carefully chosen to include members of various categories like SHG members, MGNREGS job card holder, old age pensioners and educated unemployed etc. making the sample size of 120 people from first village which was 21 per cent of total adult population and 40 (29% of adult population) from second village (Table 17.1). In these cases, the percentage of BPL category of respondents was 87 and 92.5 respectively. Besides, informal discussions were held with school teachers, Sarpanch, Panchayat executive officer, Anganwadi supervisor, Asha Karmi, and Gram Sathi. The field study was conducted during August 15—September 25, 2012.

Table 17.1: Sample Size

Category	*Village One*		*Village Two*	
	Total Sample	*% of BPL Families in Sample*	*Total Sample*	*% of BPL Families in Sample*
SHG Member	35	90	10	90
MNREGS Job Card Holder	45	100	17	100
Old Age Pensioners	15	100	6	100
Educated Unemployed	10	50	2	50
Others	15	60	5	80
Total	**120**	**80**	**40**	**84**

Considering the complex nature of the field study, the data so collected were manually processed and tabulated using computer for analysis and interpretation.

Discussions and Findings

The analysis of the reseaıch revolves around three factors i.e. (i) structure and demographic features of the villages; (ii) impact measurement on knowledge and awareness; and (iii) awareness mechanism.

Structure and Demographic Features

Table 17.2 gives the detailed structure and demographic profile of the sample villages. Table 17.2 contains population with breakup of BPL, old age pensioners, MNREGS job card holders, infrastructure and communication support services, educational environment and socio-economic livelihood projects:

(i) The most interesting feature found was that in the first village all the BPL families had at least 1 mobile phone but only 53 mobile handsets had subscriber identity module (SIM) card and rest were having only memory card used for listening music. Further, 97.22 per cent BPL families got power connection under RGGVY and the rest were waiting to get connection. Electricity enabled 37 families (54.17%) had television with DTH connection. Out of 15 motor bikes in these families, 11 were reported to have been purchased and other 4 were received as dowry. On the other hand, 21 out of 23 BPL families in second village had power connection. In the second village all BPL families had power supply and only one cell phone was found.

(ii) For safe drinking water 11 tubewells in different locations were found in first village and 5 in second village. This was reported to be adequate. The daily wage earners under MNREGS were 147 and 63 in the two villages respectively.

(iii) As regards educational infrastructure both the villages were found to have *Anganwadi* centres with 20 and 10 pre-school going kids. For elementary education, first village had a school with 5 teachers, 170 students were enrolled and studying up to class eight and second village had school with 2 teachers, 30 students and classes up to fifth. Consumer clubs were established in these schools in 2007 but reported to be defunct since 2008 due to non-availability of funds.

(iv) Educated youths numbering 69 in 18-35 years age group and 17 above 35 years age group in the first village were found to have seasonal employment outside home particularly in cotton mills in Surat and in construction related works in Hyderabad. This was reported to be the main reason that BPL families had at least one mobile phone in their house. Only 5 youth in the second village similarly went outside for seasonal employment. People with at least graduate level education were employed in public sector or Government in first village but no one with such education was found in the second village.

(v) Ten self-help groups (SHGs) were working in the first village whereas two were found in the second village. All the groups went for small savings and individual business with the loans from banks.

(vi) Village development workers like Anganwadi assistant, Asha Karmi, Krushak Sathi and Gram Sathi were working in the first village but in the second village no Asha Karmi or Gram Sathi worked.

(vii) The significant feature in the second village was that villagers planted and preserved 62.30 hectares of forest land under social forestry in participatory mode. The project was launched in 2004 with Government grant of Rs. 5 lakh. This project not only provided them employment and earnings but also made them to learn about sustainable consumption and environment protection. On the other hand, the first village was trying to follow the path of the second village but could not register for the project, even though they had 23 hectares of forest land, due to conflicting political interests and squabbling.

Table 17.2: Structure and Demographic Profile

Sl. No.	*Items*		*Village*			
			One		*Two*	
1.	Total Adult Population/No. of Voters		574		147	
2.	No. of Electoral Administrative Wards		2		1	
3.	No. of BPL Card Holder		72		23	
4.	No. of Old Age Pension Holder		51		14	
5.	MNREGS Job Card Holder		147		62	
6.	Electric connection	BPL	70		21	
		General	11		3	
7.	TV	BPL	43 (12 dowry)		2	
		General	10 (3 dowry)		2	
8.	Mobile	BPL	114		–	
		General	28		1	
9.	Motorbike	BPL	15 (1 dowry)		–	
		General	7 (1 dowry)		1 (Dowry)	
10.	Auto rickshaw		9		–	
11.	Tractor		3		–	
12.	Pump set		5		–	
13.	Tubewell		11		5	
14.	Education	(a) Anganwadi	Yes/20		Yes/10	
		(b) School	Up to 8th class		Up to 5 class	
		(c) Student strength	170		30	
		(d) No of teachers	5		2	
		(e) Consumer club	Est–2007		Est–2007	
15.	Educational Attainment for Employability	Standard	Age		Age	
			18–35 yrs	Above 35 yrs	18–35 yrs	Above 35 yrs
		Up to 10th	30	6	–	3
		10–12	16	5	–	2
		Undergraduate	15	1	–	–
		Graduates	8	4	–	–
		Above		1	–	–
16.	Salaried Employment	(a) Private sector	6		1	
		(b) Public sector	8		–	
17.	SHGs		10		1	
18.	Govt. Social Worker/Employee	(a) Anganwadi	2		2	
		(b) Asha	1		–	
		(c) Krushak Sathi	1		–	
		(d) Grama Sathi	2		1	

(Contd.)

Sl. No.	Items	Village	
		One	Two
19.	Social Project with People's Participation	Unrecognized social forestry conservation (disputed) 23 hectares	Recognized social forestry plantation and conservation 62.30 hectares
20.	Diary co-operative	Existing	Membership with first village dairy co-operative
21.	Newspaper subscribed	8	–

Source: Official Records from Panchayat and Field Data.

Impact Measurement on Knowledge and Awareness

The study analyses the impacts of development projects on the knowledge and awareness of the villagers on subjects like political empowerment and environment, economic empowerment, social empowerment, environment and climate change, corruption perception and consumer rights and protection. Table 17.3 exhibits their level of knowledge and awareness on these subjects in three parameters, i.e. 'basic', 'understanding' and 'clarity'.

(i) Villagers from both the villages understood their political rights. The clarity level of respondents of first village was as high as 92 per cent against 63 per cent in second village. This is an obvious trend because the second village was backward in educational infrastructure and attainment. During interaction it was admitted by many respondents that though they were committed to their political leader(s), irrespective of their income level, most of them accepted money ranging from Rs. 100 to Rs. 200 to cast their votes in the last Panchayat election. There was conflict and factionalism in both the villages but it was more visible in the first village. The social forestry project in the village suffered due to factionalism. The meeting of the Village Development Committee for undertaking or maintaining hygiene and welfare works was not held in April 2012 and it was deferred many times due to conflict of interests.

Table 17.3: Results of Impact Measurement: Knowledge and Awareness (%)

Level of Understanding / *Subject*	*Village One*			*Village Two*		
	Basic	Moderate	Clear	Basic	Moderate	Clear
Subject A: Political empowerment and environment	–	8	92	–	37	63
Subject B: Economic empowerment	7	42	51	29	57	14
MNREGS	–	38	62	34	60	–
Self-help group approach						
Subject C: Social empowerment	–	27	73	11	33	56
Foods security (PDS,	–	19	81	11	52	37
NRLM)	–	34	66	8	51	41
Shelter (IAY)	12	28	60	18	69	13
Education (TLC)	17	32	51	29	54	17
Health and Sanitation (NRDWP)	11	36	53	27	51	22
Power (RGGVY)						
Roads (PMGSY)						
Subject D: Environment and Climate change (Forest conservation)	–	68	32	–	14	86
Subject E: Corrupt practices	–	26	74	5	57	38
Subject F: Consumer protection	66	27	7	82	18	–

Source: Field Data.

(ii) As regards economic empowerment of poor people, MNREGS was working well and the respondents had no complaints. But their level of knowledge and understanding of the subject in the first village was spread over 'moderate' and 'clear' levels whereas in second village it was between 'basic' and 'moderate level'. Respondents from second village invariably felt that they needed work and timely payment of wages. Villagers from first village did not experience any such problem. Further, regarding economic activities under SHGs scheme for women, it was found in both villages that the loan amount taken from bank was equally distributed among the group members and used for purposes like goat/sheep rearing, agriculture, debt payment, medical expenses and creating assets. Spending on non-income generating activities were more, so the repayment of loan was mostly from sale of agricultural and forest produces.

(iii) It was found that the level of understanding among PDS beneficiaries was high in both thc villages. It was understood from the in-depth interaction with the respondents that they had little complaint about the PDS delivery mechanism after the agency system was removed about six months back. However, feedback received from 22 respondents showed that they had sold the rice after de-husking at higher price for money in some urgency.

(iv) All BPL families had IAY in both the villages but the quality of work was poor needing renovation/major repair in many cases. Getting allotment of a house under IAY needed payment of bribe ranging between Rs. 2000 to Rs. 5000.

(v) The total literacy campaign had impact in both the villages. About 90 per cent respondents in both villages had either 'understanding' or 'clarity' level on various aspects of literacy campaign. However, nearly 85 per cent respondents in first village and 64 per cent in second village affirmed that they could read, write and sign their name.

(vi) It is disheartening to note that health and sanitation was lacking in the villages under study. Malaria was known to be a common disease. 16 cases were reported to have repeated malaria during last one year. The level of their understanding on the subject suggested that they needed more education and awareness on this front.

(vii) It was found that all BPL people had power connection under RGGVY. It was reported that Rs. 100 was collected from each consumer by the official concerned at the time of giving power connections. Respondents were happy that nobody bothered to give monthly bill and collect dues or they volunteered to pay the fixed monthly dues of Rs. 30. Unauthorised hooking was known to be common with non-BPL families who were not consumers. For BPL consumers who were in default, their lines were disconnected. However, the promising impact of power connection to BPL families under RGGVY is that more DTH services were found with them for entertainment and penctration of mobile services requiring power recharge improved ease and effective communication.

(viii) As regards road connectivity, the first village had high level *pucca* road built primarily to prevent the carnage of frequent flood whereas second village had poor road and they suffered in rainy season. A new approach road from main road was being constructed as promised during last panchayat election.

(ix) Social forestry plantation and conservation in the second village had high impact on the life of the villagers. It provided regular wages, and other forest products like free firewood, bamboo and logs for house construction on regular basis. Out of the grants of Rs. 5 lakh, a small community hall was constructed. Out of the sale proceeds of bamboo, they created a tent house. A mike set and some electrical appliances worth Rs. 2 lakh were also purchased. These were used during festivals and given on rent to nearby villages at a reasonable rate.

(x) As regards corrupt practices, respondents felt that getting things done was not easy without a bribe—be it a matter with police or revenue or forest department officials. They knew about corruption, talked and debated the subject but expressed helplessness in fighting against it.

(xi) Consumer protection in the villages under study was found to be a non-issue. They lacked knowledge on consumer issues. Consumer clubs established in their respective schools in 2007 were defunct. No one remembered what programmes were conducted in the schools. Products of daily use were consumed in small quantity preferably in pouches/sachets. They all relied more on weekly local *haats* and daily market in the nearby town and mostly preferred cheaper products. Chinese products were cheaper and dominated the market. Hardly anyone purchased with a cash memo/money receipt. No one purchased any product based on TV advertisement. Consumer issues on technology, banking, insurance, financial services, medicines, real estate, education, travel services, energy saving, financial inclusion, census and *aadhar* numbers were frequently telecast in TV under "Jago Grahak Jago" campaign but hardly one could tell anything about the campaign.

Consumer Protection Awareness Mechanism

There was rigorous discussion with the respondents about how as sensible consumers they could be enlightened about their rights, duties and responsibilities—be it developmental projects or their daily consumption of products and services. About 57 per cent of the respondents in first village and 41 per cent in second village viewed that educated youth, school teachers, social development workers and local bodies could play a key role in educating them. Other suggestions were that on the date of distribution of old age pension, all beneficiaries could be seated in Panchayat community hall and film(s) on consumer protection could be shown. Such short film show could also be organised in monthly meetings of Anganwadi workers/Asha Karmi/Gram Sathi/Krushak Sathi who, in turn, would help in educating other villagers. People would not ordinarily like to come to meetings for discussions but at least once in a month, such film shows could be arranged for the parents in the school. *Gram Sabha* meetings could also discuss these issues. *Panchayats* with the involvement of Government officials could organise rallies/meeting on all important occasions like Gandhi Jayanti, National Consumers' Day, World Consumer Rights' Day, Mother's Day etc. The *Panchayat* ward members in the village need to be trained about their role as facilitator. The respondents were positive when asked whether they would approve and participate in any work undertaken by public-private partnership mode to improve their knowledge and awareness.

Implication and Conclusion

The issues covered in this study are not area/region specific as similar situations can be found in many parts in the rural areas. Review of the 12th Plan documents suggests that the 12th Plan priorities among others include promotion of socio-economic movement to protect consumer rights. As such, Government has decided to address the problems of rural consumers by aggressively launching awareness programmes. Another impediment in this direction is that 'consumer clubs' established in many schools across states during 2005-06 are more or less defunct/ inactive due to want of financial support. Debate has been going on to involve local bodies for promotion of consumer movement in general and consumer awareness in particular. With the present socio-economic conditions strategies to awaken the rural consumers, it is strongly advocated and the "consumer clubs" should be reactivated, restructured and adequate financial support be provided. Local bodies and educational institutions of higher learning should be involved in execution of the scheme.

REFERENCES

ASSOCHAM, 2012, Rural Development in India: State Level Experiences, www.assocham.org, Accessed on August 25.

Consumer International, *Consumers International Asia Pacific Consumer*, Vol. 41, 3/2005, 2005, pp. 24, 27.

Kumar Basant, Mohanty Brajraj, 2012, *Public Distribution System in Rural India: Implications for Food Safety and Consumer Protection*, under publication in Procedia Social and Behavioural Sciences.

Kumar, Basant, Mohanty Brajraj, 2005, "Impact of Microfinance through SHG-Bank Linkage in India: A Micro Study", *Vilakshana*, Issue No. 2, September 2005, pp. 1-22.

MART, More Power to Rural Consumers, 2012 http://www.livemint.com/2012/03/22213109/More-power-to-rural-consumer.html, Accessed on September 14.

Michael Johnston, Poverty and Corruption, 2009, http://www.forbes.com/2009/01/22/corruption-poverty-development-biz corruption09-cx_mj_0122 johnston.html, Accessed on September 30, 2012

Planning Commission, *Report of the Working Group on Consumer Protection*, Twelfth Five Year Plan (2012-17), Volume II, Government of India, 2012, www.planningcommission.nic.in, Accessed on September 24, 2012.

World Bank, 2010, *Empowering Rural India: Expanding Electricity Access by Mobilizing Local Resources*.

Zikmund, W.G., 2003, *Business Research Methods* (7th Ed.). Ohio: South Western a division of Thomson Learning.

18

Changing Tastes and Preferences of the Rural Consumers

Opportunities and Challenges Ahead of Oil Marketing Companies (OMCs) in India

KAUSHAL KISHORE

Introduction

Petroleum products and Indian economy are highly interrelated with each other. It is well-known fact that India's energy basket is heavily dependent on imports of crude oil. In any circumstance, if prices of crude oil goes up, the price of petroleum products has to go up leading to high price of commodities and high inflation as well. Because of this, the Government of India took more time to deregulate the sector though most of the sectors were opened for the private and foreign players in the 1991. The lubricants were deregulated in 1993 and private players entered in the Indian market without delaying further. The entry of private players like Essar, Reliance and Shell in 2003-04 in petro-retailing business has changed the overall scenario. In fact, all private players are waiting for Government's decision to decontrol the pricing of all petroleum products. The Government intention is also to do the same as subsidies burden and fiscal deficit are creating huge pressure on Indian economy.

In June 2010, on the recommendations of Parikh Committee's Report the price of petrol was deregulated and the recent price high in diesel has given positive signals to all private and foreign players. So far Public Sector Undertakings (PSUs) like Indian Oil Corporation Ltd. (IOCL), Bharat Petroleum Corporation Ltd. (BPCL), Hindustan Petroleum Corporation Ltd. (HPCL) are selling petroleum products at lower prices as compared to private players due to Government support. Once the pricing of petroleum products will be deregulated the overall marketing strategies would be different for rural and urban customers.

The entry of private players in petro-retailing business and partial decontrol of pricing of petroleum products in India altogether has created pressure on Oil Marketing Companies (OMCs) to revisit and redesign the policies for rural and urban customers as both customers have different tastes and preferences. Keeping in view the above context, an attempt has been made to understand the changing tastes and preferences of rural consumers and initiatives taken by OMCs accordingly. In this context, three main objectives have been identified:

1. To understand the preferences of the rural consumers as compared to urban consumers in the context of petro-retailing;
2. To understand the rural marketing initiatives by Oil Marketing Companies in India; and
3. To understand opportunities and challenges ahead of Oil Marketing Companies in rural markets.

Rural Consumers *vs.* Urban Consumers in the Context of Petro-Retailing

OMCs in India are selling petroleum products mainly petrol, diesel and lubricants through the dedicated petrol pumps. In general, selling petroleum products to the consumers through the petrol pumps is termed as 'petro-retailing'. Petro-retailing is the face of OMCs. Ramanathan (2007), confirms that the word 'retailing' has its origin in the French verb 'retailer' which means to cut up, and refers to one of the fundamental retailing activities, which is to buy in larger quantities and sell them in smaller quantities.

Sinha (2008) identified the characteristics of rural consumers; like value systems, religion, family and group dynamics which varies from state-to-state; rural consumers have brand loyalty and stick with tried and tasted products, they have desire to upgrade their lifestyles and are highly influenced by the opinion leaders. Shukla and Tandan (2011) confirm that rural customers are fundamentally different from their urban counterparts and different rural geographies display considerable heterogeneity, calling for rural-specific categories. Kumar and Bishnoi (2007) find that as literacy rate has improved the rural consumers have become more aware of product offerings, and the demand for products as well as the discriminatory nature of purchase has increased. Sehrawet and Kundu (2007) highlighted that a significant feature of the Indian rural middle class is its rapid growth in terms of volume and value. This provides a potentially huge untapped market. Kumar and Bishnoi (2007) confirm that due to increase in literacy rates and the penetration of conventional media, the perception and attitude of the rural consumer is changing, moving towards new consumerism. Attitude and consumption habits of rural consumers are also changing and becoming more modern in an urban sense.

Urban customers and rural customers are more or less two sides of a scale. The urban customers are highly educated; enjoy better living standards because of better per capita income, better employment opportunities and opportunities to access better facilities than the rural consumers. Undoubtedly, the marketers have understood the huge opportunities available in rural markets and are trying to create and deliver products/services according to their needs and wants. The identifications of need and wants are becoming easier as marketers pay attention to the overall lifestyle, income and consumption patterns of the rural consumers. The marketers are also trying to understand the factors which influence the behaviour of rural consumers like economy, socio-cultural, technological and demographic factors in details. In general petro-retailing companies are offering fast food restaurants, gifts store, florists, ATM, car wash, pharmacy, and oil change services to the urban consumers and for rural consumers they provide fertilisers, pesticides, seeds and other agro-products/services along with quality fuels.

Rural Marketing Initiatives by Oil Marketing Companies in India

Rao and Tagat (1985) define rural marketing as a process of delivering better standards of living and quality of life to the rural environment. Paninchukunnath (2010) defines urban myopia as a factor when a firm sees only the urban market to participate, in a country where rural market is dominantly present. He also explains that adopting inclusive approach to marketing is the need of the hour. Marketers suffering from urban myopia are not only blind to the big opportunity existing in rural market but are also undertaking a risk of offering the same to a competitor on platter. McGregor (2005) suggested that the conventional approach assumes that consumers are empowered if they have information, advice and lots of competition in the marketplace. Taylor (2001) said that marketing is essential to gain the attention of prospective consumers, building demand for products or services and winning customers. Marketing includes having right merchandise or service, enacting effective sales programmes and promoting the company and its services to the buyers. Aithal and Vaswani (2005) suggest a framework with four components like task environment, rural retailing, distribution strategy and product characteristics. Interestingly, they clarify that product characteristic influences the choice of distribution strategy and retail outlets. Kumar and Bishnoi (2007) suggest that there is a need to understand that what appeals to urban customers may not be appropriate for their rural counterparts owing to their different lifestyle. Therefore, one has to be sensitive to the customers. They also confirm that advertisers have attempted to improve the sales of products by changing purchasing behaviour, which involves changing traditional values and creating desires for new products.

Sarkar (2009) divides the Indian petroleum shopper into four distinct segments, namely routine chore doer, time poor, trust seeker and prestige seeker etc. The routine chore doer seeks additional services like vehicle repairs and maintenance along with hassle free fuelling at the pump. Time poor customers seek quick and non-fuel services, trust seeker customers seek 'quality guarantee' and prestige seekers are brand conscious and have high levels of emotional needs.

In early days, OMCs role was confined only to the distribution of petroleum products. The entry of private players in the sector and shifting tastes and preferences forced OMCs to redesign the policy to retain the existing consumers and to find out new ones. Petro-retailing companies in India took some initiatives and started campaigning in early 2000 when BPCL came with 'Pure for Sure', HPCL with 'Club HP', IOCL with 'Xtracare' etc. The overall objective of such campaigns were to create a better image as adulteration was a concern and offer different branded products and services (Non-Fuel) to the consumers as per their need and wants. Anirvana and Ravi (2011) also identified in similar studies that BPCL launched 'Pure for Sure' campaign in 2001 and later on HPCL planned to come up with 'Club HP' and IOCL with 'XTRACARE' to make sure that petroleum products were delivered properly in terms of quality and quantity.

IOCL's Rural Marketing Strategies

During the year 2010, IOCL's sales turnover (inclusive of excise duty) touched an all-time high of Rs. 3,28,744 crore while profit after tax touched Rs. 7,445 crore. The Earning per Share for the year was Rs. 30.67. IOCL has been consistently declaring dividend for the past 44 years and this year too, the Board of Directors has recommended a dividend of Rs. 9.50 per equity share of Rs. 10 each. With 19,463 retail outlets (46.4% of the industry), 5,456 LPG distributors (51.8% of industry), 3,960 SKO/LDO dealers (60% of industry) and 140 terminals/depots; IOCL is committed to serve the people of India. Realising that its rural customers have to still travel long distances to take supplies of fuel, IOCL has taken the initiative of launching its Retail Outlets in rural areas under the brand "Kisan Seva Kendras" (KSKs). 3517 KSKs are already under operation and the programme is being expanded to have a significant presence in the rural segment. Making cooking fuel (LPG) available in rural areas is another initiative taken by IOCL. Even today millions of Indians are underserved with energy products and still continue to use fuel-wood in their smoky *chullahs*. Expanding the reach of LPG availability in rural areas and serving the hitherto unserved areas is a priority programme undertaken by IOCL through the scheme of Rajiv Gandhi Gramin LPG Vitran Yojana.

Foreseeing enhanced competition from private fuel retailers in aftermath of petrol prices decontrol, state-run Indian Oil Corporation Limited (IOC), will adopt a vertical growth plan to expand its retail network. This will be part of its plan to maintain market leadership position in the fuel retailing segment. It also confirms that Kisan Seva Kendra (KSK) is a retail outlet model pioneered by IOC to cater to the needs of customers in the rural segment. At present, IOC operates over 2,700 KSK outlets. ToI (2007) confirms that Indo Gulf products such as fertilisers, seeds, agrochemicals, at present marketed through their Birla Shaktiman Krishi Seva Kendra and Birla Shaktiman Kisan Swayam Rojgar Krishi Seva Kendras, will now also be retailed through Indian Oil's low-cost outlets called Kisan Seva Kendras.

Indian Oil has tied up with Indo-Gulf for fertilisers, National Seeds Corporation for marketing seeds and agricultural inputs as well as alliances with NABARD, Oriental Bank of Commerce and Bank of Baroda for banking products. Some KSK have installed internet kiosks, communication facilities etc. Business alliances have been signed to market products from Dabur, Airtel, Tata Chemicals, Godavari Fertilisers, Gokulam Fertilisers, Hindustan Unilever and Godrej Agrovet. Other alliance partners are Emami for personal care products, Money Gram for money transfer, MILMA and COMFED for milk products, and Supplyco for convenience stores. Indian Oil has separate positioning for the urban and highways market segments through Xtra Care and Swagat brands. Indian Oil's Xtra Premium and Xtra mile are the leading automotive fuel brands in the country. IOCL (2012) confirms that the NFR model developed will provide for sharing of revenue streams with the dealer network to enable unlocking of existing retail space value that both Indian Oil and its dealers command. Several alliances have already been forged with leading brands like Hindustan Unilever Ltd., Dabur, ICICI Bank, Ferns and Petals, MTR Foods, PVR Cinema, UAE Exchange, Reliance Capital and DHL.

IOCL as a leading OMC has taken great initiatives to provide all basic needs of the rural consumers while providing agriculture products and services at the nearest retail-outlets. Rural consumers need and demands are confined to agro-products and services, FMCG products and short-term loans etc. Having tied up of IOCL with leading agro companies, FMCG companies and bankers are certainly helping consumers to get basic needs at one place and help companies to enhance the profitability and faster return on investment (ROI).

HPCL's Rural Marketing Strategies

The turnover of HPCL increased by 22 per cent to Rs. 1,32,670 crore during the year 2010-11. Even profit after tax increased to Rs. 1539 crore comparison to Rs. 1301 crore in the year 2009-10. HPCL's new-found aggression has been demonstrated through its Club HP and Hamara Pump initiatives. So far, BPCL had energised the marketplace with its "Pure for Sure" campaign, while Indian Oil has spread its magic with the "XTRA" branding. Mahindra Finance (2005) confirms that HPCL has set up low cost rural retail outlets called "Hamara Pumps" which have been improvised as multipurpose "Kisan Vikas Kendras", offering a "single window" supply point for the farmers to source their fuel, seeds, pesticides and other needs.

HPCL's 'Club HP' is a great initiative for urban and highway consumers where the outlet assures the availability of quality fuels and other non-fuel services like car wash, oil changes, ATM facilities, fast food restaurants etc. at affordable prices. To cater to the need of rural consumers and better penetration in rural markets, HPCL has introduced "Hamara Pump" which is a low cost pump and offers various products and services apart from quality fuels to consumers. The retail outlets provide agro products/ services, microfinance and input for better agriculture output.

BPCL's Rural Marketing Strategies

BPCL group's gross revenue for the year 2011-12 was Rs. 2,23,314.64 crore as compared to Rs. 1,66,104.22 crores in the year 2010-11. However, the profit after tax stood at Rs. 851.28 crores in 2011-12 as compared to Rs. 1742.06 crore in the year 2010-11. BPCL started marketing its petro-products using e-Choupal network in Uttar Pradesh and Madhya Pradesh. In the long-run apart from the distribution of LPG and other accessories the e-Choupal hubs would also be used for marketing lubricants, petrol and diesel through pumps set-up by BPCL at these locations as part of creating a village super store. According to Moneycontrol (2007) BPCL has aimed at exploring the huge potential of the rural market through adopting an innovative approach which will benefit the customers. BPCL has entered the booming rural retail segment with tie up with Godrej Aadhaar, which is an agri-service cum retail initiative of Godrej Agrovet Ltd. Both companies plan to extend their association by launching Aadhaar Express in BPCL petro-outlets situated in semi-urban and rural areas.

BPCL is known as most innovative OMC in India and credit for Brand-Building exercise in petro-retailing goes to them only. After introducing "Pure for Sure" campaign, BPCL introduced premium products and loyalty programme as an agent of change. To help the rural consumers, the company took initiatives to offer several products and services related to agricultural implements, pesticides and herbicides apart from FMCG, grocery and apparels etc. The domestic petroleum companies are keen on such tie-ups with rural retail chains as it helps them curb the widespread practice of adulteration in diesel and petroleum products. An urban petrol pump costs between Rs. 1.5 to 2 crore, while rural pumps (have vending machines and air pressure gauge only) cost between Rs. 15-20 lakh and the output is over 80 KL per month of diesel, which really shows good ROI.

Essar's Rural Marketing Strategies

Currently, Essar is operating with 1,635 retail outlets and 254 are underway. Simultaneously, Essar has increased focus on non-fuel retailing; tie-ups with more than 20 brands in segments like lubricants, food and beverages, agro products, telecom, banking and finance for setting-up points of sale at Essar Oil retail outlets. Essar has already introduced Auto LPG and CNG pumps in outlets, in association with Aegis Logistics and Sabarmati Gas Ltd. During financial year 2010-11 Essar's revenues increased by Rs. 10,717 crore representing a 25 per cent growth year on year, from Rs. 42,402 crore in FY 2009-10 to Rs. 53,119 crore in FY 2010-11, this is primarily due to record refinery output and increased product prices.

Cafe Coffee Day has entered into a tie-up with Essar Oil Ltd. for setting-up cafeterias at petrol pumps controlled by the oil company. The first such outlet has come up at Essar's petrol pump located on the Pune-Ahmednagar highway. The tie-up is an attempt to increase the share of non-fuel revenues for the oil major. On the other hand, Essar has joined hands with Gujarat Cooperative Milk Marketing Federation (GCMMF) which owns Amul, the popular butter brand, which is India's biggest food product marketing organisation. Amul stores also sell ice-cream, bread spreads, chocolates, milk products and confectioneries through its specific outlets known as Amul Parlours and Amul Cafe. Now, Amul Parlours and Cafe are available with Essar petrol pump in Gujarat and Rajasthan.

As private OMC in India, Essar is facing severe challenges in finding and retaining consumers for their outlets as pricing of petroleum products are higher than PSUs. The survival of franchisee that own and operates the petrol pump is always a concern for the company and franchisee. The overall strategies of Essar is to serve the best to the consumers and enhance the profitability and sustain growth through non-fuel services like selling lubricants of all major companies. It also offers ice-cream, fast food products and provides financial support through the ATMs in the premises and other arrangements which enhances consumer's satisfaction levels.

Narayan and Jayaswal (2010) have highlighted that Reliance Industries' (RIL) fuel retail business is currently operating with only 600 pumps, mainly in Rajasthan, West and South India. However, the total number of retail outlets is about 1,400. As far as marketing strategies of Reliance and Shell are concerned, both are waiting for Government's decision to deregulate the price of petroleum products in India. On the other hand, country's only international fuel retailer Shell India has silently increased its petrol pump network to 74, a 50 per cent jump in just one year, even as other private retailers complain about the lack of level playing field in the retailing business between the private players and government-owned companies.

Shell's presence is mainly confined to few States of India and that too in urban or semi-urban kind of markets. However, they are operating with more than 75 outlets in India and have licensed to increase up to 2000 outlets. The expansion may be in the rural markets but it all depends on pricing policies of Government of India.

Opportunities and Challenges

Clean cooking fuel like natural gas, LPG and Kerosene are merit goods. These merit goods replace the use of biomass-based fuels such as firewood and dung. These biomass based fuels create indoor air pollution that causes respiratory diseases, eye infections and result in many premature deaths, particularly of women and children in rural areas. Also, use of firewood encourages deforestation and dung is better used as a fertiliser. Moreover, the task of gathering these fuels keeps girls away from schools. Thus, use of clean cooking fuel has many social and environmental externalities, and it is merit goods. OMCs in India have started focusing on rural consumers only recently. The rural economy is nothing without agriculture and that is why all OMCs are providing products and services required to support agriculture outputs. To provide clean and quality fuel like LPG is also an opportunity to increase the presence in the rural markets and a challenge to meet the demand as more consumption will lead to higher import and high losses. Here, the role of the Government is also important.

The OMC's immediate challenges are many; like retaining its market share, retaining its existing consumers, eliminating the adulteration issues and provide the best quality and quantity of fuels to the rural as well as urban consumers. Consumers are paying the right price as decided by companies or Government in the case of PSUs than they have rights to get right quality and quantity. From the strategic marketing point of view, brand fight in a saturated market (most of the urban markets) is a loss game. Most of the firms in such a market are market followers. Competition in a developing market is creating new markets.

Consumer educators have always been concerned with empowering consumers in the marketplace. This has traditionally meant that educational programmes tended to give consumers information and advice, teach them how to make rational, efficient choices, and sensitise them to their rights. Shukla and Tandan (2011) said that the rural markets are full of challenges because of its characteristics like literacy, distances, vast market potential, communication, rail and road transportation, distribution of products and services, understanding consumer behaviour, socio-cultural factors, languages and lack of infrastructure facilities etc.

Consumer's satisfaction is the key to success in any market. The OMCs in India are offering various products and services to rural consumers but due to various reasons rural consumers lack awareness about such services. Hence, OMCs must educate the consumers about how the offers are different from others. Having information about products and services is a matter of confidence and power for consumers. As researchers suggested that quality offerings will lead to consumer satisfaction and it expands the willingness of consumers to buy more and consume more. The rural market is emerging market for OMCs as rural infrastructure is improving, employment opportunities are growing and people started enjoying luxurious life.

Conclusion

The highly regulated oil marketing companies in India are trying to differentiate their offering from others. They are also positioning themselves in different market (urban, rural and highways) in different ways. As per the tastes and preferences, OMCs are changing their offers to the consumers. India as an economy is growing faster but the emerging market is rural market. It means if OMCs in India seek sustainable growth, they have to understand the economical, socio-cultural, demographical, geographical and technological factors which influence the rural consumers. The rural consumers are being empowered by seeking information about products, services and their immediate rights.

The Government of India has gradually started decontrolling the price of petroleum products especially petrol and diesel. When the price would be fully deregulated, private OMCs will have equal playing field and then the survival of OMCs would be more or less dependent on who serves the best to the consumers. It means consumers will have all options to decide the future of OMCs and empowering rural consumers are not solely in the hand of OMCs but also depends on Government's policies.

Hence, we may say that the oil marketing companies in India playing a role in protecting the interest of the rural consumers. But at the same time, they need to be in constant touch with the rural consumers as tastes and preferences are changing in fractions of second.

Acknowledgements: The author likes to acknowledge the guidance and support of Dr. Rajnikant P. Patel, Professor at G.H. Patel Postgraduate Institute of Business Management, Sardar Patel University, Vallabh Vidyanagar, Gujarat.

REFERENCES

"BPCL to do biz on e-Choupal", *Economics Times*, June 22, 2004, retrieved from http://articles.economictimes.indiatimes.com/2004-06-22/news/27410033_1_choupal-bpcl-sources-lpg

"CCD Cafes at Essar fuel outlets", *Business Line*, August 30, 2012, retrieved from http://www.thehindubusinessline.com/companies/article 3840727.ece?css=print

"HPCL races to 2nd slot in Marketing", *Times of India*, November 9, 2004, retrieved from http://articles.timesofindia.indiatimes.com/2004-11-09/india-business/27164169_1_club-hp-hpcl-plans-hamara-pump

"Joins with Godrej Aadhaar to Draw Rural Customers", *Moneycontrol*, October 16, 2007 retrieved from http://www.moneycontrol.com/news/business/bpcl-joinsgodrej-aadhaar-to-draw-rural-customers_308306.html

"Petrol Pump at Godrej Aadhaar Outlets Soon", *Financial Express*, May 29, 2006. http://www.financialexpress.com/news/petrol-pumps-at-godrej-aadhaar-outlets-soon/94113/0

AGM, 2011, "Address of the Chairman and Managing Director at the 59th Annual General Meeting held on 29th September, 2011 at Mumbai", retrieved from http://www.hindustanpetroleum.com/Upload/En/Chairmans Specch/files/ C&MD–Speech–59th–AGM.pdf.

AGM, 2012, "Chairman's Address at Indian Oil's 52nd Annual General Meeting", Indian Oil Corporation Ltd., September 2012, retrieved from http:// www.iocl.com/InvestorCenter/ChairmanSpeech.aspx

Aithal, K.R. and Vaswani, 2005, "*K.L. Distribution Channel Structure in Rural Areas: A Framework and Hypothesis, Decision*", Vol. 32, No. 1, January-June, pp. 191-206.

Anirvana, C. and Ravi, V. N., 2011, "An analysis of Marketing and Consumption Trends in Indian Oil Industry", *Internationally Indexed Journal*, Vol. II, Issue 1, January 2011, pp. 33-46.

Fornell, C., Rust, T.R., and Dekimpe, G.M., 2010, "The Effect of Customer Satisfaction on Consumer Spending Growth," *Journal of Marketing Research*, Vol. XLVII, February, 2010, pp. 28-35.

IOCL, R., 2012, "Kisan Seva Kendra", Indian Oil Corporation Ltd., retrieved on September 10, 2012 from http://www.iocl.com/Aboutus/PetrolDiesel Stations.aspx

IOCL, 2012, "Retail (Non-Fuel) Alliances", Indian Oil Corporation Ltd., retrieved on September 10, 2012 from http://www.iocl.com/Services/ MarketingRetailBusiness.aspx

Jayaswal, R., 2012, "Essar Oil banks on Tie-ups to Keep Petrol Pumps Afloat", *Economics Times*, June 25, 2012, retrieved from http://articles. economictimes.indiatimes.com/2012-06-25/news/32409402_1_petrol-pumps-essar-oil-amul-parlours

Kumar, S. and Bishnoi, V.K., 2007, "Influence of Marketer's Efforts on Rural Consumers and their Mindset: A Case Study of Haryana", *The ICFAI Journal of Brand Management*, Vol. IV, No. 4, pp. 28-50.

Mahindra Finance, 2005, "HPCL and Mahindra Finance tie-up for Rural Financing", *Mahindra Finance*, October 4.

McGregor, S., 2005, "Sustainable Consumer Empowerment Through Critical Consumer Education: A Typology of Consumer Education Approaches",

International Journal of Consumer Studies, 29, 5, September 2005, pp. 437-447.

Narayan, S. and Jayaswal, R., 2010, Shell Ramps Up Fuel Retail Network to 74", *The Economic Times*, February 15, 2010, retrieved from http://articles.economictimes.indiatimes.com/2010-02-15/news/27606474_1_retailers-psu-oil-companies-ramps

Paninchukunnath, A., 2012, "3P Framework: Rural Marketing in India", *SCMS Journal of Indian Management*, January-March 2012, pp. 54-67.

Petrol Plaza. "Indian Oil Company Eyes Rural Market to Expand its Retail Network", July 8, 2010 retrieved from http://www.petrolplaza.com/news/print/browse/MiZlbiY5OTczJiYx

Ramanathan, V., 2007, "Retailing Channel Enhancement Strategies Adopted by FMCG Companies in South Indian Rural Markets", *The ICFAI Journal of Management Research*, Vol. VI, No. 11, pp. 64-70.

Rao, K.L.K. and Tagat, R.G., 1985. "Rural Marketing: A Developmental Approach", *Vikalpa*, 10(3), pp. 315-326.

Sarkar, A., 2009, *Petro Economics*. First Edn., New Delhi: Pentagon Energy Press.

Sehrawet, M. and Kundu, S. Subhash, 2007, "Buying Behaviour of Rural and Urban Consumers in India: the Impact of Packaging", *International Journal of Consumer Studies*, 31, ISSN, 1470-6423, pp. 630-638.

Shukla, S. and Tandan, N., 2011, "Rural Marketing—Exploring New Possibilities in the Rural India", *Gurukul Business Review*, Vol. 7 (Spring 2011), pp. 125-130.

Sinha, M., 2008, "Walk Their Walk, and Talk Their Talk: The Mantra of Success in the Hinterland", *The ICFAI Journal University Journal of Marketing Management*, Vol. VII, No. 4, pp. 7-23.

Taylor, L. Donna, 2001. "Telling It Like It Is: Marketing Maneuvers for Rural Telecos", *Rural Telecommunications*, September/October, pp. 52-57.

ToI. Indo Gulf Fert., "IOC in Rural Marketing Tie-up", *Times of India*, January 15, 2007, retrieved from http://articles.timesofindia.indiatimes.com/2007-01-15/india/27870548_1_rural-marketing-xtracare-kisan-seva-kendras

SECTION IV

Service Sector and the Rural Consumers

19

Protection of Consumers' Interest in Insurance Sector

A Study of Belgaum District in Karnataka State

S.F. TANGADE

Introduction

Insurance is a form of risk management in which the insured transfers the cost of potential loss to another entity in exchange for monetary compensation known as the premium. Insurance in India is not a new thing. Since, 1818, Insurance has firmly established in India. It has a deep-rooted history. The Insurance sector in India has gone through number of phases and heavy changes, particularly after 1990, insurance sector in India has a full circle with private players, when the Government of India opened up the insurance sector to allow the private insurance companies to solicit insurance. This is the main reason, Indian insurance sector is considered as a booming market and varieties of global players have entered to grab a share of the pie in Indian Insurance sector. At present, India's largest insurance company is owned by the Government of India, i.e. LIC of India.

Today, there are 24 General Insurance Companies and 23 Life Insurance Companies operating in India. The insurance sector is growing at a speedy rate of 15-20 per cent. Insurance sector is adding about 7 per cent to the country's GDP. A well developed and evolved insurance sector is a boom for economic development as it provides long-term funds for infrastructure development and also strengthening the risk taking in the country. To strengthen the insurance sector in India, the Government has set-up a Committee in 1990 under the chairmanship of R.N. Malhotra, former Governor of RBI, to propose recommendations for reforms in the Insurance Sector. The committee submitted its report in 1994 and recommended that the private sector including foreign companies can also be permitted to enter the Insurance sector.

Insurance Regulatory and Development Authority (IRDA)

Following the recommendations of the Malhotra Committee report, in April 2000, the IRDA was constituted as an autonomous and statutory body to regulate and develop the Insurance industry. The main objectives of the IRDA are to promote competition in Insurance sector so as to enhance customer satisfaction through increased choice and lower premiums and to ensure financial security of the insurance market. Even after establishment of IRDA in 2000, so many dissatisfied insurance policy-holders of different insurance companies have filed their complaints in different Consumer Forums and also in complaint cell of different insurance companies. Hence, the present study is undertaken to know the response of dissatisfied insurance policy-holders in the Belgaum District of Karnataka State.

The research work is based on empirical data collected from primary and secondary sources. Primary data is collected from 300 aggrieved insurance policy-holders. Secondary data is collected from District Consumer Forum, and from other Insurance Companies in Belgaum District of Karnataka.

Objectives of the Study

Following are the important objectives of the study:

- To study the grievances of policy-holders in the study area.
- To observe the problems faced by the policy-holders.
- To study the role of consumer forum in mitigating the hardship of policy-holders.
- To observe findings and make suggestions for improving the Insurance sector.

During the last five years, total 2303 complaints have been filed in the District Consumer Forum, Belgaum. Out of the total complaints filed, 334 complaints are related to insurance sector, which includes both life

Insurance as well as General Insurance. It means around 15 per cent of complaints are relating to insurance sector. The researcher has approached 300 complainant respondents and collected necessary information relating to the study by using questionnaire.

Table 19.1: Year-wise Cases Filed since its Inception in District Consumer Forum, Belgaum

Sl. No.	Particulars	2007	2008	2009	2010	2011
1.	Banks	378	452	566	636	647
2.	Railway	43	44	45	46	47
3.	Airlines	9	9	10	10	12
4.	Insurance	764	862	970	1030	1098
5.	Telecom	228	228	228	229	230
6.	Postal	72	74	75	77	81
7.	Housing	110	112	113	113	115
8.	Electricity	262	267	276	279	285
9.	Medical	110	119	121	128	138
10.	Defective goods	417	425	430	431	453
11.	Education	57	57	57	60	62
12.	Road Transport	140	144	146	146	146
13.	Miscellaneous	3285	3674	4310	4957	5588
	Total	**5875**	**6467**	**7347**	**8142**	**8902**

Table 19.2: Cases Filed and Disposed in District Consumer Forum, Belgaum (During the years 2007-2011)

Sl. No.	Particulars	Cases filed during the period	Disposed of during the period	Pending as on 31-12-2011
1.	Banks	269	294	24
2.	Railway	4	4	–
3.	Airlines	3	3	–
4.	Insurance	334	346	12
5.	Telecom	2	2	-
6.	Postal	9	11	2
7.	Housing	5	1	4
8.	Electricity	23	25	2
9.	Medical	28	28	–
10.	Defective goods	36	18	18
11.	Education	5	5	–
12.	Road Transport	6	6	–
13.	Miscellaneous	1579	1368	22
	Total	**2303**	**2111**	**84**

Source: Records of District Forum, Belgaum.

Table 19.3: Area-wise Complaints Filed by the Insured Consumers in the District Forum, Belgaum

Area	*Years*					
	2007	*2008*	*2009*	*2010*	*2011*	*Total*
Rural	22	27	33	23	36	141
Urban	34	38	36	37	48	193
Total	**56**	**65**	**69**	**60**	**84**	**334**

Source: Records of District Forum, Belgaum.

It is observed from Table 19.3 that every year urban consumers have filed more number of complaints (58%) rather than rural consumer (42%). This shows that awareness about consumer forum is less among rural consumers. But it is satisfactory.

Table 19.4: Age-wise Complaints Filed by the Insured Consumers in the District Forum, Belgaum

Age	*Years*					
	2007	*2008*	*2009*	*2010*	*2011*	*Total*
Below 20	0	–	2	17	3	5
20-40	7	18	21	17	25	88
40–60	34	28	32	28	34	156
Above 60	15	19	14	15	22	85
Total	**56**	**65**	**69**	**77**	**84**	**334**

Source: Records of District Forum, Belgaum.

Table 19.4 revealed that majority of the complaints (47%) belongs to the age group of 40-60 years. Whereas, least numbers of complaints (1.5%) are filed by the age group of below 20 years aged consumers.

Table 19.5: Gender-wise Complaints Filed by the Insured Consumers in the District Forum, Belgaum

Gender	*Years*					
	2007	*2008*	*2009*	*2010*	*2011*	*Total*
Male	48	52	54	51	68	273
Female	8	13	15	9	16	61
Total	**56**	**65**	**69**	**60**	**84**	**334**

Source: Records of District Forum, Belgaum.

Table 19.5 shows that out of the total complainants, 82 per cent complainants are male. Whereas, only 18 per cent female complainants have filed their cases in the consumer forum. It shows that the main decision-maker in the family is men.

Table 19.6: Occupation-wise Complaints Filed by the Insured Consumers in the District Forum Belgaum

Occupation	*Years*					
	2007	*2008*	*2009*	*2010*	*2011*	*Total*
Business	11	15	8	12	18	64
Agriculture	8	7	22	8	11	56
Profession	14	21	19	13	25	92
Service	17	12	8	17	16	72
Household	6	10	12	8	14	50
Total	**56**	**65**	**69**	**58**	**84**	**334**

Source: Records of District Forum, Belgaum.

Table 19.6 shows that majority of the complaints are relating to professionals and service holders. Out of the total complaints filed in the District Forum, 28 per cent complainants were professionals like advocates, doctors etc. 22 per cent complainants were service holders, 19 per cent complainants were businessmen, 17 per cent complainants belonged to agriculture sector and only 15 per cent complaints belonged to households. In 2009, 32 per cent complaints have been filed by farmers against Agricultural Insurance companies.

Table 19.7: Insurance Organization-wise Complaints Filed by the Insured Consumers in the District Forum, Belgaum

Year	*Type of Insurance Organisation*				
	Life Insurance		*General Insurance*		*Total*
	Govt.	*Private*	*Govt.*	*Private*	
2007	15	5	20	16	56
2008	12	8	22	23	65
2009	6	6	29	28	69
2010	12	13	24	11	60
2011	11	14	32	27	84
Total	**56**	**46**	**127**	**105**	**334**

Source: Records of District Forum, Belgaum.

It is observed from Table 19.7 that more number of complaints have been filed against General Insurance companies (69%) out of which

39 per cent related to Government sector and 30 per cent related to private sector. General Insurance Companies includes New India Assurance Company, United India Insurance Company, National Insurance Company, Oriented Insurance Company, Agricultural Insurance Company, and other private Insurance Companies.

Out of total complaints filed, 31 per cent related to Life Insurance Sector, out of which 14 per cent related to private and 17 per cent related to Government organizations. Life Insurance Companies included Life Insurance Corporation of India, and other private owned Life Insurance Organizations.

Table 19.8: Complaints Filed and Dismissed at District Forum, Belgaum

Complaints	*Years*					
	2007	*2008*	*2009*	*2010*	*2011*	*Total*
Allowed	43	45	48	41	62	239
Dismissed	13	20	21	19	22	95
Total	**56**	**65**	**69**	**60**	**84**	**334**

Source: Records of District Forum, Belgaum.

It is observed from Table 19.8 that every year on an average 29 per cent complaints were dismissed by the consumer forum due to different technical reasons. Only 71 per cent complaints have been allowed by the forum, which have been disposed of within a stipulated period of time.

Findings of the Study

Following are the important findings of the study:

(1) It is observed from the study that out of the total complaints filed in the District Forum, majority of complaints (69%) related to miscellaneous sector, only 15 per cent complaints are against Insurance sector and remaining complaints related to banks and others goods and services.

(2) The study shows that 58 per cent of urban consumers and 42 per cent of rural consumer have filed complaints against Insurance sector.

(3) It is revealed from the study, that out of total complaints filed against Insurance sector majority of them are related to General Insurance (80%) and only 20 per cent are related to Life Insurance Sector.

(4) Occupation-wise complaints filed shows that majority of complaints filed by professional consumers like Doctors, Advocates etc.

Suggestions

Following are the important suggestions of the study:

(1) It is suggested that the IRDA should have strict control on all Insurance companies, which will minimise filing of complaints in the Consumer Forum and quick justice can be availed by all consumers.
(2) All Insurance companies are suggested to solve the problems of Insured policy-holders at their end only to avoid hindrances to the consumers.

Conclusion

Insurance is a form of risk management in which insured transfers their risk of loss to other organisations. But in reality it is not so happening. Majority of the Insurance Companies are exploiting the consumers and making money from large number of insured policy-holders. When the time comes to pay back the amount to the insured, then the Insurance Companies start playing hide and seek with the insured consumers, which is against the rule and assurance given by them at the time of starting of insurance business. Hence, all consumers are requested to read and follow all the instructions carefully before making any commitment with insurance companies. They should submit all the documents and keep the records in their custody.

REFERENCES

Different Websites

Harrington and Niehaus, 2011, *Risk Management and Insurance*, New Delhi: Tata McGraw-Hill Publication.

Mark S. Dorfman, 2009, *Introduction to Risk Management and Insurance*, New Delhi: PHI Publication.

Saharay, H.K., 2010, *Text Book on Consumer Protection Law*, New Delhi: Universal Law Publishing Company.

Taxmanns, 2008, *Consumer Protection Law Manual with Practice*, New Delhi: Taxman Allied Services (P) Ltd.

20

Service Quality in Telecom Services in Rural Areas

A Study with Reference to BSNL in Chittoor District, Andhra Pradesh

K.S.S. HARI PRASAD

Introduction

In the twenty-first century the planet earth has become a global village and this is due to prompt, easy and accessible communication. Due to telecom revolution, geographical distances seem to have lessened. As one of the fastest growing industries, telecommunications is at the core of the Information Society. The dissemination of information and progress of culture go hand-in-hand with the possibility of interacting and sharing ideas, again putting telecommunications at the centre stage. That makes it an interesting area of study.

Telecommunications is one of the few sectors in India, which has witnessed the most fundamental structural and institutional reforms since 1991. The entire sector is now open to unrestricted competition. The opening of the sector has not only led to rapid growth but also helped a great deal towards maximisation of consumer benefits. Growth in this industry is fuelled by the increased competition that has arisen due to globalisation and deregulation. The tariffs have been falling continuously across board as a result of healthy and unrestricted competition and today India has one of the lowest tariffs in the world.

Urban-Rural Divide

India is an agriculture-based country with vast rural background. In respect of telecom services, urban subscribers have been growing significantly; similar growth has not been seen on the rural front. However, with introduction of mobile services in rural areas, the rural subscribers are increasing.

Mobile Services—Competition

In India, the mobile telephone service is one of the fastest growing (40% annual growth) service segments in telecommunications. This sector is experiencing rapid changes technologically. The economic liberalization policy of the Government of India (GoI) has paved the way for the entry of new cellular service companies in India. In the cellular mobile telecommunication services, there are many service providers in India in different circles, in addition to the public sector giant BSNL, offering services to users with three different digital transmission systems: GSM (Global System for Mobile Communications), CDMA (Code Division Multiple Access) and WLL.

Service Quality in Telecom Service Sector

Service quality is essential and important for telecommunication service provider Company to ensure the quality service for establishing and maintaining loyal and profitable customers. The service delivery systems have the ability to allow managers of company to identify the real customer feedback and satisfaction on their telecommunication service. Since, quality reflects the customers' expectations about a product or service. Lovelock (1996) stated that this customer driven quality replaced the traditional marketing philosophies which was based on products and process. Service quality is different from the quality of goods. Since, services are intangible, perishable, produced and consumed simultaneously and heterogeneous (Zeithaml and Bitner, 2000). So, it is a major problem for the telecommunication service providers, especially for the mobile telecommunication service providers to deliver quality service consistently. Rahman (2006) measured the service quality at cellular retail outlets in the Indian environment with a focus on perception and expectation of service quality from the customer's perspective. Arora *et al.* (2007) conducted a study which focused on generating a customised index to measure service quality based on the dimensions of SERVQUAL scale of GSM service provides in the Punjab Circle of Indian Telecom Industry and measurement of their service quality level.

The study is based on the customers' survey consisting of a sample of 200 respondents. After screening the 22 items across, four dimensions—appearance, performance, knowledge and courtesy, and responsiveness—were selected to measure the service validity. Seth *et al.*, (2008), in their study, identified that most of the studies reported on service quality in the cellular mobile services were focused on the service delivery aspects and ignored the role of technical quality. They developed a valid and reliable instrument to measure customer perceived service quality by incorporating both the service delivery and technical quality aspects.

BSNL—Chittoor in Andhra Pradesh

Chittoor District is located in Rayalaseema Region of Andhra Pradesh State. The total population of the Chittoor District is 3.26 million, with 66 Mandals and 1292 Panchayats, 1540 revenue villages with 22 BSNL Customer Service Centres (CSCs). Chittoor Secondary Switching Area (SSA) is covered by 16 Short Distance Charging Areas (SDCA) served with 172 telephone exchanges with equipped capacity of 1,77,084 lines. Total working lines as on February-2011—land-lines 86,551, Wireless in Local Loop (WLL) connections 16,490, internet connections 7658 and broadband connections are 11,516. 2,14,285 prepaid mobile connections and post paid mobile connections are 5,918.

Objectives and Methodology of the Study

Specifically, the study is designed with the following objectives:

- To measure the perceived importance of service offer elements.
- To measure the overall service quality and satisfaction levels of BSNL services and across demographics—among the rural and semi-urban areas of Chittoor District, Andhra Pradesh.

A four pages questionnaire covering aspects like the perceived importance of service offer elements, service quality (reliability, responsiveness, tangibles, empathy and assurance), is canvassed among the rural and semi-urban (semi-rural) customers of BSNL. The questionnaire is designed based on a rational construct criterion method drawing questions from earlier studies. This method assured content validity and reliability of the questionnaire. For these questions, a 5-point scale of agreement/satisfaction—5 indicates strongly agree/very satisfied and—1 indicates strongly disagree/very dissatisfied is used.

In view of the mass customer base, it was decided to take a large sample of 500 customers based on convenience method. The questionnaire was administered to 500 BSNL customers within Chittoor District, out of which 485 completely filled in questionnaires were sorted out for final evaluation. In administering the questionnaire care was taken, (i) to cover both rural and semi-urban customers, and (ii) all major villages and small towns to make the study geographically representative. The data collected has been analysed and presented in the form of simple and bivariate tables. First, reliability of the instrument constructs are measured by using Cronbach's alpha. For all the variables, in the research instrument, descriptive statistics presented using means, standard deviations and variances. Statistical tools are used with the help of software package SPSS 16.

Limitations of the Study

The study is limited to cellular telecom services of BSNL in some of the rural and semi-urban areas of Chittoor District of Andhra Pradesh. The study is limited to the measurement of service quality of cellular services of the customers and the perceived importance of service offer elements. A detailed study of other service offer elements has not been included in this chapter, as this is mainly focused on the service quality elements. Language is a limitation in rural areas. The questionnaire developed in English was translated into local language and this limitation was overcome. The responses are from different categories of people. The diversity has given a wide range of answers and scaling technique has helped capture the extremes. In the analysis means and standard deviations are computed to even out the extreme cases.

Profile of the Respondents

The data was collected from a sample of 485 respondents both urban (59%) and rural respondents (41%). About 65.6 per cent of the respondents were male customers. Only 34.4 per cent were female customers. The respondents belonged to different age groups. However, most of the respondents were youngsters. About 39.4 per cent of the respondents were below 30 years of age.

Table 20.1: Perceived Importance of Service Offer Elements (N=485)

Sl. No.	Offer Dimension	Mean*	S.D.
1.	Tangibles (the appealing nature of physical environment, recharge cards etc.)	4.08	0.74
2.	Reliable (Competence to give timely, reliable services and truthful to promises)	4.08	0.84
3.	Responsive (attending to customer needs and complaints promptly at any time)	4.02	0.78
4.	Assurance (assurance of efficiency, variety and in time delivery of services)	4.16	0.68
5.	Empathy (Showing of respect, care and understanding to customers' needs)	4.16	0.68
6.	Price Perception (view on price as a value for money offer)	3.97	0.71
7.	Value Offers (worthwhile promotional offers, discounts and rebates)	3.96	0.75
8.	Brand Image (having a good reputation for brand name, successful and socially responsible)	4.01	0.78

Responses on a 5-point scale of importance. 5—very important. 1—not at all important.

About 27.6 per cent respondents were in the age group of 30-39 years, 20.6 per cent of the respondents were in the age group of 30-49 years, and 12.4 per cent of the respondents were in the age group of 50 and above. From the responses, it is clear that all the eight variables are important and BSNL has to address all of them to stay competitive in the marketplace.

Service Offer Elements

Table 20.2 gives the perceived importance of service offer elements of the semi-urban and rural respondents. Z test reveals that differences in the opinions are not significant in many cases. The opinions of respondents significantly differed at 0.05 level in respect of three service offer elements, namely Responsiveness, Empathy and Price perception.

Service Quality Ratings by Respondents

How are the service quality factors offered by BSNL perceived? Are they rated positively or negatively by the respondents? The analysis of the perceptions of the respondents on five service quality factors is presented here.

Table 20.2: Perceived Importance of Service Offer Elements—Across Area (N=485)

Sl. No.	*Statement*	*Area*				*Z*
		Urban (N=286)		*Rural (N=199)*		
		Mean	*S.D*	*Mean*	*S.D*	
1.	Tangibility	4.05	0.76	4.12	0.69	0.96
2.	Reliability	4.07	0.87	4.11	0.80	0.25
3.	Responsiveness	4.11	0.79	3.90	0.76	8.68*
4.	Assurance	4.18	0.72	4.13	0.63	0.66
5.	Empathy	4.22	0.72	4.08	0.61	5.34*
6.	Price perception	4.04	0.74	3.87	0.65	6.59*
7.	Value offers	4.00	0.79	3.91	0.68	1.55
8.	Brand Image	4.05	0.80	3.95	0.75	1.71

Responses on a 5-point scale of importance. 5—Very important, 1—Not at all important

* Significant at 0.05 level.

(i) Perceptions on Tangibles

Table 20.3: Service Quality—*Tangibles* (N=485)

Sl. No.	*Statement*	*Mean**	*SD*
1.	BSNL's office/CSCs having modern looking equipment.	3.31	0.83
2.	BSNL's office, showrooms, customer service centres (CSCs) are visually appealing with physical facilities like provision of water, magazines, newspaper, sitting chairs etc.	3.15	0.76
3.	BSNL's showrooms/CSCs provided with pamphlets, displays or statements showing tariffs/schemes, plans	3.27	0.83
4.	Front desk employees have neat and professional appearance.	3.20	0.84

Responses on a 5-point scale of agreement 5—strongly agree, 1—Strongly disagree.

Table 20.3 presents opinions of respondents on service quality element-tangibles of the BSNL. Respondents have taken a neutral stance (mean value is above 3) on all the statements as shown in the table.

Influence of Demographics—Across Area

Table 20.4 examines the views of customers on Service quality element—Tangibles across area. Respondents belonging to urban and rural area did not differ significantly. The mean differences are not significant at 0.05 levels.

Table 20.4: Service Quality—*Tangibles*—Across Area (N=485)

Sl. No.	Statement	Area				Z
		Urban (N=286)		Rural (N=199)		
		Mean	S.D	Mean	S.D	
1.	BSNL's office/CSCs having modern looking equipment.	3.30	0.82	3.33	0.84	0.16
2.	BSNL's office, showrooms, customer service centers (CSCs) are visually appealing with physical facilities like provision of water, magazines, newspapers, sitting chairs etc.	3.15	0.78	3.17	0.72	0.07
3.	BSNL's showrooms/CSCs provided with pamphlets, displays or statements showing tariffs/schemes, plans etc.	3.30	0.83	3.22	0.83	1.16
4.	Front desk employees have neat and professional appearance.	3.26	0.87	3.13	0.79	2.95

Responses on a 5-point scale of agreement 5—strongly agree, 1—strongly disagree.

* Significant at 0.05 level.

(ii) Perceptions on Reliability

Table 20.5 presents the opinions of respondents on service quality element—Reliability. Respondents have taken a neutral stance on all the statements.

Table 20.6 provides the views of respondent customers on the service quality element—Reliability across area. Z-test is conducted to test the significance of differences in mean values at 0.05 levels. The differences are not significant.

(iii) Perceptions on Responsiveness

Table 20.7 presents the opinions of respondents on service quality

Table 20.5: Service Quality—*Reliability* (N=485)

Sl. No	*Statement*	*Mean**	*SD*
1.	Products of BSNL such as recharge cards, top-up cards, India Telephone Card (ITC) etc., are available in any retail outlet.	3.04	0.98
2.	BSNL is truthful towards keeping its promises to customers.	2.80	0.84
3.	BSNL is dependable in solving customers' complaints.	2.78	0.84
4.	BSNL services are reliable.	3.30	0.88

Responses on a 5-point scale of agreement 5 Strongly agree, 1—Strongly disagree.

Table 20.6: Service Quality—*Reliability*—Across Area (N=485)

Sl. No.	*Statement*	*Area*				*Z*
		Urban (N=286)		*Rural (N= 199)*		
		Mean	*S.D*	*Mean*	*S.D*	
1.	Products of BSNL such as recharge cards, top-up cards, India Telephone Card (ITC) etc., are available in any retail outlet.	3.01	1.03	3.08	0.83	0.53
2.	BSNL is truthful towards keeping its promises to customers.	2.81	0.84	2.78	0.85	0.14
3.	BSNL is dependable in solving customers' complaints.	2.81	0.92	2.75	0.72	0.57
4.	BSNL services are reliable.	3.35	0.91	3.23	0.84	2.31

Responses on a 5-point scale of agreement 5—strongly agree, 1—strongly disagree

* Significant at 0.05 level.

element—Responsiveness. Respondents have taken a neutral stance on some statements.

- BSNL staff conducts telephonic conversation with someone else, while serving a customer (3.03).
- BSNL staff hurries you, when the break time approaches (lunch/shift/closing hours) (3.02). They are not happy with services and disagreed with the statements.

Table 20.7: Service Quality—*Responsiveness* (N=485)

Sl. No.	*Statement*	*Mean**	*SD*
1.	Delivery of SMS, activations, voice message and other services of BSNL mobile services is timely	2.73	0.99
2.	Customers receive telephone bills in time	3.58	1.08
3.	BSNL gives prompt customer services by attending to customer needs and problems	2.88	0.94
4.	BSNL officials respond promptly and politely over telephone	3.33	1.15
5.	BSNL employees are approachable and easy to contact	3.22	0.93
6.	BSNL staff conducts telephonic conversation with someone else, while serving a customer	3.03	0.93
7.	BSNL staff hurries you, when the break time approaches (lunch/shift/closing hours)	3.02	0.94

Responses on a 5-point scale of agreement 5—strongly agree, 1—strongly disagree.

* Significant at 0.05 level.

- Delivery of SMS, activations, voice message and other services of BSNL mobile services is timely (2.73).
- "BSNL gives prompt customer services by attending to customer needs and problems" (2.88).

With regard to approachability and courteous response of employees weak agreement is found.

- BSNL officials respond promptly and politely over telephone (3.33).
- BSNL employees are approachable and easy to contact (3.22). Regarding prompt billing there is agreement.
- Customers receive telephone bills in time (3.58).

Table 20.8 represents the views of respondents on responsiveness—as a service quality element across area. Significant difference is observed in the opinions of the respondents in respect of one statement only. As such it is concluded that the area has little influence on responsiveness factor.

(iv) Perceptions on Empathy

Table 20.9 presents the opinions of respondents on Service quality element—Empathy. Respondents agreed (4.09) with the statement "BSNL staff communicates in the language you can understand". However, they have taken a neutral stance (3.32) and mildly neutral stance on the remaining statements as shown in the Table 20.9

Table 20.8: Service Quality—*Responsiveness*—Across Area (N=485)

Sl. No.	*Statement*	*Area*				*Z*
		Urban (N=286)		*Rural (N=199)*		
		Mean	*S.D*	*Mean*	*S.D*	
1.	Delivery of SMS, activations, voice message and other services of BSNL mobile services is timely	2.69	0.99	2.80	0.97	1.70
2.	Customers receive telephone bills in time	3.55	1.06	3.69	1.11	0.43
3.	BSNL gives prompt customer services by attending to customer needs and problems	2.91	0.98	2.84	0.87	0.72
4.	BSNL officials respond promptly and politely over telephone	3.36	1.30	3.28	1.18	0.55
5.	BSNL employees are approachable and easy to contact	3.30	0.98	3.11	0.84	5.13*
6.	BSNL staff conducts telephonic conversation with someone else, while serving a customer	2.96	0.90	3.13	0.96	3.83*
7.	BSNL staff hurries you, when the break time approaches (lunch/shift/closing hours)	2.91	0.92	3.18	0.94	9.59*

Responses on a 5-point scale of agreement 5—strongly agree 1—strongly disagree

* Significant at 0.05 level.

Table 20.9: Service Quality—*Empathy* (N=485)

Sl. No.	*Statement*	*Mean**	*SD*
1.	BSNL staff communicates in the language you can understand	4.09	0.79
2.	BSNL is having the customer's best interest at heart	3.32	0.85
3.	BSNL is making many efforts to understand customer specific needs	2.92	0.95
4.	BSNL apologizes for inconvenience caused to customers.	2.79	0.98

Responses on a 5-point scale of agreement 5—strongly agree, 1—strongly disagree.

Table 20.10 examines the opinions of customers on the Empathy parameter of service quality element across area. Their views differ on the statement "BSNL apologizes for inconvenience caused to customers" at 0.05 level. Since, the differences on the rest of the items are not significant, it can be concluded that area has no influence on views of the customers.

Table 20.10: Service Quality—*Empathy*—Across Area (N=485)

Sl. No.	Statement	Area				Z
		Urban (N= 286)		Rural (N=199)		
		Mean	S.D	Mean	S.D	
1.	BSNL staff communicates in the language you can understand	4.04	0.82	4.16	0.73	2.63
2.	BSNL is having the customer's best interest at heart	3.32	0.87	3.33	0.83	0.01
3.	BSNL is making many efforts to understand customer specific needs	2.90	0.98	2.96	0.89	0.64
4.	BSNL apologizes for inconvenience caused to customers	2.70	0.98	2.91	0.98	5.37*

Responses on a 5-point scale of agreement 5—strongly agree, 1—strongly disagree.

* Significant at 0.05 level.

(v) Perceptions on Assurance

Table 20.11 presents opinions of respondents on Assurance, a parameter of Service Quality element. Respondents have taken a neutral stance (mean value of about 3) on all the statements that express confidence in employee support and provision of a variety of value added services. The response indicates the need to create better assurance standards by BSNL.

Table 20.12 examines the opinions of semi-urban and rural customers on the services of BSNL pertaining to service quality element—Assurance. Their opinions are almost similar. The Z values are not significant at 0.05 level. Evidently, area has no significant influence on customers.

Customer Satisfaction

Customer satisfaction is an important theoretical as well as practical issue

Table 20.11: Service Quality—*Assurance* (N=485)

Sl. No.	*Statement*	*Mean**	*SD*
1.	BSNL is able to provide variety of value added services—Music, access to internet, SMS, MMS etc.	3.20	0.88
2.	Behaviour of employees is instilling confidence in customers to remain with and enjoy the BSNL services	3.00	0.92
3.	Employees of BSNL using required skills and knowledge to answer customers' questions	3.34	1.01

Responses on a 5-point scale of agreement 5—strongly agree, 1—strongly disagree.
* Significant at 0.05 level.

Table 20.12: Service Quality—*Assurance*—Across Area (N=485)

Sl. No.	*Statement*	*Area*				*Z*
		Urban (N= 286)		*Rural (N= 199)*		
		Mean	*S.D*	*Mean*	*S.D*	
1.	BSNL is able to provide variety of value added services—Music, access to internet, SMS, MMS etc.	3.25	0.87	3.14	0.89	1.91
2.	Behaviour of employees is instilling confidence in customers to remain with and enjoy the BSNL services	2.97	0.94	3.05	0.89	0.89
3.	Employees of BSNL using required skills and knowledge to answer customers' questions	3.29	0.97	3.41	1.07	1.70

Responses on a 5-point scale of agreement 5—strongly agree, 1—strongly disagree.

for most marketers and consumer researchers (Dabholkar *et al.,* 2000; Fournier and Mick, 1999; Meuter *et al.,* 2000). Lovelock & Wirtz, 2007); Burnham, (2003) provided a similar view. Customer satisfaction is "an experience-based assessment made by the customer of how far his own expectations about the individual characteristics or the overall functionality of the services obtained from the provider have been fulfilled." Customer satisfaction measurement (CSM) enables organisations to evaluate their abilities and capabilities to meet customers' expectation, desires and needs effectively.

Table 20.13 shows the opinion of customers on customer satisfaction. Respondents have taken neutral stance (2.98) as shown in Table 20.13. How are the respondents distributed on this aspect? About 34 per cent of the customers are satisfied with overall services of BSNL. About 32.58 per cent of the customers have taken neutral stance on the services of BSNL; they are neither satisfied nor dissatisfied about the services. About 5.78 per cent of the customers are very dissatisfied, whereas 27.62 per cent of respondents are dissatisfied with the services of BSNL.

Table 20.13: Perceptions on Customer Satisfaction with Overall BSNL Services (N=485)

Sl. No.	*Satisfaction level*	*f*	*%*
1.	Very dissatisfied	28	5.78
2.	Dissatisfied	134	27.62
3.	Neutral	158	32.58
4.	Satisfied	148	30.52
5.	Very satisfied	17	3.50
	Overall mean and (SD)	**2.98 (0.98)**	

Responses on a 5-point scale of satisfaction 5-very satisfied, 1—very dissatisfied.

From this it is clear that BSNL has a task of converting about one-third of its customers into satisfied and remove dissatisfaction in about one-third of its respondents. Once the customer satisfaction achieved, customer loyalty can be expected.

Analysis across Demographics

Who are more dissatisfied? Table 20.14 shows the views of customers of rural and semi-urban areas.

Table 20.14: Perceptions on Overall Services of BSNL—Across area (N=485)

Factor	*Categories*	*Mean*	*SD*	*F/Z*
Area of residence	Semi-urban (N=286)	2.94	1.02	1.35
	Rural (N=199)	3.05	0.91	

Results of Survey-Customers

The findings of the study can be summarized as under:

Service Quality

The study ascertained importance of service quality first and sought rating on performance later.

Perceived Importance of Service Quality

Respondent customers have rated all the elements of service quality—tangibles, reliability, responsiveness, assurance and empathy were important. However, rural people perceived responsiveness and empathy were more important than others.

Ratings on Service Quality Offered

- Respondent customers have rated the offer-service quality-positively. Rating is "neutral" for tangibility, reliability, responsiveness (with some exceptions), assurance and mixed for empathy.
- Customers are not happy with services and disagreed with the following statements relating to service quality elements.

Reliability

- BSNL is truthful towards keeping its promises to customers (2.80).
- BSNL is dependable in solving customers' complaints (2.78).

Responsiveness

- Delivery of SMS, activations, voice message and other services of BSNL mobile services is timely (2.73).
- "BSNL gives prompt customer services by attending to customer needs and problems" (2.88).
- In addition, rural customer groups expressed their displeasure by agreeing with the following statements:
  - BSNL staff conducts telephonic conversation with someone else, while serving a customer.
  - BSNL staff hurries you, when the break time approaches (lunch/shift/closing hours).

Empathy

- BSNL is making many efforts to understand customer specific needs (2.92).
- SNL apologizes for inconvenience caused to customers (2.79).

Customer Satisfaction

Only one-third of customers are satisfied. Satisfaction level and dissatisfaction level are somehow the same.

Suggestions

In order to improve the service quality of the BSNL services, the following suggested improvements are to be implemented for better results.

Exhibit 20.1: Areas and Nature of Improvement

Areas of Improvement	*Nature of Improvement*
Reliability	To be truthful towards keeping its promises to customers.
	To be dependable in solving customers' complaints.
Responsiveness	To make timely delivery of SMS, activations, voice message and other services.
	To give prompt customer services by attending to customer needs and problems.
	To avoid telephone conversations and hurrying when break time approaches.
Empathy	To make efforts to understand customer specific needs and be polite (learn to apologize for inconvenience caused to customers).
Customer Satisfaction	To improve customer satisfaction in both semi-urban and rural areas.

Conclusion

Based on the results and findings of the study, it is concluded that marketing initiatives such as availability, affordability, awareness on products (e.g. tariffs, rebates, plans and concessions to rural customers) and positive service quality parameters may have impact on customer satisfaction which may lead to customer loyalty. Demographically area has less or no influence on the service quality parameters, as per this study. No rural area or customer should be ignored, as rural markets are potentially contributed to the overall customer base and market of the cellular services. In order to encourage and develop the rural customer base, certain rural packages, rebates, tariffs are specially designed and made available to the BSNL customers in general and customers of BSNL, Chittoor District in particular.

LIST OF ABBREVIATIONS

BSNL	Bharat Sanchar Nigam Limited
CDMA	Code Division Multiple Access
CSC	Customer Service Centre
CSM	Customer Satisfaction Measurement
GoI	Government of India
GSM	Global System of Mobiles
MMS	Multimedia Messaging Service
PSU	Public Sector Undertaking
SDCA	Short Distance Charging Area
SMS	Short Messaging Service
SSA	Secondary Switching Area
WLL	Wireless in Local Loop

REFERENCES

Arora, Parvinder, Garg, Ajay, and Singh, Amritha (2007), "Service Quality in Punjab Telecom Circle", *The ICFAI Journal of Services Marketing*, Vol. 5, No. 2, pp. 19-40.

Burnham, T.A., Frels, J.K. and Mahajan, V., 2003, "Consumer Switching Costs: A Typology Antecedents, and Consequences", *Journal of the Academy of Marketing Science,* 32 (Spring 2003), pp. 109-126.

Dabholkar, P.A., Shepherd, C.D. and Thorpe, D.I., 2000, "A Comprehensive Framework for Service Quality: An Investigation of Critical Conceptual and Measurement Issues through a Longitudinal Study", *Journal of Retailing*, Vol. 76, No. 2, pp. 139-173.

Johnson, W.C. and Sirikit, A., 2002, "Service Quality in Thai Telecommunication Industry: A Tool for Achieving a Sustainable Competitive Advantage", *Management Decision*, Vol. 40, No. 7, pp. 693-701.

Leisen, B. and Vance, C., 2001, "Cross-National Assessment of Service Quality in the Telecommunication Industry: Evidence from the USA and Germany", *Managing Service Quality*, Vol. 11, No. 5, pp. 307-317.

Lovelock C. and Wirtz, J., 2007, "*Services Marketing: People, Technology, Strategy*", 6th Ed., New Jersey: Pearson Prentice Hall.

Meuter, M.L., Ostrom, A.L., Roundtree, R.I. and Bitner, M.J. 2000, "Self-Service

Technologies: Understanding Customer Satisfaction with Technology-based Service Encounters", *Journal of Marketing*, Vol. 64, No. 3, (July), pp. 50-64.

Rahman, Zillur, 2006, "Superior Service Quality in Indian Cellular Telecommunication Industry: A Source of Sustainable Competitive Advantage in an Emerging Economy", *Services Marketing Quarterly*, Vol. 27, No. 4, pp. 115-139.

Sheth, J.N., 1998, June, "Creating Value through Relationship Marketing: A New Business Model", Paper presented at the 1998 Conference on Relationship Marketing, Creating Partnerships that Enrich Customer Value and Boost Marketing Productivity, Atlanta, GA.

Zeithaml, V. and Bitner, M.J., 2003, *Services Marketing: Integrating Customer Focus across the Firm*, 3rd ed., McGraw-Hill, New York.

21

Banking and Insurance Services for the Rural Consumers

Special Reference to State Bank of India (SBI) Village Chas–District Ahmednagar (Maharashtra)

ARAVIND SUHAS INGOLE

Introduction

The State Bank of India is the oldest and largest bank in India, with more than $250 billion (USD) in assets. It is the second-largest bank in the world in number of branches; it opened its 10,000 branch in 2008. The bank has 84 international branches located in 32 countries. SBI traces its heritage to the 1806 formation of the Bank of Calcutta. The bank was renamed the Bank of Bengal in 1809 and operated as one of the three premier "presidency" banks (the presidency banks had the exclusive rights to manage and circulate currency and were provided capital to establish branch networks). In 1921, the Government consolidated the three presidency banks into the Imperial Bank of India. The Imperial Bank of India continued until 1955, when India's Central Bank, the Reserve Bank of India, acquired the majority interest in the bank and changed its name to the State Bank of India (SBI). In 1959, the Government of India passed the State Bank of India Act, resulting in the acquisition (majority shareholding) of eight state-affiliated banks and the creation of the State Bank of India Group (SBI Group). The SBI itself is now majority owned by the Government of India, which purchased the shares held by the Reserve Bank of India.

The customer orientation of the banking sector has significantly increased in recent times. The introduction of a variety of new products and services with emphasis on quality of services clearly indicates how banks address the issue of customer needs and requirements through a customer centric approach. The Banking and Insurance services are planned and implemented for rural consumers on high priority and the technology helps the SBI to provide the latest services to rural consumers. The State Bank of India has achieved its goal of offering its full range of products and services to rural consumers at all its branches and customers, spreading economic growth to rural areas and providing financial inclusion for all of India's citizens. India has a rural population of about 900 million with limited or no access to financial services. The branch banking route apparently is not very practical due to the huge cost of opening the branches *vis-à-vis* volumes expected, high costs of operations, limited banking hours, illiteracy, non-availability of alternate channels in rural centres etc.

Services of SBI to Empower Rural Consumers

The State Bank of India has its presence in most parts of rural India. It has its trust and faith in rural consumer's mind and soul. The empowerment of rural consumers mostly relates to agricultural sector, but this trend is changing with the application of technology, which has changed the rural banking scenario. The Chas Village Branch of Ahmednagar district of Maharashtra is using technology to empower rural consumers. Some of the major services are discussed below.

Financial Literacy and Credit Counselling Centres (FLCCs)

In order to provide Financial Literacy and Credit Counselling, the SBI has set up 87 FLCCs and 88 FLCs are planned to be set-up by 31st December. 2012. The Chas village branch is organising Financial Literacy programmes and workshops to empower the rural consumers. Every three months the branch is organising such programmes and workshops in which the Branch Manager or the Zonal Head guides the rural consumers (in local Language, i.e. Marathi) about the Banking facilities and services available to rural consumers.

Formation of Farmers Club

The Bank has formed the Farmers Club in the village. In this Club retired

Government officers, teachers, ex-army men, business owners, sarpanchs, LIC Agents and the Branch Manager of SBI Chas village branch are the prime members. These members help or assist the rural people and solve their various problems.

Providing Loans for Rural Consumers

Disbursement of agricultural loan is the major banking service that is being provided. Through this the bank is providing loans for various innovative and specialised pre-designed agricultural schemes of the State and Central Government.

Customer Specific Products/Offerings

The Bank has especially designed the marketing strategies and services as per the customer specific needs which the customer can avail. These kinds of services are customer savvy and offered on a regular basis. (e.g. financing for organic farming and green houses for plantation)

Rural Multi-Purpose Kiosks/Village Knowledge Centre

These services in rural banking are at inception stage and mainly relate to Information Technology. But slowly this will enable and empower the rural consumers to a large extent.

Automatic Teller Machine (ATM)

Automatic Teller Machine is the most popular device in India and especially in the rural areas of the district. This has empowered the rural consumers as it enables them to withdraw their money 24 hours a day' 7 days a week. It is a device that allows a customer who has an ATM card to perform routine banking transactions without interacting with a human teller. In addition to cash withdrawal, ATMs can be used for payment of utility bills, funds transfer between accounts, deposit of cheques and cash into accounts, balance enquiry etc.

Commercial Banking for Rural HNI (High Networth Individuals)

This covers services such as cash management (money transfers, payroll services, and bank reconcilement), credit services (asset-based financing, lines of credits, commercial loans or commercial real estate loans), deposit services (checking or savings account services) and foreign exchange.

Connect with Customer at Marketplace: A Market and Service Strategy

The Banking Sector adopts various service strategies to connect with the customer at the marketplace. The banks are making their presence and doing good business in spite of huge competition, this service strategy will drive the attention of rural customers. The service will also help SBI Bank to retain their rural consumers.

Reaching to Masses: Need to Customise the Services

The Banking Industry needs to customise its marketing and services strategies for better progress. Instead of reaching only to the masses, the banks need to be reached to the rural customised customers as it will help the bank to understand the mindsets of rural consumers and reframe their strategies based on the feedback.

Grow through Alliances: Marketing Strategy and Services for Rural Consumers

Marketing has reached beyond the limits of services and strategies. Banks are growing through various kinds of alliances with other sector providers, like other financial service providing companies, educational institutions, housing/construction companies, automobiles, consumer durables, hospitality, Indian Post etc.

Faster Service/Reduced TATs

Due to the rising demand, the Banking Industry is focusing its strategy more and more on providing the services effectively and efficiently in a very short time. This is really helping the rural consumers to get their work done within a stipulated time.

Real Time Gross Settlement (RTGS)

Real Time Gross Settlement system has been introduced in India since March 2004. It is a system through which electronic instructions can be given by banks to transfer funds from their account to the account of another bank. The RTGS system is maintained and operated by the RBI and provides a mean of efficient and faster funds transfer among banks, facilitating their financial operations. As the name suggests, funds transfer between banks takes place on a 'Real Time' basis. Therefore, money can reach the beneficiary instantaneously and the beneficiary's bank has the responsibility to credit the beneficiary's account within two hours.

Electronic Funds Transfer (EFT)

Electronic Funds Transfer (EFT) is a system whereby anyone who wants to make payment to another person/company etc. can approach his bank and make cash payment or give instructions/authorisation to transfer funds directly from his own account to the bank account of the receiver/ beneficiary. Complete details such as the receiver's name, bank account number, account type (savings or current account), bank name, city, branch name etc. should be furnished to the bank at the time of requesting for such transfers so that the amount reaches the beneficiaries' account correctly and faster. RBI is the service provider of EFT.

Electronic Clearing Service (ECS)

Electronic Clearing Service is a retail payment system that can be used to make bulk payments/receipts of a similar nature especially where each individual payment is of a repetitive nature and of relatively smaller amount. This facility is meant for companies and Government departments to make/receive large volumes of payments rather than for fund transfers by individuals.

Electronic Payment Services—E-Cheques

Now-a-days, we are hearing about e-governance, e-mail, e-commerce, e-tail etc. In the same manner, a new technology is being developed in US for introduction of e-cheque, which will eventually replace the conventional chapter cheque. India, as harbinger to the introduction of e-cheque, the Negotiable Instruments Act has already been amended to include truncated cheque and E-cheque instruments.

Point of Sale Terminal

Point of Sale Terminal is a computer terminal that is linked online to the computerised customer information files in a bank and magnetically encoded plastic transaction card that identifies the customer to the computer. During a transaction, the customer's account is debited and the retailer's account is credited by the computer for the amount of purchase (DEBIT/CREDIT Cards).

Advisory Services Empowering Rural Consumers

The banks have to take on the role of an adviser for the poor and disadvantaged sections of the society, as the right advice at a difficult time can be of great help to them. This approach recognises the close two-way links between poverty and deprivation on the one hand and being unable to find and use appropriate financial products and services on the other. The banks must advise on reducing the vulnerability of low income families to financial exclusion and multiple debts in order to prevent them from becoming overindebted and/or to lift them out of poverty. Improving access to high quality services for the most disadvantaged groups and individuals in rural communities should be a priority of the banks which includes managing debt and other interlinked difficulties that people often face. Protection from loan sharks, information about where to go to get expert help when people are in difficulty is the need of the hour. The banks should also provide advice on business related issues, such as best insurance deals, availability of raw material, plant and machinery, agri inputs, helping in forming forward and backward linkages and markets related information.

Life Insurance and General Insurance Services

Every individual and all activities connected with him/her be it life, profession, business, travel etc. or any other pursuit are subject to unforeseen circumstances. Insurance is a mechanism that ensures an individual to thrive on adverse consequences by compensating the individual his/her loss financially. The life insurance services are empowering the rural consumers by protecting their families from uncertainties in life, and also helping them to plan for their Child's education and many more such activities.

Insurance Services by SBI

The SBI Bank is empowering the rural consumer by providing Life and

General Insurance services also through its various channels and associated group companies. These services have reached the rural consumers due to rising prosperity in the rural areas.

General Insurance

Fire, Motor, Health etc. Insurance

It is an Insurance against loss/damage of property/material caused by fire generally happens in rural area. The rural consumer can take insurance on his property/material for a maximum amount of its present value. It is also noted that there is a considerable increase in the Motor Vehicles and Agricultural Equipment's insurance in the rural areas. The bank is providing all types of motor insurance. Moreover, within the district it has also been observed that Health Insurance that pays for medical expenses is still not very popular among the rural consumers. Rural consumers are still not interested in buying any such insurance policies but it is now increasing gradually.

Special Insurance for Farming Equipments

Farming equipment is an integral part of the rural life and forms the major asset of the rural people. Considering these aspects the bank in association with other partners and companies of general insurance are providing such services to the rural consumers.

Crop Insurance

Crop Insurance is very important for farmers and the bank is providing good facilities and services to protect the agricultural crops of the rural consumers. It is purchased by agricultural producers, including farmers, ranchers, and others to protect themselves against either the loss of their crops due to natural disasters, such as hail, drought, and floods, or the loss of revenue due to decline in the prices of agricultural commodities. The two general categories of crop insurance are called crop-yield insurance and crop-revenue insurance.

Crop-yield Insurance

There are two main classes of crop-yield insurance: Crop-hail insurance is generally available from private insurers (in countries with private sectors) because hail is a narrow peril that occurs in a limited place and its accumulated losses tend not to overwhelm the capital reserves of private insurers. In early 1820s, crop-hail insurance was available to farmers in France and Germany. That is among the earliest forms of hail insurance from an actuarial perspective. It is possible to implement the hail risk into financial instruments since the risk is isolated.

Multi-peril Crop Insurance (MPCI)

Coverage in this type of insurance is not limited to just one risk. Usually, multi-peril crop insurance offers hail, excessive rain and drought in a combined package. Sometimes, additional risks such as insect or bacteria-related diseases are also offered. The problem with the multi-peril crop insurance is the possibility of a large scale event. Such an event can cause significant losses beyond the insurer's financial capacity. To make this class of insurance, the perils are often bundled together in a single policy, called multi-peril crop insurance (MPCI). In India, a multi-peril crop insurance called National Agriculture Insurance Scheme (NAIS) was implemented. This scheme is being implemented by Agriculture Insurance Company of India, the Government of India owned company. The scheme is compulsory for all farmers who take agricultural loans from any financial institution. It is voluntary for all other farmers. The premium is subsidised for farmers who own less than two hectares of land. This insurance follows the area approach.

This means that instead of individual farmers, a specific area is insured. The area may vary from gram panchayat (an administrative unit containing 8-10 villages) or block or district from crop-to-crop or state-to-state. The claim is calculated on the basis of crop cutting experiments carried out by agricultural departments of respective states. Any shortfall in yield compared to past 5 years average yield is compensated.

Crop-revenue Insurance

Crop-yield minus the crop price gives the crop-revenues. Based on farmer's revenues, crop-revenue insurance is based on deviation from the mean revenue. RMA uses the futures prices on harvest-times listed in the commodity exchange markets, to determine the prices. Combining the future price with farmer's average production gives the estimated revenue of the farmer. Accessing the future market offers enables revenue protection even before the crop is planted. There is a single guarantee for a certain number of dollars. The policy pays an indemnity if the combination of the actual yield and the cash settlement price in the futures market is less than the guarantee.

Life Insurance for Rural Consumers

The State Bank of India is spreading the importance of Life Insurance to rural consumers. The purpose of SBI Bank in association with SBI Life Insurance is to provide life cover to rural consumers and secure their lives. The Bank and the concerned Group Insurance Company is providing low cost insurance to groups of economically weaker sections of society particularly those people who are funded by Micro-Financial Institutions or NGOs or avail loan from bank/financial institutions through SHG. SHG is a group of rural poor who have volunteered to organise themselves into a group for eradication of poverty of members. "Grameen Super Suraksha" is a low cost group term assurance plan for rural people who can seek life insurance protection without maturity benefit. There are many Life Insurance Services and Policies which are available with the State Bank Group to help rural consumers to fulfil their future needs and wants.

Conclusion

To accelerate the pace of development of the rural areas expansion of banking services is very important. Goods and a variety of customer services are equally important. It is a fact that only a satisfied customer returns to the business and ensures that healthy profits are made. They also help to build a good reputation of the service provider thereby enabling the service provider to provide better services to the customers. Rural consumers need more knowledge about the products and services and therefore, more emphasis must be given to educating them about the various services and products that are available with the bank. The technology is helping the rural consumers in so many ways. There is no doubt that Banking and Insurance are the most beneficial services to the rural consumers and if these services are provided to them efficiently in a low cost manner and also catering to the need and requirements then it will definitely improve the quality of life of the rural consumers. Moreover, it will also help them to strengthen their financial background.

The study of the various services that the State Bank of India (SBI) is providing in Village Chas of District Ahmednagar in Maharashtra indicates that the rural consumers are looking for various services which were mainly meant for the urban consumers. Banking and insurance is picking up in the rural areas due to the rise in the income level of the farmers of Ahmednagar District. The SBI has played an important role in delivering these services thereby helping the rural consumers to improve their quality of life. Use of technology by the Bank has transformed the life of rural consumers to a large extent.

REFERENCES

India Rural Banking 2010—Towards a High Performing Sector (McKinsey & Co.).
Kotler, Philip *Marketing Management*, 13th Edition.
PPT Presentation of Mrs. Soundara Kumar (GM Personal Banking, State Bank of India).
Reddy, Y.V., *Future of Rural Banking*, Reserve Bank of India.
The Indian Banking Sector—On the Road to Progress, G.H. Deolalkar Formerly Managing Director, State Bank of India.
www.google.com
www.rbi.org.in
www.sbi.com
www.sbigeneral.in
Yang, Jiaqin E., *Banking—Recent Trend and Development: A Case Study.*

22

E-Banking Service in Rural Punjab

Emerging Issues, Challenges and Potential Strategies to Create Awareness among Rural Masses

R.K. UPPAL AND ADITI BAGHLA

Introduction

The tremendous advances in technology and the aggressive infusion of information technology had brought a paradigm shift in banking operations. For the banks, technology has emerged as a strategic resource for achieving higher efficiency, control of operations, productivity and profitability. For customers, it is the realisation of their anywhere, anytime, anyway banking dream. This has prompted the banks to embrace technology to meet the increasing customer expectation and face the tough competition.

The recent trends show that most brick and mortar banks are shifting from a product-centric model to a customer-centric model as they develop their new e-banking capabilities. They have, over a long time been wing electronic and Telecommunication networks for delivering a wide range of value added products and services. With the popularity of pc, easy access to internet and World Wide Web (www), banks increasingly use internet as a channel for receiving instructions and delivering their product and services to their customers. This form of banking is generally referred to as internet banking, although the range of product and services offered by different banks vary widely both in their content and sophistication.

Internet banking involves customers wing the internet to access their bank account and to undertake banking transaction. E-banking is becoming more and more popular today, as is banking *via* digital television. Beyond doubt, a substantial part of the future of banking business lies and less branch-based and where customers are able to access banking services remotely. E-banking has become a necessary survival weapon and is fundamentally changing the banking industry worldwide. Today, the click of the mouse offers customers banking services at a much lower cost and also empowers them with unprecedented freedom in choosing vendors for their financial service needs.

No country today has a choice whether to implement e-banking or not given the global and competitive nature of the economy. Banks have to upgrade and constantly think of new innovative customised packages and services to remain competitive. The invasion of banking by technology has created an information age and communisation of banking services.

India is still in the early stages of e-banking growth and development. Competition and change in technology and lifestyle in the last five years have changed the face of banking. India has been able to take one step in this direction—physical cash has been replaced by anytime and anywhere money. But these are more pronounced in multinational and private sector banks. The public sector banks are far behind in the technology integration. The major problem lies in the fact that Indian banks specially public sector banks lack the basic infrastructure needed for internet banking, smart cards, electronic cash transfer etc. in order to become high-tech banks, they will have to adopt the combination of bricks and clicks strategy exhaustively.

Objectives, Data Source and Research Methodology

The objectives of the study are:

1. To assess the current status of e-banking services in rural Punjab; and
2. To explore the potential strategies to create awareness among the rural masses.

Data Collection

Data has been collected from the rural sector of Punjab in August 2012.

Findings of the Survey

Profile of Respondent

The present study shows that gender-wise (Table 22.1) maximum

Table 22.1: Profile of Respondents

Group	Number	%
Area		
1. Rural	100	33.33
2. Semi-Urban	100	33.33
3. Urban	100	33.33
Age Group (Yrs.)		
1. Below 25	100	33.33
2. 25-35	102	34.00
3. 35-45	70	23.33
4. Above 45	45	9.33
Income (Rs.)		
1. Below 1 Lakh	56	18.67
2. 1-2 Lakh	154	51.33
3. Above 2 Lakh	90	30.00
Gender		
1. Male 18662.00	186	62.00
2. Female 11438.00+	114	38.00
Education		
1. High School 3812.67	38	12.67
2. Graduate 17056.67	170	56.67
3. Post Grad. 9230.67	92	30.67
Occupation		
1. Service 8929.67	89	29.67
2. Business 9030.00	90	30.00
3. Professional 93.00	9	3.00
4. Industry 113.67	11	3.67
5. Agriculture 4816.00	48	16.00
6. Others 5317.67	53	17.67
All Data	300	100.00

respondents are males similarly 34 per cent respondents are in the age group of below 35. The young blood has quick decision-making and easy to move alternative. 51 per cent of the respondent's family earn between Rs. one lakh to Rs. two lakh and 30 per cent respondents family earn above Rs. two lakh. Those who are earning more, their expectation and perception level will vary with those who are earning less. Income affects the thinking of the customers in the present study because we have taken the samples from the 3 segments of the economy.

The total sample size was 300. 33.33 per cent of the respondents have been analysed from the rural sector of Punjab and remaining 200 respondents (33.33 per cent each) from the semi-urban segment and urban respectively. Occupation-wise 30 per cent respondents are from business class and 29.67 per cent respondents belonged to the service class. Based on income level, educational qualifications, age group, designation and their family setup like qualification, need, wants, desire vary so also respondent's designation also disturbs the service preferences. The individual behaviour has lots of differences based on their education profile. This study found that 56.67 per cent of the respondents were graduates and 36.67 per cent respondents were post-graduates.

Availability of Products and Services

Banks in India have traditionally offered mass banking products. Most common deposit products being Savings Bank, Current Account, Term Deposit Account and lending products being Cash Credit and Term Loans. In view of several developments in the 1990s, the entire banking products structure has undergone a major change. As part of the economic reforms, banking industry has been deregulated and made competitive. New players have added to the competition. IT revolution has made it possible to provide ease and flexibility in operations to customers. Rapid strides in information technology have, in fact, redefined the role and structure of banking in India. Further, due to exposure to global trends after Information explosion led by Internet, customers—both Individuals and corporate—are now demanding better services with more products from their banks. Financial market has turned into a buyer's market. Banks are also changing with time and are trying to become one-stop financial supermarkets.

Market focus is shifting from mass banking products to class banking with introduction of value added and customised products. Customised banking products like Investment Advisory Services, Photo-credit cards, Cash Management services, Investment products and Tax Advisory services. Banks also offer advisory services termed as 'private banking'—to "high relationship—value" clients. Products like debit cards, flexi deposits, ATM cards, personal loans including consumer loans, housing loans and vehicle loans have been introduced by a number of banks. The survey revealed that whether it is a rural segment, semi-urban or urban sector, the availability of more products and services is an important factor for bank customers. The people of different age-group, different income level, different sex, different education level and different occupation level considered that availability of more products and services are important for customers who are availing bank services.

The chi-square test exhibits that the difference in opinion of customers is insignificant age group-wise, annual income-wise, gender-wise and occupation-wise. It is significant at 1 pc LOS segment-wise and education level-wise. Overall 58.33 per cent customers considered that the availability of more products and services is an important factor for bank customers while 37 per cent customers considered it most important.

Table 22.2: Perception: Availability of More Products/Services

Summary	Most UnImportant		Unimportant		Undecided		Important		Most Important		
Group/Sub-Group	**N**	**%**	**N**	**%**	**N**	**%**	**N**	**%**	**N**	**%**	**Chi-square**
Area											
1. Rural							78	78.00	22	22.00	Chi^2=
2. Semi-Urban			14	14.00			61	61.00	25	25.00	72.98**
3. Urban							36	36.00	64	64.00	(df:4)
Age Group (Yrs.)											
1. Below 25							60	60.00	36	36.00	Chi^2=8.10
2. 25-35			4	4.00			62	60.78	32	31.37	(df:6)
3. 35-45			8	7.84			40	57.14	28	40.00	
4. Above 45			2	2.86			13	46.43	15	53.57	
Annual Income (Rs.)											
1. Below 1 Lakh			6	10.71			28	50.00	22	39.29	Chi^2=6.78
2. 1-2 Lakh			6	3.90			91	59.09	57	37.01	(df:4)
3. Above 2 Lakh			2	2.22			56	62.22	32	35.56	
Gender											
1. Male			6	3.23			105	56.45	75	40.32	Chi^2=3.94
2. Female			8	7.02			70	61.40	36	31.58	(df:2)
Education Level											
1. High School			6	15.79			19	50.00	13	34.21	Chi^2=17.06**
2. Graduate			2	1.18			107	62.94	61	35.88	(df:4)
3. Post Graduate			6	6.52			49	53.26	37	40.22	
Occupation											
1. Service			6	6.74			50	56.18	33	37.08	Chi^2=14.09
2. Business			6	6.67			45	50.00	39	43.33	(df:10)
3. Professional							4	44.44	5	55.56	
4. Industry							6	54.55	5	45.45	
5. Agriculture							37	77.08	11	22.92	
6. Others			2	3.77			33	62.26	18	33.96	
All Data			**14**	**4.67**			**175**	**58.33**	**111**	**37.00**	

Better Customer Relationship Management (CRM)

Technology, People and Customers are the three elements on which depends the success of banking in the fast changing economic environment. The ultimate performance of a bank depends upon the satisfaction of its customers. In the emerging competitive and technological driven banking era, banks have to strive hard for retaining and enlarging their customer base.

E-CRM, which is the latest buzzword in the corporate sector, is perceived as one of the effective tool in this direction by the banks. Its emphasis is on defining the customers as valuable in the long-term and on viewing customer relationships as a learning relationships. The concept of CRM, when seen in the context of e-business, it translates into e-CRM, which essentially deals with managing customer interactions over the web. The present chapter attempts to analyze the concept of e-CRM in Indian banks from its various dimensions covering specifically its need, process, present status and future prospects. The survey exhibits that whether it is a rural segment, semi-urban or urban sector all the customers from different segments want that there should be a good relationship between customers and bank employees and it is an important factor for bank customers.

Age-wise preference to CRM lies more in the age group of 35 to 45 which is 68.57 per cent followed by the age group of 25 to 35 that is 54 per cent then in the age group of above 45 that is 53.57 per cent. The preference to CRM is least in the age group of below 25 that is 51 per cent.

The people of different income level, different sex, different education level and different occupation level-wise considered that CRM is important because without CRM customers will not get any affiliation with the organisation. The chi-square test exhibits that the difference in opinion of customers is insignificant age group-wise, annual income-wise, education-wise. It is significant at 1 pc LOS segment-wise and gender-wise and occupation level-wise (*see* Table 22.3).

Overall 56.67 per cent customers considered that CRM is an important factor for bank customers while 39.67 per cent customers considered it most important.

Convenient Location of a Bank

There was a time when people were not aware about modern e-services such as ATMs, Smart cards, debit cards and credit cards. But now-a-days almost everybody is aware about modern e-services and people do not take the risk of carrying cash with them. So, they are using more and more ATM, debit card, credit card smart cards, tele-banking and mobile banking services. If the location of a bank is convenient to customers they use more and more e-banking services. Usage of more and more services is dependent upon the convenient location of a bank. In order to know the perceptions of people about the convenient location of a bank, the enquiry was made in which 77 per cent rural respondents said

Table 22.3: Perception: Better Customer Relationship Management

Summary	*Most Unimportant*		*Unimportant*		*Undecided*		*Important*		*Most Important*		
Group/Sub Group	**N**	**%**	**N**	**%**	**N**	**%**	**N**	**%**	**N**	**%**	**Chi-square**
Area											
1. Rural							82	82.00	18	18.00	Chi^2=79.9
2. Semi-Urban			5	5.00	6	6.00	57	57.00	32	32.00	6**(df:6)
3. Urban							31	31.00	69	69.00	
Age Group (Yrs.)											
1. Below 25							51	51.00	43	43.00	Chi^2=10.88(df:9)
2. 25-35			2	2.00	4	4.00	56	54.90	41	40.20	
3. 35-45			3	2.94	2	1.96	48	68.57	22	31.43	
4. Above 45							15	53.57	13	46.43	
Annual Income											
1. Below 1 Lakh			2	3.57	2	3.57	29	51.79	23	41.07	
2. 1-2 Lakh			1	0.65	2	1.30	84	54.55	67	43.51	Chi^2=6.36
3. Above 2 Lakh			2	2.22	2	2.22	57	63.33	29	32.22	(df:6)
Gender											
1. Male			2	1.08			112	60.22	72	38.71	Chi^2=12.0
2. Female			3	2.63	6	5.26	58	50.88	47	41.23	2**(df:3)
Education Level											
1. High School							24	63.16	14	36.84	
2. Graduate			5	2.94	2	1.18	100	58.82	63	37.06	Chi^2=10.04(df:6)
3. Post Grad.					4	4.35	46	50.00	42	45.65	
Occupation											
1. Service			2	2.25	2	2.25	40	44.94	45	50.56	
2. Business			2	2.22			47	52.22	41	45.56	
3. Professional							4	44.44	5	55.56	Chi^2=31.1
4. Industry							8	72.73			0**(df:15)
5. Agriculture							38	79.17	3	27.27	
6. Others							33	62.26	10	20.83	
			1	1.89	4	7.55			15	28.30	
All Data			5	1.67	6	2.00	170	56.67	119	39.67	

that convenient location of a bank is very important, followed by semi-urban sector that is 72 per cent. The preference to convenient location of a bank in urban sector is 44 per cent. Gender-wise study revealed that female prefers more convenient location of a bank that is 64.91 per cent as compared to males that is 63.98 per cent.

The people of different age group, different annual income level, different education level and different occupation level-wise considered that convenient location of a bank is important to receive bank services. The chi-square test revealed that the difference in the opinion of the customer is insignificant age group-wise, annual income wise and gender-wise. It is significant at 1 pc LOS areas-wise and occupation-wise. It is significant at 5 per cent LOS education level-wise. Over-all 64.33 per cent customer wants convenient location of a bank and considered it is important while 25.33 per cent customers considered it is most important (*see* Table 22.4).

Table 22.4: Convenient Location of a Bank

Summary	Most Unimpor-tant		Unimportant		Undecided		Important		Most Important		
Group/Sub Group	**N**	**%**	**N**	**%**	**N**	**%**	**N**	**%**	**N**	**%**	**Chi-square**
Area											
1. Rural			17	17.00			77	77.00	6	6.00	Chi^2=91.00**(df:6)
2. Semi-Urban			10	10.00	4	4.00	72	72.00	14	14.00	
3. Urban							44	44.00	56	56.00	
Age Group (Yrs.)											
1. Below 25			8	8.00			71	71.00	21	21.00	Chi^2=7.23(df:9)
2. 25-35			11	10.78	2	1.96	64	62.75	25	24.51	
3. 35-45			6	8.57	2	2.86	42	60.00	20	28.57	
4. Above 45			2	7.14			16	57.14	10	35.71	
Annual Income (Rs.)											
1. Below 1 Lakh			8	14.29			31	55.36	15	26.79	Chi^2=8.34 (df:6)
2. 1-2 Lakh			9	5.84	2	3.57	105	68.18	38	24.68	
3. Above 2 Lakh			10	11.11	2	1.30	57	63.33	23	25.56	
Gender											
1. Male			19	10.22	2	1.08	119	63.98	46	24.73	Chi^2=1.13(df:3)
2. Female			8	7.02	2	1.75	74	64.91	30	26.32	
Education Level											
1. High School			6	15.79	2	5.26	21	55.26	9	23.68	
2. Graduate			17	10.00	2	1.18	113	66.47	38	22.35	Chi^2=12.64*(df:6)
3. Post Grad.			4	4.35			59	64.13	29	31.52	
Occupation											
1. Service					2	2.25	65	73.03	22	24.72	
2. Business			6	6.67	2	2.22	53	58.89	29	32.22	Chi^2=40.39**(df:15)
3. Professional							3	33.33	66	6.67	
4. Industry			2	18.18			6	54.55	3	27.27	
5. Agriculture			11	22.92			31	64.58	6	12.50	
6. Others			8	15.09			35	66.04	10	18.87	
All Data			**27**	**9.00**	**4**	**1.33**	**193**	**64.33**	**76**	**25.33**	

Convenient High Rate of Interest on Deposits

The term deposits means to lay down in particular place, store or entrust for keeping. It means money deposits in banks are known as bank deposits. Deposits are the chief source of the funds of the banks. Deposit Management consists of the activities involved in obtaining funds from depositors. In E-Banking Deposit cash means depositing cash in the Bank *via* Internet. Customers can deposit cash in Banks from their sitting places. Today Banks only think about customer's convenience. E-banking has made easy and convenient for the customers to deposit cash *via* Internet and banks are paying high rate of interest on deposits. The study revealed that occupation-wise Agriculturist respondents are satisfied that there is a high interest on deposits, i.e. 72.92 per cent as compared to other respondents, i.e. 39.62 per cent. Area-wise Urban respondents, i.e. 64 per cent considered it most important as compared to Semi-Urban, i.e. 25 per cent. People from different Age group, different Annual Income, different gender, different education level are satisfied that there is a high interest on deposits.

Table 22.5: Perception: High Rate of Interest on Deposits

Summary	*Most Unimportant*		*Unimportant*		*Undecided*		*Important*		*Most Important*		
Group/Sub Group	**N**	**%**	**N**	**%**	**N**	**%**	**N**	**%**	**N**	**%**	**Chi-square**
Area											
1. Rural	8	8.00	35	35.00	6	6.00	57	57.00	2	2.00	Chi^2=123.07
2. Semi-Urban	3	3.00	14	14.00	4	4.00	49	49.00	25	25.00	**(df:8)
3. Urban					6	6.00	27	27.00	64	64.00	
Age Group (Yrs.)											
1. Below 25	1	1.00	12	12.00	10	10.00	42	42.00	35	35.00	Chi^2=33.76
2. 25-35	9	8.82	15	14.71	2	1.96	55	53.92	21	20.59	**(df:12)
3. 35-45	1	1.43	16	22.86	1	1.43	25	35.71	27	38.57	
4. Above 45			6	21.43	3	10.71	11	39.29	8	28.57	
Annual Income											
(Rs.)	1	1.79	6	10.71	3	5.36	29	51.79	17	30.36	Chi^2=6.01
1. Below 1 Lakh	6	3.90	25	16.23	10	6.49	70	45.45	43	27.92	(df:8)
2. 1-2 Lakh	4	4.44	18	20.00	3	3.33	34	37.78	31	34.44	
3. Above 2 Lakh											
Gender											Chi^2=11.02
1. Male	10	5.38	33	17.74	5	2.69	83	44.62	55	29.57	*(df:4)
2. Female	1	0.88	16	14.04	11	9.65	50	43.86	36	31.58	
Education Level											
1. High School	3	7.89	6	15.79	4	10.53	22	57.89	3	7.89	Chi^2=34.57
2. Graduate	8	4.71	37	21.76	4	2.35	73	42.94	48	28.24	**(df:8)
3. Post Grad.			6	6.52	8	8.70	38	41.30	40	43.48	
Occupation											
1. Service	4	4.49	8	8.99	9	10.11	37	41.57	31	34.83	Chi^2=85.48
2. Business	6	6.67	6	6.67	5	5.56	35	38.89	38	42.22	**(df:20)
3. Professional	1	1.89	8	72.73	2	3.77	4	44.44	5	55.56	
4. Industry			13	27.08			1	9.09	2	18.18	
5. Agriculture			14	26.42			35	72.92	15	28.30	
6. Others							21	39.62			
All Data	**11**	**3.67**	**49**	**16.33**	**16**	**5.33**	**133**	**44.33**	**91**	**30.33**	

The chi-square test reveals that difference in opinion of customers is insignificant Annual Income-wise. It is significant at 1 Pc LOS Area-wise, Age group-wise, Education level-wise and occupation-wise.

E-Channels Don't Ensure Privacy

Technological innovations witnessed by the corporate sector during the Nineties have changed the way business needs to be conducted. I.T has introduced new business paradigms and is increasingly playing a significant role in improving the services in the banking industry. E-Banking is becoming more and more popular today, as is banking *via* digital television. E-Banking has become a necessary survival weapon and is fundamentally changing the banking industry worldwide today. The click of the mouse offers customers banking services at much lower cost and also empowers them with unprecedented freedom in choosing vendors for their financial service needs. But only single drawback is E-channels don't ensure privacy and privacy is super most important while conducting a business.

The study concludes that 68 per cent of the urban segment and 15 per cent of the Semi-Urban segment strongly agree that e-channels do not ensure privacy. Occupation-wise 66 per cent of the professionals strongly agree that e-channels do not ensure privacy as comparative to business sector, industry sector and agriculture sector that is 40 per cent, 18 per cent and 12 per cent respectively. All people from different age group, different Annual Income, different Gender, different Education level agree that e-channels do not ensure privacy.

Table 22.6: E-channels do not Ensure Privacy

Group	*Sub-Group*	*Strongly Dis. Ag.*	*Disagree*	*Undecided*	*Agree*	*Strongly Agree*	*Chi-Square Value*
Area	Rural		55		33	12	
	Semi-Urban	8	24		53	15	
	Urban		7		25	68	Chi^2=131.24**
Age Group (In Years)	Below 25	3	24		45	28	
	25-35	5	33		37	27	
	35-45		29		30	42	
	Above 45		33		29	40	Chi^2=13.05
Annual Income (In Lakhs)	Below 1 Lakh	6	22		45	29	
	1-2 Lakh	4	29		33	36	
	Above 2 Lakh		34		40	27	Chi^2=9.46
Gender	Male	3	27		35	36	
	Female	3	32		41	26	Chi^2=3.36
Education Level	High School	8	48		27	19	
	Graduate	3	28		44	26	
	Post Grad.		23		30	48	Chi^2=28.26**
Occupation	Service		31		33	38	
	Business	6	18		37	40	
	Professional				34	67	
	Industry		19		64	19	
	Agriculture		61		28	13	
	Others	6	23		50	23	Chi^2=52.96**
All Data		**3**	**29**		**37**	**32**	

The chi-square test concludes that difference in opinion of customers is insignificant age-wise, annual income-wise, gender-wise. It is significant at 1 Pc LOS Area-wise, Education-wise, Occupation-wise. Overall 31.67 per cent respondents strongly agree with that e-channels do not ensure privacy.

E-Channels: Bright Future in Global-Age

Banks have come to realise that survival in the new e-economy depends on delivering some or all of their banking services on the Internet while continuing to support their traditional infrastructure. Without any doubt, the international scope of E-banking provides new growth perspectives and Internet business is a catalyst for new technology and new business process. The study concludes that occupation-wise industry sector agrees that the E-Channels have bright future in global age that is 72.73 per cent as compared to agriculture sector and other sector that is 58.33 per cent, and 39.62 per cent respectively. Similarly, area-wise 71 per cent of Urban respondents and 18 per cent of Semi-Urban respondents strongly agree with the same. According to Annual Income-wise, Age group-wise, Education-wise, Gender wise respondents agree with that E-Channels have bright future in global-age.

Table 22.7: E-channels have Bright Future in Global Age

Group	*Sub-Group*	*Strongly DisAg.*	*Disagree*	*Undecided*	*Agree*	*Strongly Agree*	*Chi-Square Value*
Area	Rural		41		51	8	
	Semi-Urban	6	33	6	37	18	
	Urban	3	4		22	71	Chi^2=129.53**
Age Group (In Years)	Below 25	6	18	3	43	30	
	25-35	2	39	3	28	30	
	35-45	2	28		35	38	
	Above 45		8		54	40	Chi^2=27.00**
Annual Income (In Lakhs)	Below 1 Lakh	4	29	6	38	25	
	1-2 Lakh	2	29	2	30	39	
	Above 2 Lakh	5	20		49	27	Chi^2=17.53*
Gender	Male	3	22	2	39	35	
	Female	4	33	3	34	29	Chi^2=5.06
Education Level	High School	6	43	3	32	19	
	Graduate	3	28	3	42	26	
	Post Grad.	3	18		31	50	Chi^2=25.54**
Occupation	Service	7	25		26	43	
	Business	2	19	4	32	46	
	Professional				23	78	
	Industry				73	28	
	Agriculture		38		59	5	
	Others	4	40	6	40	12	Chi^2=75.05**
All Data		**3**	**26**	**2**		**33**	

The chi-square concludes that difference in the opinion of the respondents is insignificant Gender-wise. It is significant at 1 Pc LOS Area-wise, Age group-wise, Education-wise and Occupation-wise. While it is significant at 5 Pc LOS Annual Income-wise. Overall study reveals that 36.67 per cent respondents agree that e-channels have bright future in global age while 32.33 per cent strongly agree with the same.

Suggestions

- E-banking services should be more customer-centric than the service-centric as dreamt earlier.
- The rise of E-banking is redefining business relationship and the most successful banks will be those that can truly strengthen their relationship with the customers.
- Banks should also offer sufficient price incentives for customers to use bank online in their efforts to build a sound E-banking business.
- Just enrolling customers for online banking may not be sufficient until and unless they use the site actively, banks must make the efforts to increase their site usage by customers and effectively co-ordinate the online channel with branches and call centres. Then only they will be able to derive maximum value that includes cost reduction, cross-selling opportunities and higher customer retention.
- It is found that awareness of rural customers about the E-services of banks is hence not adequate. There is a need to educate them about the E-channels provided by banks as well as about the benefits of E-banking. Now need is to aware the consumers about the E-age products and how to use them.

Conclusion

In the era of E-banking and severe competition, the expectations of the bank customers have increased. Due to this bank should offer a broad range of deposits, investments and credit products through diverse distribution channels including upgraded branches, ATMs, telephone and internet. For this banks should become more customer-centric, offering a wide range of products through multiple delivery channels, becomes proficient in managing assets and liabilities according to risk and return and pay greater attention to profitability including cost reduction and increased fee-based income.

It can be concluded that mere introduction of IT alone will not be sufficient to bring necessary performance improvement and to get the competitive edge. Intelligent people are required to use such intelligent tools. Awareness programmes should be conducted to spread awareness to usage of more E-channels.

REFERENCES

Avasthi, G.P. and Sharma, M., 2000-01, "Information Technology in Banking: Challenges for Regulators". *Prajanan.* XXIX(4). 17.

Deniel, Amor, 2000, *"the E-business (r) evolution", Pearson Education,* New Delhi.

Hua, G., 2009, "An Experimental Investigation of Online Banking Adoption in China". *Journal of Internet Banking and Commerce.* 14(1). April. Accessed on 20th January, 2010 on http://www.arraydev.com/commerce/jibc/

Joseph, P.T., 2002, *E-commerce: A Managerial Perspective, New Delhi:* Prentice-Hall of India Pvt. Ltd.

Kalakota, Ravi and Whinston, Andrew B., 1999, "Frontiers of Electronic Commerce", *Pearson Education,* New Delhi.

Mittal, R.K. and Sanjay, 2007, "Technology in Banking Sector: Issues and Challenges", *Vinimaya,* Vol. XXVII, No. 4, (January-March), pp. 14–22.

Padhy, K.C., 2007, *Banking Future,* (ed.book) New Delhi: Dominant Publishers and Distributors.

Schaechter Andrea, 2002, "Issues in Electrnic Banking: An Overview", IMF policy discussion paper No. 02/6 (Washington: Informational Monetary Fund).

Shastri, R.V. (2003), "Recent Trends in Banking Industry: IT Emergence", *Analyst,* (March), pp. 45-46.

Shetty, V.P. (2000), "E-Banking", *IBA Bulletin,* Vol. XXI, No. 3 (March Special Issue), pp. 31-34.

Uppal, R.K. & Kaur, R. (2007), "Indian Banking Moving Towards IT", *Journal of Commerce and Trade,* Vol. 2, No. 1 (April), pp. 26-32.

23

Problems in the Banking Service Marketing in the Mofussil

With Special Reference to HDFC Bank of Anand District

JAYESH POOJARA AND SEJAL CHRISTIAN

Introduction

With the spread of banking habits and banking facilities to mofussil corners of the country the banking services marketing has become an important factor. It is no longer a residual matter but requires a careful attention of bankers as inflow and outflow of cash which is an important part of the bankers, has become highly unpredictable. Cash being a crucial inventory item for banking operations, is one of the most liquid assets owned by banks. Like other assets excluding non-performing ones, cash does not yield direct or indirect benefits to the bank. Therefore, efficient management of cash, as bank services marketing, has become a necessity for banks, that too at a time when profit margins are shrinking. This calls for managing the operations with minimum cash which in turn requires managerial acumen and efficient systems and procedures in banks. The managerial acumen demands the efficiency not only in meeting the needs of the cash of customers but also in reducing the idle cash to the barest minimum. This has special significance especially in the present-day geographical spread of branches in mofussil areas. However, banks, as commercial organisations cannot keep idle cash for meeting the expected demand and incur loss. The large idle cash is neither available to meet CRR requirements nor for profitable deployment. In this way, cash management is one of the most difficult problems in bank service marketing.

The bank together with its group of affiliates has been making a multi-pronged attack on the intractable problems of economic development in mofussil areas. By adopting flexible methods of financing, by sponsoring local development finance institutions for mobilizing and channelling both domestic and external capital for production purpose, by helping member countries in the planning of their development projects and by furnishing technical assistance and by forming international consultation groups to co-ordinate the provision of foreign aid the banks have endeavoured to fulfil the role assigned by their charter to uplift the people of mofussil areas.

Concept of Mofussil Bank Marketing

Banking industry is the key for restructuring the economic scenario of the country. Today banks have been recognised as an effective instrument for the socio-economic development of the country. This has cast new tasks and responsibilities on the banks. The traditional function of banks is accepting deposits and granting loans, has given way to a more dynamic one. Banks are now required to mobilise savings from all sectors of the community and utilise the same for productive use so as to bring about a rapid increase in national income and living standards of the people. Till 1960s Indian Banks were more conservative and inward looking, concerned with their profits. As a matter of fact, competition was not in existence. Majority of the banks were private commercial banks, local oriented and primarily serving the business community. They had limited range of activities. Banks were serving the needs of a colonial economy and hence confined to urban and industrial centres. They basically concentrated on selling their loans, positive appropriation of their liabilities to keep their funds safe and giving moderate interest on deposits.

Banking industry is necessarily a service industry which provides various types of banking services to its clients. The bank customer may be deposit customer or a borrower customer or customer using some ancillary service of the bank. These customers come from different strata of economy, from different population groups like rural, semi-urban, urban, metropolitan etc. from different geographical locations and from different professions and businesses. There is total heterogeneity in customer character. Naturally, the need of each group of customer is different from that of other. The banker has to identify the diversified needs of these different groups of customers. Products or services should be designed to satisfy their particular needs and delivered to them in the best possible manner. These days private banks like HDFC, ICICI, Axis Bank, Kotak Mahindra and IDBI have realised these key-factors and executed accordingly.

Rational and Significance of the Study

In India more than 70 per cent of households live in rural area. Therefore, the rural bank marketing assumes a significant importance. A rural bank is one which serves a population of less than 10,000. The most notable transition in the post-nationalisation period has been from class banking to mass banking. This means that lending to the select elite in the urban areas gave way to lending to the rural masses. Of late, it is recognised that the potentiality of rural India should not be underestimated. The five year plans have been laying much emphasis on raising the level of economic activity in the rural areas. Banks—commercial or private—have to play a dual role in rural areas. Firstly, for institutionalise the activities as a part of banking. Secondly, help in the social upliftment of the poor as a part of social banking. India follows a multi-agency approach in rural credit. The flow of credit to rural areas are from cooperatives, commercial, private and regional rural banks. All these agencies receive active financial and non-financial assistance from Central and State government and other institutions like RBI, NABARD etc. Ever since nationalisation, a good number of bank branches are being operated in rural areas. As at the end of March 1972, there were 60,528 branches of commercial banks including RBIs in the country of which 35,275 or 53.3 per cent were in rural areas as against 22.3 per cent at the time of bank nationalisation in July 1969.

In spite of huge branch expansion in rural areas and developmental policies of the governments, it is to be noted that the commercial banks have not made systematic marketing efforts to squeeze the rural business as compared to private banks. The foregoing discussion reveals that bank marketing is an organisation imperative and identification of customers' needs and the development of service which will satisfy those needs. In the Indian context, bank marketing strategy should be developed to achieve not only the commercial objectives of the banks, but also the social objectives. It is especially so in the case of rural bank marketing. While designing the marketing mix for rural customers, their needs, inspirations, opinions and problems should be taken into consideration.

Specific Objectives of the Research Work

Specific objectives of the research work are as follows:

1. To study the concept of Banking Service Marketing in the mofussil.
2. To study the services rendered by private banks particularly HDFC Bank.
3. To study identify problems in the Banking Service Marketing in the mofussil.
4. To study the responses of customers to private bank marketing in rural areas.
5. To study whether there is change in people's or users' attitude towards Banking Service Marketing in the mofussil.

Hypotheses of the Present Study

The following hypotheses have been formulated for the study:

1. Private Banks are active in rendering service marketing in mofussil.
2. Rural people are benefited from banking service marketing.
3. Services of private banks have increased the per capita income and thus helped the downtrodden farmers of mofussil.
4. Services of private banks have attracted rural people towards themselves.
5. Overcoming and nullifying problems in banking service marketing in the mofussil will increase the efficiency of private bank and fulfil the social objectives.

Research Methodology of the Present Study

Primary Data and Research Design

Primary survey was undertaken to study the perception of Account Holders or the customers. Questionnaires of 100 respondents were used for the study. To analyse the collected data, statistical techniques like weighted average, mean, median, mode, chi-square, ANOVA, indexation, correlation and technique of factor analysis was applied. Secondary data was collected with the help of following sources: Reference books on concerned topic, Articles published in periodicals, Annual Reports of

Government of India, banks, and other sources and websites of various banks, RBI, and issuers of corporate fields.

Major Research Findings Regarding Problems in the Banking Service

Table 23.1: Gender-wise Classification of Respondents

Particulars	*Frequency*	*Percentage*
Male	52	52
Female	48	48
Total	**100**	**100**

Source: Compiled and calculated from the primary data by the author.

Table 23.1 displays the classification of gender. The frequencies of male having bank accounts are 52 out of 100 and that of female are 48. The percentage of male having bank accounts is 52 and that of female is 48. So, it can be concluded that there is a little difference between the percentage of male and female having bank accounts.

Table 23.2: Age-wise Classification of Respondents

Particulars	*Frequency*	*Percentage*
18-25	36	36
26-35	33	33
36-45	20	20
46-55	8	8
Over 55	3	3
Total	**100**	**100**

Source: Compiled and calculated from the primary data by the author.

Table 23.2 shows the age groups of the respondents. There are total 5 age groups. The percentage of this age group from age of 18 to 25 is 36. The second age group is from 26 to 35 years and it has 33 respondents.

Table 23.3 displays the educational qualifications of the respondents. There are total 7 groups, namely—Illiterate, Primary Education, Secondary Education, Higher Secondary Education, Under Graduate, Graduate and Post-Graduate. There are 6 respondents who are illiterate (6%). Three respondents have Primary education. This group has 3 per cent respondents with Secondary education are 4 and it has 4 percentage. There are 15 respondents who are having Higher Secondary education and its percentage is 15. Eleven respondents are having Under Graduate education which displays 11 per cent of total percentage. There are 34 Graduates having 34 per cent of share and 27 Post-Graduate with 27 per cent. Here, the Graduates are 34 per cent while respondents with Primary education are only 3 per cent. So, Table 23.3 concludes that higher educated respondents are having more bank accounts as compared to lower educated respondents.

Table 23.3: Educational Qualification of Respondents

Particulars	*Frequency*	*Percentage*
Lliterate	6	6
Primary	3	3
Secondary Education	4	4
Higher Secondary Education	15	15
Under Graduate	11	11
Graduate	34	34
Post-Graduate	27	27
Total	**100**	**100**

Source: Compiled and calculated from the primary data by the author.

Table 23.4: Use of Banking Service Particulars like Net Banking, NEFT, Phone Banking and Online Payments etc.

Particulars	*Frequency*	*Percentage*
Never	5	5
Rarely	11	11
Sometimes	16	16
Often	6	6
Very Often	62	62
Total	**100**	**100**

Source: Compiled and calculated from the primary data by the author.

Table 23.4 displays the use of net banking service indicating that 5 per cent of the respondents had never used net banking service. There are 11 respondents who rarely use this service. The percentage of it is 11. Sixteen respondents (16%) sometimes use net banking service. Six respondents (6%) often use this service. There are 62 respondents (62%) use this service very often. It is clear from the Table 23.4 that the net banking service is customer friendly.

Table 23.5: Various Selected Banking Services Provided by HDFC Bank

Particulars	*Percentage*
SMS News	26
Stop payment	7
Minimum Balance Alerts	8
Mobile Bank Transfers	7
Bill Payment	8
Credit/Debit Alerts	28
Account Statement Enquiry	10
Financial Services like share trading	4
Enquire on Your Account Details—your balance, account activity, unclear fund details and cheque status	2

Source: Compiled and calculated from the primary data by the author.

Table 23.5 confirms the mobile banking services offered by banks. According to Table 23.5, 26 per cent wanted SMS news service and highest number of users for SMS are Debit Card as well as Credit Card holders.

Other Important Findings

- ATM, At Par Cheque, Net Banking, Phone Banking, Debit Card and Credit Card services are the major innovative technology based services being used by HDFC Bank in Anand district under the study.
- It was found in discussion with branch managers that HDFC Bank use following innovative technology based products and services for rural area to attract the customers, these include:
  - (a) ATM Services.
  - (b) At par Cheque Facility.
  - (c) e-Banking.
  - (d) Phone Banking.
  - (e) Doorstep Services.
  - (f) Debit Card Facilities.
  - (g) Credit Card Facilities.
  - (h) RTGS Facility.
- It is found that more difficulties regarding products or services like phone banking, net banking etc. are faced by rural customers as compared to customers of urban areas.
- Branch Managers and Managers are aware of problems faced by the customers. According to them, Network problem,

Technical problem, Problem of fraud, Hacking of account, Security of the ATM centres, Shortage of talented manpower, expensive technology are the major problems faced by customers.

- It is found that innovative technology based services are used more by young customers in Anand district. Less than 1 per cent customers using innovative technologies are having age more than 55 years. This is another problem.
- Customers are afraid of using net banking because of fraud, chances of account hacking and fast changing IT technologies.
- During the study it is found that—
  - (a) Loss of ATM Cards of customers was observed in 73.23 per cent cases.
  - (b) No money in ATM was observed in 26.66 per cent cases at various places.
  - (c) Fraud cases up to 5 times in a month were observed
  - (d) Original account hacking in case of Net banking.
- 51 per cent respondents use Net Banking, 21.53 per cent respondents use Debit and Credit Card very often. While 14.48, 4.70 and 27.20 per cent respondents never use the services like Net banking, Phone banking and Debit/Credit cards respectively.
- Testing of the hypothesis proved that Innovative Techniques are helpful for marketing of the bank services.
- The Innovative Techniques enable the Private Sector Banks in providing more efficient and effective services to the customers.
- According to Binomial employed test hypothesis was tested at 5 per cent level of significance and as is accepted we conclude that the customers of Private Sector Banks are satisfied with present innovative techniques used by the banks.
- Rural customers are facing more problems in using innovative services of the Private Sector Banks as compared to urban customers.
- Senior citizen do not use sufficient innovative technology, so for them banks should arrange some training programmes and teach them how to use innovative technology to gain better services from the banks.
- The study reveals that high charges, intolerable interest rate, furious penalty, high renewable fees and unbelievable charges of credit card are the complexities faced by the customers.
- One remarkable observation of the present study is that 53 per

cent customers use computer although they are rural side while dealing with the bank at the same time 15 per cent customers are also associated with bank who are not computer familiar with computer.

- Testing of the hypothesis proved that Innovative Techniques are helpful for marketing of the bank services but not at urban side only.

Identification of Problems in the Banking Service Marketing

1. In rural areas, suitable accommodation is not readily available.
2. Lack of adequate security to the branch and its staff.
3. Lack of rural–oriented staff and an effective training programme.
4. It entails high establishment costs and consequent low profitability.

REFERENCES

Arora, R.C., 1979, *Intergrated Rural Development*, New Delhi: S. Chand & Sons.

Badi, R.V. and Badi, N.V., *Rural Marketing*, Mumbai: Himalaya Publishing House.

Chandra Prakash, *Financial Management,* New Delhi: Alpha Publishers.

Chunawalla, S.A. and Sethia, K.C.,1997, *Foundations of Advertising Theory and Practice,* 4th edition, Mumbai: Himalaya Publishing House.

Kohok, M. A., *Financial Services in India,* Nashik: Digvijay Publications.

Financial Management; 2001, ICFAI Press.

Fraser, Donald R. Ga., Benton E., Kolavi James W.: *Commercial Banking*, England: West Publishing Co.

Hempel, George H. and Simonson, Donald G., *Bank Financial Management*, New York: John Wiley & Sons.

Hempel, Simonson and Coleman, *Bank Management,* (4th Ed.) London: John Wiley & Sons.

Ins. John, P. Alings, *Marketing Research Application Prcedures and Cases*, New York: Pentice Hall.

John H. Methews, *Problem in Marketing*. New Delhi: McGraw Hill Book Company.

John Marsh, *Managing Financial Service Marketing,* London: Pitman Publishing, Co. Long Area.

Kishore, R. M., *Financial Management*, New Delhi: Taxmann's Publications.

Koch, Timothy W., *Bank Management,* New York: The Dryden Press.

Kothari, C.R. (2009), *Research Methodology*, New Delhi: Vikas Publishing House.

Kotler, Philip, *Marketing Management*, New Delhi: Prentice Hall of India Pvt. Ltd.

Laelock Christophen H., *Services Marketing Text, Cases and Readings,* New Jersey: Prentice Hall Inc. Englewood Cliff.

Lovelock, Christopher H., *Managing Services: Marketing Operations and Human Resources*, Englewood Cliffs, New Jersey: PHI.

Porter, Michael, E., 1980, *Competitive Strategy,* New York: Free Press.

Rao, K. Ketshwar, *Management of Commercial Banks,* New Delhi: Delta Publishing House.

Rao, P. Subha, *Principles and Practice of Bank Management,* New Delhi: Himalaya Publishing House.

Index